THE DEEDS OF
PHILIP AUGUSTUS

THE DEEDS
OF PHILIP
AUGUSTUS

AN ENGLISH TRANSLATION OF RIGORD'S *GESTA PHILIPPI AUGUSTI*

Translated from the Latin by Larry F. Field
Edited by
M. Cecilia Gaposchkin and Sean L. Field
Foreword by Paul R. Hyams

CORNELL UNIVERSITY PRESS
Ithaca and London

First published 2022 by Cornell University Press
Printed in the United States of America

Library of Congress Cataloging-in-Publication Data

Names: Rigord, approximately 1145–approximately 1209, author. | Field, Larry F., translator. | Gaposchkin, M. Cecilia (Marianne Cecilia), 1970– editor. | Field, Sean L. (Sean Linscott), 1970– editor.
Title: The deeds of Philip Augustus : an English translation of Rigord's "Gesta Philippi Augusti" / Rigord ; translated from the Latin by Larry F. Field ; edited by M. Cecilia Gaposchkin and Sean L. Field ; foreword by Paul R. Hyams.
Other titles: Gesta Philippi Augusti. English
Description: Ithaca, [New York] : Cornell University Press, 2022. | Includes bibliographical references and index.
Identifiers: LCCN 2021052230 (print) | LCCN 2021052231 (ebook) | ISBN 9781501763144 (hardcover) | ISBN 9781501763151 (paperback) | ISBN 9781501763168 (epub) | ISBN 9781501763175 (pdf)
Subjects: LCSH: Philip II, King of France, 1165–1223. | France—History—Philip II Augustus, 1180–1223.
Classification: LCC DC90 .R5413 2022 (print) | LCC DC90 (ebook) | DDC 944/.023092—dc23/eng/20220105
LC record available at https://lccn.loc.gov/2021052230
LC ebook record available at https://lccn.loc.gov/2021052231

Contents

CONTENTS

ILLUSTRATIONS

Maps

Figures

Maps

Figures

FOREWORD

My acquaintance with Rigord is long-standing but began rather fortuitously. When I was still new at Cornell University, I started to create a course with two main aims. First, it would introduce students, who preferably had some knowledge of the Middle Ages already from my survey course, to the great watershed "moment" of the long twelfth century through an in-depth study of the French hexagon and the Capetian monarchy. Second, it would offer a variety of translated source texts, whole works where possible, to display the extra richness of primary materials over secondary studies.

This array of primary texts would illustrate key themes, including chivalry; the emergence of vernacular literature, especially French, and the transition from epic to romance with its new notions of love, continence, and binding marriage; and the myths about Arthur and the Grail. My students would have the opportunity to see what they could make of some masterpieces of medieval culture, not merely as beautiful works in themselves, but also as ways into the harsher realities arising with the systems of power within which everything operated. I looked especially for narrative texts on the twelfth-century resurgence of a nation-state in France. Suger's *Life of Louis the Fat* (d. 1137) was an obvious choice for the one bookend, as it were, but there was no evident equivalent on Philip Augustus (d. 1223) in English. I would have to provide something myself. Rigord's life of Philip Augustus seemed an enticing proposition because of its unusual mixture of topics, among them the paving of Paris streets, the Third Crusade, Rigord's obsession with the Jews, and his apparent fascination with eclipses. Additionally, I thought he offered a more than average number of passages to provoke fertile class discussion. What puzzles me is usually a good place to start such discussion.

One cannot rush a translation that must bridge the gulf between minds of the twenty-first century and the twelfth. My rough-and-ready translation only reached so far (the first ten years of Philip II's reign) before the looming semester made me stop, "for the time being." I hoped to return and complete the job, perhaps with a grad student partner who might use a first publication to impress the academic employment market. The first ten years was quite enough for a week's reading anyway, and it quickly found its way beyond my campus via the Internet, where it remains to this day, my small contribution to the cooperative Internet I had always wanted to see. Though my effort was never completed, we now have something much better than I, no French historian, would have produced. This book is the real thing: a readable, accurate rendering of Rigord's Latin presented in a form that one can certainly enjoy, but also use in the multifarious ways that a sound scholarly translation makes possible.

But possession of the book takes us only halfway. I have always felt that we scholars fail to remember from our own pasts how hard it is for readers new to the Middle Ages to make sense of its writings. The gulf between our minds and those of Rigord and his contemporaries remains massive. As someone once remarked, even if people could speak the language of lions, they would never experience a satisfying conversation with one. Still, a translation as carefully prepared as this one is a good place from which to prise our way into the France of Rigord and his king, especially if there is on hand a capable professorial guide to help. To get the best out of this text, students should actively look out for the passages that make *no* sense to them, grapple with these, and then—but *only then*—challenge their instructors to lead them on to a deeper understanding of what to make of the words. A generation before Rigord took up his pen, one great Parisian, Peter Abelard, encouraged *his* students to challenge *him*, telling them that by doubting they could be led to question, and through their questions hope to reach toward truth. So, ask on. If that is what a real-life professor in the first great university to emerge in northern Europe taught his students, we should hope for nothing less from ours, if they first give Rigord full enough attention to single out the most perplexing difficulties.

Let me end with one such passage that I only noticed late in my own reading, when I realized it presented questions I could not answer. The passage in question is found at the end of chapter 61 about the disastrous Third Crusade:

> And note that in the very same year of our Lord when the Lord's Cross in Outremer was captured by this same Saladin [1187], babies who were born since that time have only twenty-two teeth, or only twenty, when before then they would usually have thirty or thirty-two.

Any critical appraisal of this passage throws up all kinds of questions. What if anything could Rigord's intended readership have made of it? Where did he get his information, and why did he bother? Did he really believe that God would change His global child development schedule to punish the crusaders in so esoteric a fashion for this specific default among so many? Why did Rigord even notice so minute a change? Numbers are otherwise scarce in his work. He shows no great interest in observation and causal explanations elsewhere. Where did he get these confidently precise ones?

A "preliminary" Internet search sheds some light, by confirming that whereas most adults do indeed possess thirty-two teeth, young children normally have no more than twenty milk teeth. Then, prompted by a friend, I searched for "babies" and "twenty-two teeth." The results brought me to some later writers who peddled exactly the same numbers as Rigord, but used them to make sense of putatively punitive plagues without any mention of him or his cross. There must be a larger story here, one perhaps known to his few literate peers but not more widely. It seems unlikely that it began with Rigord. While it is not inconceivable that he had picked up his dental information orally, it more probably reached him from something he had read, possibly during his medical training. The next step is to pursue his words back into the early Middle Ages, which I can and will do in due course by using—this being the twenty-first century—searchable databases. Naturally being in Latin, these resources are open to me, but not to everybody.

Few people will go to such lengths of course. But every intelligent person can keep a weather eye open for statements that contravene common sense, a mystic substance that is sometimes in shorter supply among scholars than the rest of us! And any students who do persist richly deserve a modicum of special credit from their instructor, plus some special assistance to confirm whether they really are on to a small discovery of their own. A good translation like this one opens up the joyous sport of reading between the lines to far more people than the few specialists who can read it in Latin. May it help you to enjoy your Rigord as much as I have.

Paul R. Hyams

Acknowledgments

The editors and translator would like to thank Mahinder Kingra at Cornell University Press for supporting this project from its inception, Marian Rogers for fine copy editing, and William North and the Press's anonymous readers for helpful suggestions and corrections. We also warmly thank Paul Hyams for his much-appreciated encouragement and suggestions and for contributing the foreword. Others to whom we owe a debt of gratitude for answering questions or lending their expertise include Elizabeth A. R. Brown, Anne Lester, and Walter Simons.

We thank our students who have, at various stages, read the manuscript in production. Sean Field thanks the members of his History 103 class at the University of Vermont for giving a draft of the translation its first trial run in spring 2020; Cecilia Gaposchkin thanks Valentina Jaramillo as well as the students of History 3.01 at Dartmouth College in fall 2020 for the same. Even a plague year has its rewards.

Cecilia Gaposchkin thanks her uncle and aunt, Bernard and Christine Myers, for walking the walls of Philip Augustus in Paris with her in 2017.

Finally, the editors would like to thank the translator for generously sharing his energy and expertise. The translator in turn would like to thank the editors for having the vision to perceive the need for this project and the courage to accomplish it. He dedicates his translation *Tamarae, animae meae.*

Abbreviations

Baldwin, *GPA*   John W. Baldwin, *The Government of Philip Augustus:*
Foundations of French Royal Power in the Middle Ages
(Berkeley: University of California Press, 1986)

Baldwin, *KLL*   John W. Baldwin, *Knights, Lords, and Ladies: In Search*
of Aristocrats in the Paris Region, 1180–1220, foreword
by William Chester Jordan (Philadelphia: University of
Pennsylvania Press, 2019)

BAV   Vatican City, Biblioteca Apostolica Vaticana

BL   London, British Library

BnF   Paris, Bibliothèque nationale de France

HPA   Rigord, *Histoire de Philippe Auguste,* ed. and trans. Élisabeth
Carpentier, Georges Pon, and Yves Chauvin (Paris: CNRS
Éditions, 2006)

Œuvres   Henri-François Delaborde, ed., *Œuvres de Rigord et de*
Guillaume le Breton, historiens de Philippe-Auguste, 2 vols.
(Paris: Renouard, 1882–85)

RHGF   Martin Bouquet et al., eds., *Recueil des historiens des Gaules*
et de la France, 24 vols. (Paris, 1738–1876)

CAST OF CHARACTERS

The Capetians

Louis VII of France (b. 1120, r. 1137–80).

[1] married **Eleanor of Aquitaine** (ca. 1124–1204) in 1137; divorced 1152.

Daughters **Marie of France** (1145–98, m. **Henry I of Champagne**) and **Alix of France** (1150–98, m. **Thibaut V of Blois**).

[2] married **Constance of Castile** (ca. 1136–60) in 1154.

Daughters **Marguerite of France** (1158–97, m. **Henry the Young King of England** in 1160, m. **King Bela III of Hungary** in 1186) and **Alix of France** (1160–1220, betrothed to **Richard I** in 1169, m. **William IV of Ponthieu** in 1195/6).

[3] married **Adele of Champagne** (ca. 1145–1206) in 1160.

Son **King Philip II** (b. 1165, r. 1180–1223).

Philip II "Augustus" of France (b. 1165, r. 1180–1223).

[1] married **Isabelle of Hainaut** (1170–90) in 1180.

Son **Louis VIII** (1187–1226, r. 1223–26), m. **Blanche of Castile** (1188–1252) in 1200.

[2] married **Ingeborg of Denmark** (1174–1237) in 1193.

[3] married **Agnes of Méran** (ca. 1175–1201) in 1196.

Daughter **Marie** (1198–1224, betrothed to **Arthur of Brittany**, m. **Philip of Namur** in 1211, m. **Henry I of Brabant** in 1213). Son **Philip Hurepel** (1200–1235, m. Mathilde II of Boulogne in 1223).

Daughter **Agnes of France** (1171–after 1204, m. **Emperor Alexius II Comnenus** in 1180).

The Plantagenets

Henry II of England (b. 1133, r. 1154–89), married Eleanor of
Aquitaine (ca. 1124–1204) in 1152. Sons William (1153–56); Henry
the Young King (1155–83, m. Marguerite of France in 1160, co-
crowned in 1170); Richard (1157–99, r. 1189–99, m. Berengaria
of Navarre in 1191); Geoffrey, Count of Brittany (1158–86, m.
Constance of Brittany in 1181, son Arthur); John (1166–1216,
r. 1199–1216, m. Isabella of Gloucester in 1189, m. Isabelle of
Angoulême in 1200, son King Henry III).

The House of Blois-Champagne (siblings)

Henry I "the Liberal," Count of Champagne (b. 1127, r. 1152–81).
Married Marie of France (1145–98) in 1165 (betrothed since 1159).
Sons Henry II, Count of Champagne (1166–97, r. 1181–97, m. Isabelle
of Jerusalem in 1192), and Thibaut III, Count of Champagne
(1179–1201, r. 1198–1201, m. Blanche of Navarre in 1199); daughters
Marie (1171–1204, m. Baldwin VI of Hainaut in 1186) and
Scholastique (1172/3–1221, m. William V, Count of Mâcon, in 1184).
Thibaut V, Count of Blois (r. 1152–91), Seneschal of France in 1164,
m. Alix of France (1150–98) in 1164. Son Louis I, Count of Blois
(r. 1191–1205).
Stephen, Count of Sancerre (1133–91, r. 1152–91).
William "of the White Hands" (1135–1202), bishop-elect of Chartres
(1165–68), archbishop of Sens (1168–75), archbishop of Reims
(1176–1202), named cardinal and papal legate in 1179.
Adele (ca. 1145–1206), m. Louis VII of France in 1160. Son Philip II of
France.

The House of Flanders (siblings)

Philip of Alsace, Count of Flanders (1143–91, r. 1168–91), m. Elizabeth
of Vermandois (1143–82) in 1159 (no heirs).
Marguerite, Countess of Flanders (ca. 1145–95, r. 1191–95), m. Ralph II
of Vermandois in 1160, m. Count Baldwin V of Hainault in 1169.
Daughter Isabelle of Hainaut married King Philip II in 1180; sons
Baldwin VI, Count of Hainaut (r. 1195–1205), Count of Flanders
(r. 1195–1205), and Emperor of Constantinople (r. 1204–5), m. Marie
of Champagne (sister of Henry II of Champagne) in 1186; Philip I of
Namur, m. Marie, daughter of King Philip II and Agnes of Méran, in 1211.

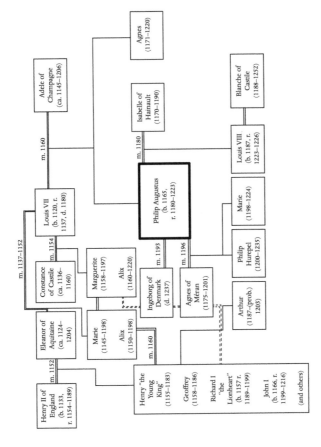

FIGURE 1. Genealogy of the French and English royal houses

CHRONOLOGY

25 July 1137	Marriage of Louis VII and Eleanor of Aquitaine
1 August 1137	Death of Louis VI
21 March 1152	Annulment of marriage between Louis VII and Eleanor of Aquitaine
18 May 1152	Eleanor marries future Henry II of England
Fall 1154	Louis VII marries Constance of Castile
19 December 1154	Henry II crowned king of England
4 October 1160	Death of Constance of Castile
12 October 1160	Maurice of Sully elected bishop of Paris
2 November 1160	Marriage of Marguerite of France and Henry the Young King of England
13 November 1160	Marriage of Louis VII and Adele of Champagne
Sept. / Oct. 1164	Marriage of Alix of France and Thibaut V of Blois
November 1164	Thomas Becket arrives in France
21 August 1165	Birth of Philip II
14 June 1170	Henry the Young co-crowned as king of England
29 December 1170	Assassination of Thomas Becket
8 August 1176	William of the White Hands elected archbishop of Reims
1 November 1179	Coronation of Philip II
28 April 1180	Marriage of Philip II and Isabelle of Hainaut
29 May 1180	Coronation of Isabelle of Hainaut
18 September 1180	Death of Louis VII

14 February 1181	Expulsion order for all Jews of the royal domain
1183	Philip II undertakes urban development projects in Paris
11 June 1183	Death of Henry the Young King of England
May 1186	Hugh Foucaud elected abbot of Saint-Denis
19 August 1186	Death of Geoffrey, count of Brittany
Fall 1186	Marriage of Marguerite of France to Bela III of Hungary
4 July 1187	Saladin victorious over Frankish forces at Battle of Hattin
10 July 1187	Saladin captures Acre from the Franks
5 September 1187	Birth of Louis VIII
2 October 1187	Saladin takes Jerusalem
19 October 1187	Pope Gregory VIII calls the Third Crusade
19 December 1187	Clement III elected pope (through 1191)
21 January 1188	Philip II and Henry II take the cross near Gisors
March 1188	Philip II issues the Saladin tithe in France
10 February 1189	Rigord at Argenteuil
6 July 1189	Death of Henry II
3 September 1189	Coronation of Richard I
1190	Philip II begins construction of the walls around Paris
15 March 1190	Death of Queen Isabelle of Hainaut
10 June 1190	Death of Emperor Frederick I
24 June 1190	Philip II at Saint-Denis for blessing before crusade
5 July 1190	Philip II and Richard I reach Vézelay
16 September 1190	Philip II arrives in Sicily
30 March 1191	Celestine III becomes pope (through 1198)
20 April 1191	Philip II arrives in Acre
12 May 1191	Marriage of Richard I to Berengaria of Navarre
8 June 1191	Richard I arrives in Acre
12 July 1191	Acre falls to crusading armies
31 July 1191	Philip II sails from Acre
December 1191	Philip II returns to France

March 1192	Philip II orders burning of Jews at Brie
9 October 1192	Richard I sails from Acre
December 1192	Richard I in custody of Emperor Henry VI
4 March 1193	Death of Saladin
14 August 1193	Marriage of Philip II to Ingeborg of Denmark
15 August 1193	Ingeborg's coronation; Philip II seeks to annul his marriage
5 November 1193	Council of Compiègne annuls Philip II's marriage to Ingeborg
February 1194	Richard I released from captivity
March 1194	Richard I reaches England
3 July 1194	Richard I defeats Philip II at Battle of Fréteval, captures baggage train
13 March 1195	Celestine III overturns decision of Council of Compiègne
June 1196	Marriage of Philip II to Agnes of Méran
11 September 1196	Death of Maurice of Sully, bishop of Paris
October 1197	Hugh of Milan elected abbot of Saint Denis
28 September 1197	Death of Emperor Henry VI
8 January 1198	Innocent III elected pope (through 1216)
11 March 1198	Death of Marie of France, countess of Champagne
July 1198	Philip II readmits Jews to the kingdom
15 August 1198	Innocent III calls the Fourth Crusade
26 March 1199	King Richard I wounded
6 April 1199	Death of King Richard I
27 May 1199	Coronation of King John
Jan.–Sept. 1200	France under interdict
11 May 1200	Treaty of Le Goulet between Philip II and King John
22 May 1200	Marriage of Prince Louis to Blanche of Castile
24 August 1200	Marriage of King John to Isabelle of Angoulême
May/June 1201	King John in Paris and at Saint-Denis
18/19 July 1201	Death of Agnes of Méran

2 November 1201	Innocent III legitimates Philip II's two children with Agnes of Méran
28 April 1202	King John condemned by French royal court; Philip II begins conquest of Normandy
1 August 1202	King John captures his nephew Arthur, who is never seen again
7 September 1202	Death of William of the White Hands
6 March 1204	Philip II takes Château Gaillard as part of conquest of Normandy
8 April 1204	Fourth Crusade captures Constantinople
24 June 1204	Philip II takes Rouen, effectively completing conquest of Normandy
1205	Philip II gives relics sent from Constantinople to Saint-Denis
4 June 1206	Death of Queen Adele
27 July 1214	Philip II's victory over English, Flemish, and German forces at Bouvines
14 July 1223	Death of Philip II

Introduction

Rigord's *Deeds of Philip Augustus* (*Gesta Philippi Augusti*) is the most important narrative source for the first twenty-five years of the reign of King Philip II of France (r. 1180–1223), and provides a vivid window onto many aspects of the late twelfth and early thirteenth centuries. The reign of Philip II "Augustus" is generally regarded as the pivotal period during which the power of the Capetian kings made its definitive leap forward.[1] Rigord, in turn, is often the best, and sometimes the only, French source for events in the first two-thirds of that period, including Philip's decisive triumph over his English rival, King John (r. 1199–1216), between 1202 and 1204. And if Philip II's reign transformed French royal power, it was Rigord who transformed contemporary writing about the nature of that power.

Philip II's reign occurred within the context of a rapidly expanding European society. The twelfth century witnessed remarkable growth in trade, urbanization, population, and the economy,[2] alongside an intellectual and

---

1. For historiography, see Sean L. Field and M. Cecilia Gaposchkin, "Questioning the Capetians, 1180–1328," *History Compass* 12 (2014): 567–85.

2. The classic overview is R. W. Southern, *The Making of the Middle Ages* (New Haven: Yale University Press, 1953). A good update is Thomas F. X. Noble and John Van Engen, eds., *European Transformations: The Long Twelfth Century* (Notre Dame: University of Notre Dame Press, 2012).

cultural flowering sometimes referred to as the twelfth-century Renaissance.[3] The success of the First Crusade and the capture of Jerusalem in 1099 gave western Europe's knightly class an aggressive swagger, the papacy's great reforming campaign (the "Gregorian Reforms") produced an ever more ambitious church hierarchy, and secular governments gained in power and sophistication.[4] Growing literacy, new opportunities in secular and ecclesiastical government, and pure intellectual curiosity drove the growth of cathedral schools and resulted, by century's end, in the emergence of the first universities at Paris and Bologna.[5] In 1100 the German emperors were still the most powerful political figures on the European landscape, but by 1200 the long battles of Emperor Frederick I "Barbarossa" (r. 1152–89) with Pope Alexander III (r. 1159–81) and his successors had diminished real imperial authority, just as the French and English monarchies were coming into their own. Ever since William, duke of Normandy, conquered the kingdom of England in 1066, the political fortunes of England and France had been intertwined.[6] The French kings of the Capetian dynasty were relatively weak in the early twelfth century, only gradually asserting real control over a small area (the Île-de-France) around Paris and Orléans during the reign of Louis VI (r. 1108–37).[7] England suffered a period of civil war ("Stephen's Anarchy") following the death of King Henry I in 1135, but through most of the middle decades of the century Henry II, king of England (r. 1154–89) as well as duke of Normandy, count of Anjou and Maine, duke of Aquitaine, and lord of Ireland, was far more powerful than the French king Louis VII (r. 1137–80).[8] When Rigord's account begins at the end of Louis's reign, the French monarchy was certainly the weaker of the two powers. By the end of Rigord's narrative, Philip II had emerged as one of the most important figures in Europe.

---

3. The classic treatment is Charles Homer Haskins, *The Renaissance of the Twelfth Century*, (Cambridge, MA: Harvard University Press, 1927); more recently, see Christopher Brooke, *The Twelfth-Century Renaissance* (New York: Harcourt, Brace & World, 1969); and R. N. Swanson, *The Twelfth-Century Renaissance* (Manchester: Manchester University Press, 1999).

4. Robert Bartlett, *The Making of Europe: Conquest, Colonization, and Cultural Change, 950–1350* (Princeton: Princeton University Press, 1993); R. I. Moore, *The First European Revolution* (Oxford: Blackwell, 2000).

5. John W. Baldwin, *The Scholastic Culture of the Middle Ages, 1000–1300* (Lexington, MA: Heath, 1971); Ian P. Wei, *Intellectual Culture in Medieval Paris: Theologians and the University, c. 1100–1330* (Cambridge: Cambridge University Press, 2012).

6. M. T. Clanchy, *England and Its Rulers 1066–1307*, 4th ed. (Malden, MA: Wiley, 2014).

7. Elizabeth M. Hallam and Charles West, *Capetian France, 987–1328*, 3rd ed. (New York: Routledge, 2020); Dominique Barthélemy, *Nouvelle histoire des Capétiens, 987–1214* (Paris: Seuil, 2012); Jean-Christophe Cassard, *L'âge d'or capétien, 1180–1328* (Paris: Belin, 2011).

8. Martin Aurell, *The Plantagenet Empire, 1154–1224*, trans. David Crouch (London: Longman, 2007).

The introduction that follows here summarizes the main events of Philip II's reign, details what we know of Rigord's career, offers context for the writing of royal history at Saint-Denis, assesses the main themes and interest of the *Deeds*, and concludes with a note on manuscripts, previous editions and translations, and our own translation policies.

The Life and Reign of Philip II

A famous manuscript illumination made at Saint-Denis in the 1270s illustrates Philip II's first nickname: "Given by God" (*Deodonatus*).[9] In this image (see figure 2) the Lord hands the already-crowned and scepter-wielding Philip down to King Louis VII and his third wife, Adele of Champagne (d. 1206), while the lords, ladies, and clergy of France look on approvingly, their hands held in prayer in such a manner that one might almost think them to be applauding.

French subjects must have been relieved when Louis VII had finally fathered a son. Since the beginnings of the Capetian dynasty with the coronation of Hugh Capet in 987, long-lived kings had crowned their sons during their lifetimes and passed on the throne without contest. In 1137, just before the death of his own father (Louis VI), Louis VII married Eleanor, heir to the duchy of Aquitaine. Prospects for the new royal couple looked bright: Louis VI's thirty-year reign had brought most of the rebellious castellans in the Île-de-France to heel, and now with Aquitaine in his grasp, Louis VII appeared poised to expand royal power and eclipse English preeminence. Moreover, Louis's leadership on the Second Crusade (1147–49) seemed to bode well for Capetian prestige.[10] But the crusade was an embarrassing failure, and—worse yet—the king's marriage to Eleanor produced only daughters: Marie in 1145 (who would marry Henry I of Champagne) and Alix in 1150 (who would marry Henry's brother Thibaut V of Blois). When in 1252 Louis and Eleanor wanted to separate, pliant French churchmen annulled the marriage on the grounds of consanguinity (being too closely related). Much to Louis's chagrin, Eleanor promptly married Henry of Anjou, who

---

9. A chronological narrative of Philip's reign can be traced in the "narrative" sections that begin each "part" of Baldwin, *GPA*. A readable but less authoritative synthesis is Jim Bradbury, *Philip Augustus: King of France, 1180–1223* (London: Longman, 1998). In French, see the concise recent treatments in Bruno Galland, *Philippe Auguste: Le bâtisseur du royaume* (Paris: Belin, 2014), and Jean Flori, *Philippe Auguste: La naissance de l'État monarchique* (Paris: Tallandier, 2007), as well the classic essay collection edited by Robert-Henri Bautier, *La France de Philippe Auguste: Le temps des mutations* (Paris: Éditions du CNRS, 1982), updated by Martin Aurell and Yves Sassier, eds., *Autour de Philippe Auguste* (Paris: Classiques Garnier, 2017). Alexander Cartellieri, *Philipp II. August, König von Frankreich*, 4 vols. (Leipzig: Dyksche, 1899–1922) is a detailed compilation of the evidence from contemporary chroniclers.

10. Michael L. Bardot and Laurence W. Marvin, eds., *Louis VII and His World* (Leiden: Brill, 2018).

FIGURE 2. Philip II being given by God to Louis VII and Adele of Champagne. Paris, Bibliothèque Sainte-Geneviève, MS 782, fol. 208r. Reproduced by permission of the Bibliothèque Sainte-Geneviève.

in 1154 became King Henry II of England. Louis in turn married Constance of Castile, but in the six years before her death, again only daughters were born: Marguerite in 1158 (who would marry Henry "the Young King," the son of Eleanor and Henry II; and then Bela III of Hungary), and another Alix in 1160 (long engaged to the future Richard I of England, she eventually married William IV of Ponthieu). When Philip was finally born in 1165, five years into King Louis's third marriage to Adele of Champagne, it really must have seemed as though God had at last seen fit to grant the king's prayers (it may also have seemed as though divine illumination was necessary to keep straight the relationships between all of Philip's half- and step-siblings; readers may consult the Cast of Characters and Genealogy).

During the fourteen years between Philip's birth (1165) and coronation (1179), his father generally seemed overmatched by his great rival Henry II, king of England as well as overlord of Ireland and much of western France, including Aquitaine by his marriage. Henry theoretically owed homage (i.e., pledged service and loyalty) to Louis VII for his "French" lands. Yet, in reality Henry was more powerful than his putative overlord, the French king. Louis did, however, play his cards adeptly, for instance by granting refuge to Henry's rebellious archbishop of Canterbury Thomas Becket in 1164, and nurturing the resentments of Henry "the Young King," crowned as co-king of England by Henry II in 1170 but increasingly resentful about his lack of real authority.[11]

Philip II was likewise crowned before the death of his father, on 1 November 1179, at Reims, by Archbishop William "of the White Hands," the brother of Queen Adele and thus Philip's uncle. Henry the Young King of England and his brothers Richard (count of Poitou) and Geoffrey (count of Brittany) attended the coronation, as did Count Philip of Flanders and Count Baldwin of Hainaut. This northern block (Flanders-Hainaut) would be largely ascendant as powerful counselors to the young Philip II, following his marriage to Isabelle of Hainaut (28 April 1180) and the death of Louis VII (18 September 1180). Their main rivals for influence at court were the siblings of Champagne: the queen mother Adele, Archbishop William, Count Henry I of Champagne (married to Marie of France), Count Thibaut V of Blois (married to Alix of France), and Count Stephen of Sancerre.[12]

The first decade of Philip's reign was characterized by his assault on the Jews and his struggles with Henry II. French Jews had participated in the twelfth century's rising prosperity, establishing or expanding communities in northern France while thriving particularly in Paris.[13] But in Philip II's generation a Christian backlash was epitomized by the "blood libel," the utterly spurious claim that Jews ritually murdered Christian babies. Following its emergence in England after 1144, by the 1170s the ritual murder accusation was deployed in France by Philip's brother-in-law Count Thibaut V of Blois, and then by Philip himself.[14] The Jews of the Capetian royal domain

---

11. Matthew Strickland, *Henry the Young King, 1155–1183* (New Haven: Yale University Press, 2016).

12. Theodore Evergates, *Henry the Liberal Count of Champagne, 1127–1181* (Philadelphia: University of Pennsylvania Press, 2016); Evergates, *Marie of France, Countess of Champagne, 1145–1198* (Philadelphia: University of Pennsylvania Press, 2019).

13. Robert Chazan, *The Jews of Medieval Western Christendom, 1000–1500* (Cambridge: Cambridge University Press, 2007); Chazan, *Reassessing Jewish Life in Medieval Europe* (Cambridge: Cambridge University Press, 2010).

14. E. M. Rose, *The Murder of William of Norwich: The Origins of the Blood Libel in Medieval Europe* (Oxford: Oxford University Press, 2015).

(essentially the Île-de-France) were arrested in (probably) 1181 and expelled in 1182, and their properties and a portion of their outstanding loans were absorbed into the royal treasury.[15]

If many French churchmen, like Rigord, must have regarded this "defense" of the realm by the most Christian king as a "success," Philip's military fortunes during this phase of his reign were far more mixed. After the death of Henry the Young King, in 1183, Philip continued to support the rebellions of Henry II's sons Richard and Geoffrey (the latter died in 1186). Philip gained the upper hand only in the last days of Henry II's life, in July 1189, when not only Richard but even his youngest brother, John, challenged the ailing old king. Yet any satisfaction Philip might have felt was short-lived, since Richard I "the Lionheart" proved every bit as skillful as his father in fending off French aggression.[16]

Richard took the cross as early as 1187, and Philip II pledged to go on crusade in 1188. The situation in the Holy Land was urgent. The Islamic sultan An-Nasir Salah ad-Din Yusuf ibn Ayyub, known in the West as Saladin, had annihilated the Frankish army at the Battle of Hattin and retaken the Latin Kingdom of Jerusalem in 1187. Neither Richard nor Philip would leave their lands unguarded to crusade in the East as long as the other remained behind, so the two kings negotiated a joint plan of departure. They sailed (separately) in the summer of 1190, with Philip entrusting the kingdom to his mother, Adele, and her brother Archbishop William as regents. His wife, Isabelle, had given him a son, the future Louis VIII, in 1187. But with Isabelle's death in March 1190, the royal succession was less than secure.

Philip wintered in Sicily and then arrived at Acre, in the Holy Land, on 20 April 1191, assuming leadership of the siege of the port city.[17] Richard, having stopped to attack Cyprus, arrived in June and quickly outshone Philip in wealth and military prowess. Both kings fell ill, but even so by 12 July Acre was taken. Philip declared victory and set off for home, departing by the end of the month. Prince Louis had been dangerously ill back in France, and the deaths of Count Philip of Flanders as well as the three brothers Henry of Champagne, Thibaut of Blois, and Stephen of Sancerre opened up challenges and opportunities for the king; Philip had

---

15. William Chester Jordan, *The French Monarchy and the Jews: From Philip Augustus to the Last Capetians* (Philadelphia: University of Pennsylvania Press, 1989).

16. Reliable biographies include Wilfred L. Warren, *Henry II* (Berkeley: University of California Press, 1973); John Gillingham, *Richard I* (London: Longman, 1999); and Ralph V. Turner, *King John* (London: Longman, 1994).

17. John D. Hosler, *The Siege of Acre, 1189–1191: Saladin, Richard the Lionheart, and the Battle That Decided the Third Crusade* (New Haven: Yale University Press, 2018).

had his fill of crusading. After sailing to Italy and proceeding overland, the king entered Paris, to much rejoicing, in December 1191. Meanwhile, Richard stayed in the Holy Land through October 1192, securing a series of military victories and security gains for the Kingdom of Jerusalem. On his return home, however, he was captured by Duke Leopold V of Austria, who nursed a grudge against Richard. Leopold had assumed leadership of the German forces at Acre (following the death of Frederick of Swabia), but was denied a share of the spoils upon the taking of the city, and, to make matters worse, was insulted when his battle standard was thrown to the ground, supposedly at Richard's command. Leopold now gained his revenge by turning Richard over to the German emperor Henry VI, who held him for ransom. Philip II, for his part, did everything possible to prolong Richard's captivity.

With only a single, rather sickly male heir, Philip sought a second wife. He chose Ingeborg, the sister of King Cnut VI of Denmark,[18] but set eyes on her only just before they married on 14 August 1193. The next day, Philip announced his intention of annulling the marriage. The true reasons for Philip's change of heart remain a matter of debate. The great modern historian of Philip's reign, John Baldwin, assessed simply that Philip's "reasons must have been personal and sexual, however, because he steadfastly refused to see her for seven years."[19] Philip's public claim was that he had suddenly realized he was too closely related to his new bride (the Church before 1215 insisted that a man and a woman who shared a common ancestor going back seven generations were forbidden to marry). A French church council, led by Archbishop William of the White Hands, obligingly supported this fiction. Ingeborg, in turn, fought the annulment for decades, eventually with the help of the dynamic new pope Innocent III (r. 1198–1215), who placed France under interdict (that is, a prohibition and cessation of all sacraments in the region) for much of the year 1200.[20] Philip meanwhile took a new wife (or "concubine" in the eyes of the papacy), Agnes of Méran, who bore him two children before dying in 1201.

Across the 1190s Philip's battles with King Richard seesawed, with fighting often centered on the Vexin, the borderlands between Normandy and the royal domain in the Île-de-France.[21] Philip sought alliances with Richard's

---

18. George Conklin, "Ingeborg of Denmark, Queen of France 1193–1223," in *Queens and Queenship in Medieval Europe*, ed. Anne Duggan (Woodbridge: Boydell, 1997), 39–52.

19. Baldwin, *GPA*, 83.

20. John W. Baldwin, *Paris, 1200* (Stanford: Stanford University Press, 2010).

21. For an assessment of Philip as a military leader, see Sean McGlynn, "Fighting the Image of the Reluctant Warrior: Philip Augustus as Rex-Not-Quite-So-Bellicosus," in *The Image and Perception*

younger brother John, but as long as Richard lived, the French king made no real headway against his rival. The sudden shift in French fortunes began with Richard's chance death, when shot by a crossbowman while besieging Châlus-Chabrol in April 1199. Richard was succeeded by his brother, the infamous King John ("Lackland"), who was a far less capable leader. He briefly made peace with Philip, sealed by a marriage between his niece Blanche of Castile and Prince Louis (the future Louis VIII).[22] John's undoing was his own impetuous marriage to Isabelle of Angoulême in 1200.[23] This young heiress was already betrothed to Hugh of Lusignan, count of La Marche. By swooping her up, John had denied Hugh the lands and inheritance his marriage would have entailed. John declined to make restitution, and Hugh sought justice from King Philip, who, as John's overlord, had the right to summon his vassal to his court to account for himself. John refused the summons, claiming that as king of England he was not required to appear. Philip (and Hugh) replied that he was being summoned not as king, but as duke of Aquitaine, the title by which he was both the count of La Marche's lord and the king of France's vassal. On 28 April 1202 the royal court judged John to have forfeited all his French lands by virtue of his failure to appear before his overlord, Philip of France.

This judgment would have been meaningless, if the king of France had been unable to enforce it militarily. Philip first tried supporting the claims of John's nephew, Arthur (the son of Geoffrey, late count of Brittany). But John captured Arthur, who was never seen again. Rumor at the time, very possibly correct, accused John of his nephew's murder. One after another, important French barons withdrew their loyalty from John and came over to the French cause. Philip invaded Normandy, and in December 1203 John retreated to England. In March 1204 the crucial Château Gaillard, guarding the Seine at the Norman border, fell to Philip, and by June John's remaining Norman strongholds, including Rouen, had surrendered. Philip's conquest of Normandy, the ancestral heart of the Anglo-Norman territories, was complete. By 1206 John's lands everywhere north of the Loire, including Maine and most of Anjou, had fallen. Henry II's great "Angevin Empire" had crumbled almost overnight.

of *Monarchy in Medieval and Early Modern Europe*, ed. Sean McGlynn and Elena Woodacre (Cambridge: Cambridge Scholars Publisher, 2014), 148–67.

22. Lindy Grant, *Blanche of Castile* (New Haven: Yale University Press, 2016); Catherine Hanley, *Louis: The French Prince Who Invaded England* (New Haven: Yale University Press, 2016).

23. William Chester Jordan, "Isabelle d'Angoulême, by the Grace of God Queen," *Revue belge de philologie et d'histoire* 69 (1991): 821–52.

Between 1206 (when Rigord finished writing) and 1214, John plotted revenge, building up alliances while raising funds and troops. The plan was
a joint military venture with Otto of Brunswick, claimant to the German
imperial throne; Otto would advance toward Paris from the east, while John
would land in Aquitaine and move in from the west. Philip briefly hoped to
launch a preemptive attack on England, to be led by Prince Louis. But the
French fleet was so severely damaged by a surprise attack at Damme (in Flanders) that the planned invasion was no longer feasible. Although Philip was
on the defensive, he proved capable of fending off this two-pronged attack.
John arrived in La Rochelle in February, and Prince Louis was sent south
to meet him. After several skirmishes, John retreated (as he so often did).
The decisive battle then took place in the north, at Bouvines, on Sunday, 27
July 1214.[24] In one of the rare examples of a true winner-take-all confronta-
tion between medieval monarchs, the forces of Philip Augustus decisively
routed those of Otto of Brunswick. Otto fled. Philip had lived up to the nickname "Augustus" that Rigord had first bestowed upon him twenty-five years
earlier. The Capetian fleur-de-lis had triumphed over the imperial eagle.

In these same years, between the Third Crusade and the Battle of Bouvines,
French royal government made rapid progress in its organizational sophistication. Philip had inherited from his father and grandfather a fairly rudimen-
tary system of royal officials, known as *prévôts*, who operated on the ground
as local tax collectors and dispensers of justice. By the time of the royal ordinance of 1190, issued before he departed on crusade to define the governing
of the kingdom in the king's absence, a higher level of regional officials,
called *baillis*, was implemented to oversee the *prévôts*. The *baillis* were to
report and account directly to the regents (Queen Adele and Archbishop William of the White Hands of Reims) in Paris. This moment began the steady
trend toward a more centralized system of accounting and accountability in
the nascent royal administration. Another innovation occurred when Philip
suffered a humiliating defeat against Richard at Fréteval in 1194 and lost the
royal documents that were part of his baggage train. From this time on, a
centralized royal archive, eventually known as the Trésor des Chartes, took
shape in Paris, allowing royal officials to search among earlier charters and
acts when they needed to establish royal rights and precedents. Beginning in
1204, following the seizure of Normandy, the royal court began to keep track
of outgoing correspondence, charters, and other miscellaneous documents

---

24. John W. Baldwin and Walter Simons, "The Consequences of Bouvines," *French Historical Studies* 37 (2014): 243–69; Dominique Barthelemy, *La bataille de Bouvines: Histoire et légendes* (Paris: Perrin, 2018).

in a series of registers. All in all, between the first written protoconstitu-tion of 1190, the emergence of a true bureaucracy (*baillis* and *prévôts*), and regular fiscal and legal record keeping at Paris, Philip's reign inaugurated effective royal government in France. Indeed, the highly centralized French government of the twenty-first century has its roots in innovations instituted between 1190 and 1204.[25]

Philip II declined to participate in the Fourth Crusade, which resulted in the capture of Constantinople in 1204.[26] Nor did he join in the Albigensian Crusade, beginning in 1209, for which Innocent III empowered northern French knights to invade Toulouse and the Languedoc, supposedly hotbeds of heresy.[27] Prince Louis, however, led several expeditions south as part of this crusade, and ultimately provided the royal might necessary to bring the conflict to a close. But this was after the death of his father. Philip II passed away on 14 July 1223, leaving a kingdom and capital far more powerful and prosperous (and, for the moment, peaceful) than the one he had inherited in 1180. The sour fruit of this new power was the persecution of perceived enemies—Jews and "heretics."[28] The reward was a nearly unbroken advance of royal authority under his direct descendants Louis VIII (r. 1223–26), Louis IX (r. 1226–70), Philip III (r. 1270–85), and Philip IV (r. 1285–1314).[29]

Rigord and His Works

Rigord is our best witness to many of these events. Although over the years a number of different historical or hagiographic works have been credited to Rigord,[30] we can attribute only two securely: the *Deeds of Philip Augustus* and a short chronology of and guide to the kings of France. We actually know very little about Rigord, and what we do know comes mostly from his own writings.[31] In his entry for the year 1205 in the *Deeds* (see ch. 153) Rigord

25. Baldwin, *GPA*, ch. 15.

26. Donald E. Queller and Thomas F. Madden, *The Fourth Crusade: The Conquest of Constantinople*, 2nd ed., with an essay on primary sources by Alfred J. Andrea (Philadelphia: University of Pennsylvania Press, 1997).

27. Mark Gregory Pegg, *A Most Holy War: The Albigensian Crusade and the Battle for Christendom* (Oxford: Oxford University Press, 2008).

28. R. I. Moore, *The Formation of a Persecuting Society: Authority and Deviance in Western Europe 950–1250*, 2nd ed. (Malden, MA: Wiley-Blackwell, 2007).

29. William Chester Jordan and Jenna R. Phillips, eds., *The Capetian Century, 1214–1314* (Turnhout: Brepols, 2017).

30. On these false or dubious attributions, see Henri-François Delaborde, "Notice sur les ouvrages et sur la vie de Rigord, moine de Saint-Denis," *Bibliothèque de l'École des chartes* 45 (1884): 605–9.

31. The most substantial introductions to the life of Rigord are *Œuvres*, 1:xxvii-xxxiii; Delaborde, "Notice sur les ouvrages et sur la vie de Rigord," 584–614; and *HPA*, 51–67. See also Élisabeth

says that he is "now entering old age," suggesting that he was probably born around 1145 or 1150.[32] In the prologue, he tells us that he was a doctor (*professione physicus*) and that he came from what we would today call the South of France, apparently from somewhere around Alés or Uzès in the Languedoc.[33] Perhaps he studied at Montpellier, which had a renowned school of medicine.[34] It seems clear that he was in Paris by 1180, since his descriptions of events in the first years of Philip's reign (notably the arrest and expulsion of the Jews) appear to be based on personal observation. The reason for Rigord's move from the Languedoc northward to the Île-de-France is entirely opaque to us now.[35] Presumably he was earning his living as a doctor in Paris by the beginning of the 1180s—indeed one of Philip Augustus's physicians, Giles of Corbeil, seems to mock him as a not very successful medical practitioner.[36] In his prologue, Rigord further informs us that he began writing his *Deeds* amid the "press of business" and under difficult circumstances, lacking resources and even food. Since this does not sound like the life of a monk (in spite of their vows of poverty, Benedictine monks had ample food and the resources necessary for writing), it is generally assumed that he began his work before joining Saint-Denis, the eminent Benedictine abbey just north of Paris, which was both a center of historical writing and a burial place for kings. We do not know exactly why, how, or when he made this move. It was certainly before 1189 (when he tells us he was at Saint-Denis's priory of Argenteuil) and probably by 1186, to judge by his detailed description of the abbatial election of that year. But once at Saint-Denis, Rigord self-consciously took up the role of "historian of the king of the Franks" (*regis Francorum cronographus*), as he proudly states.

The *Deeds* appears to have been written in two stages, though the details are open to debate. The first stage probably included chapters 1–76, up to Philip's departure on crusade in 1190.[37] At this point Rigord added the pro-

Carpentier and Georges Pon, "Relecture de Rigord," in Aurell and Sassier, *Autour de Philippe Auguste*, 117–28; François-Oliver Touati, "Faut-il en rire? Le médecin Rigord, historien de Philippe Auguste," *Revue historique* 305 (2003): 243–65; and Gabrielle Spiegel, *The Chronicle Tradition of Saint-Denis: A Survey* (Brookline, MA: Classical Folia Editions, 1978), 56–63.

32. *Œuvres*, 1:xxx; *HPA*, 54.

33. Rigord says that he was *natione Gothus*, meaning from the lower Languedoc. Internal references suggest familiarity with local events in the towns of Uzès and Alès. *Œuvres*, 1:xxix. Further arguments made in *HPA*, 52.

34. See *HPA*, 54–57 for discussion.

35. See *HPA*, 57 for fuller discussion of the possibilities.

36. *HPA*, 54–55.

37. This is the argument of *HPA*, which we find largely persuasive. Delaborde preferred to see the first stage extending up to 1196. The break at ch. 76 seems convincing because of a number of changes that characterize the text at that point, including the discontinuing of chapter titles. It is

logue, in which he explained his coining of the epithet "Augustus" for the king. He bemoans early challenges, and says that at one point he considered suppressing the work,[38] which had taken him ten years to write. Urged on by his abbot Hugh, he nonetheless decided to offer it to King Philip, presumably upon the king's return from crusade at the end of 1191. Working backward, this evidence suggests that Rigord began writing as early as 1180/81, perhaps corresponding with the start of Philip's reign. Then, at some point between 1192 and 1196, he took up the project again.[39] The remaining chapters (chs. 77–156), extending through 1206, were themselves written in several stages, with the dedicatory letter to the future Louis VIII probably written toward the end of that period, perhaps as the young prince was preparing for his entry into knighthood.[40] There is no evidence that the king had paid his first version any heed at all; Rigord may now have been looking for an audience in the next generation. It is also notable that in this second section of the work Rigord is at times markedly cooler toward the king, particularly in his disapproval of Philip's attempts to annul his second marriage to Ingeborg of Denmark.[41] Rigord died on 17 November (according to the abbey's necrology), perhaps in 1207 and certainly by 1209.[42]

The *Deeds* was a major accomplishment, and has received praise as both a balanced account and an invaluable source for Philip's reign, from Rigord's time to our own. Evidently Rigord had access to both a good library and, importantly, certain royal documents. In fact, we owe to Rigord our knowledge of the documents Philip Augustus issued in preparation for his departure on the Third Crusade, including the so-called Saladin tithe (chs. 64–66) and his testament-ordinance of 1190 (ch. 77), copies of which may well have been deposited in Saint-Denis's archives (since official royal archives did not come into existence until after 1194).[43] Although not widely diffused in his own time, Rigord's text was evidently consulted by a number of thirteenth-century

---

also true that one of the two manuscripts of the text, BAV Reg. lat. 930, ends at exactly this point. But since that manuscript begins with the dedicatory letter to Prince Louis, which was clearly added to the second version of the text, the question of why a scribe ceased copying at this point remains a mystery.

38. This statement, however, is in the form of a quotation from Walter of Châtillon's *Alexandreis*, and so perhaps should not be taken literally.

39. One mystery is when, exactly, he would have added ch. 77, the crucial testament-ordinance for the government of the kingdom during the crusade.

40. *HPA*, 60–67. For the dating for the dedicatory letter, *HPA*, 67, although reviewing other possibilities.

41. Carpentier and Pon, "Relecture de Rigord."

42. *HPA*, 59.

43. "At some unspecified date sometime in the sixth or early seventh century, the court began to deposit copies of royal documents at Saint-Denis," according to Sumner McKnight Crosby, *The Royal*

historians outside of Saint-Denis.[44] His contemporary and co-historian, William le Breton, spoke of Rigord's "elegant style."[45] In our own era, Gabrielle Spiegel regards Rigord as one of the most important chroniclers of Saint-Denis's long tradition of royal historiography. Her assessment is worth repeating: "Careful in his collection of materials, exact in his reportage, unafraid to make judgments both critical and moral, he represents the developing historiographic tradition of Saint-Denis at its best. His clear-sighted, somewhat sober appraisal of the Capetian monarch does not prevent him from recognizing Philip's great merits nor from exercising his historical talents in praise of the king."[46]

In addition to the *Deeds of Philip Augustus*, Rigord also composed his short history of the reigns of the kings of France, a *cronica*, dedicated to his monastery's prior John and his fellow monks, and designed as a short guide to the kings' history and the placement of their tombs in the abbey.[47] The single surviving copy of this text begins with the mythic Trojan origins of the French,[48] and runs through the reign of Louis IV (d'Outremer, d. 954), although because the folios that followed are missing we cannot know how far Rigord's chronology originally extended. In the prologue (where he identifies himself only as "R") Rigord again calls himself *natione gothus professione phisicus, regis Francorum cronographus beati dyonisii artiopagite clericorum minimus,* (a Goth in origin, a doctor by calling, historian of the king of the Franks, the least of the clergy of the blessed Denis the Areopagite),[49] echoing exactly the language he used in the *Deeds*.[50] In this prefatory section, he further explains that the text, which will untangle and delineate the genealogy of the kings of France (*regum Francorum genealogiam*) and describe the most salient features of each reign, will also designate the placement of each king's tomb held within the

---

Abbey of Saint-Denis: From Its Beginnings to the Death of Suger, 475–1151 (New Haven: Yale University Press, 1987), 9.

44. *HPA*, 98–100.

45. *Œuvres*, 1:168.

46. Spiegel, *Chronicle Tradition*, 63.

47. Soissons, Bibliothèque municipale, MS 129, fols. 130r-137v. Spiegel, *Chronicle Tradition*, 62. The account, published by Delaborde, "Notice sur les ouvrages et sur la vie de Rigord," 600–604, survives in only this one manuscript, where it is unfinished. The subsequent pages have been removed from the manuscript. Because the prior is assumed to be a certain John, who was made abbot of Corbie in 1196, it is argued that Rigord composed the work before that date. *HPA*, 64.

48. On the Trojan origins of the French, see R. E. Asher, "Myth, Legend, and History in Renaissance France," *Studi Francesci* 13 (1969): 409–19; and Elizabeth A. R. Brown, "The Trojan Origins of the French: The Commencement of a Myth's Demise, 1450–1520," in *Medieval Europeans: Studies in Ethnic Identity and National Perspectives in Medieval Europe* (Houndmills, UK: Macmillan Press; New York: Saint Martin's Press, 1998), 135–79.

49. Soissons, Bibliothèque municipale, MS 129, fol. 130r.

50. Cf. *Œuvres*, 1:1.

monastery, indicating the growing interest at Saint-Denis in royal history and its association with the abbey as the burial place for kings. In addition to these two works and in accordance with their major goals, Rigord has been identified as the person who updated a royal genealogy found in Bibliothèque Mazarine MS 2013, a manuscript representing an early interest at Saint-Denis in historical compilation, sometime before 1200.[51] Finally, Rigord may have had a hand in pulling together another historical compilation in the years around 1200, which, as with Rigord's authored works, ultimately made its way into the Latin tradition at Saint-Denis.[52]

The Historiographical Tradition at Saint-Denis

Rigord's writings were an important brick in the edifice of an influential historiographical project carried out at the abbey of Saint-Denis, which has shaped our understanding of the Capetians and the history of medieval France in general. By the end of the thirteenth century, the monks of Saint-Denis had become the quasi-official historians of the kings of France, a role they would play consistently through to the fifteenth century and beyond. Rigord and his *Deeds of Philip Augustus* were integral to the early phase of this development, which had begun to take form about a half century before Rigord joined the abbey.[53]

The monastery of Saint-Denis was (and still is) located less than six miles north of the Île-de-la-Cité, the islet at the heart of Paris where the royal palace was located. The monastery was legendarily founded upon the relics of Saint Denis (Latin, Dionysius) and his two companions, probably atop some type of oratory established as early as the fourth century.[54] Denis was the evangelizing first bishop of Paris, who suffered martyrdom under either the Roman emperor Domitian in the first century or Decius in the third

---

51. See Elizabeth A. R. Brown, "The Children of Louis VI of France and Adelaïde de Maurienne," forthcoming in *Medieval People* (2021), summarizing the unpublished work of Marc du Pouget.

52. This is BAV, Reg. lat. 550, on which see *HPA*, 64; and Bernd Schneidmüller, "Ein Geschichtskompendium des frühen 13. Jahrhunderts aus Saint-Denis (Vat. Reg. lat. 550) als Vorläufer der Grandes Chroniques," *Quellen und Forschungen aus italienischen Archiven und Bibliotheken* 67 (1987): 447–61. Elizabeth A. R. Brown's forthcoming article "Charles the Bald, the Miraculous Translation of His Remains, and the Construction of the Past at Saint-Denis" claims Rigord's involvement. Materials from BAV, Reg. lat. 550 were ultimately copied into BnF MS lat. 5925, along with our single witness of the entirety of Rigord's *Deeds of Philip Augustus*.

53. For perspective, Élisabeth Carpentier, "Les historiens royaux et le pouvoir capétien: D'Helgaud de Fleury à Guillaume le Breton," in *L'historiographie médiévale en Europe*, ed. Jean-Philippe Genet (Paris: Presses du CNRS, 1991), 129–39.

54. The legend as received in the Middle Ages is provided succinctly in Crosby, *Royal Abbey of Saint-Denis*, 3; Spiegel, *Chronicle Tradition*, 51, 66n13.

FIGURE 3.   The west facade of Saint-Denis in 2020. Wikimedia Commons, photograph in the public domain.

(the sources differ).[55] The story as it later coalesced held that Denis and his two companions—Rusticus and Eleutherius—were beheaded together on the top of Montmartre (lit., the mountain of the martyrs), and that upon its severing, the bishop-saint picked up his head and walked north down the mountain to the point where he finally collapsed, on which spot an oratory was later founded. In the ninth century, Abbot Hilduin of Saint-Denis (d. ca. 855) conflated this Denis, the patron saint of the monastery, with two

---

55. Crosby, *Royal Abbey of Saint-Denis*, 3–4.

other figures bearing the name—the apostolic Dionysius, called the Areop-agite, who had been a convert of Saint Paul, and a later sixth-century author known as Pseudo-Dionysius—elevating the apostolic antiquity and prestige of the monastery's patron saint.[56]

The monastery's association with the Frankish kings began in the Merovingian period. Saint Denis, through this association and its careful management, slowly emerged as a favorite saint of the kings of France, and ultimately came to be considered the patron saint of the kings and the king-dom.[57] It was probably the Merovingian king Dagobert (r. 629–39) who was most responsible for establishing what would become a unique relationship between king, saint, and abbey.[58] Dagobert, who had made Paris his capital, granted the abbey the rights to run a fair as early as 635 or 636, gave new prominence to the relics of Denis, Rusticus, and Eleutherius, and funded an expansion of the early church.[59] Dagobert's father, Clothar II, had called De-nis his "special patron."[60] Clothar II, Dagobert, and Dagobert's son Clovis II were all buried in the basilica, establishing the precedent of royal burial that the abbey would later cultivate.[61]

From that point onward, Saint-Denis enjoyed the periodic favor of the Merovingian, Carolingian, and Capetian kings, intensifying and solidifying as kings increasingly settled in Paris. The abbey was the site of Pepin the Short's coronation in 754, establishing the important link with the Carolin-gians.[62] Charles the Bald (d. 877), who, in addition to being Charlemagne's grandson and emperor, was also the abbot of Saint-Denis, and who called Saint Denis "our most worthy patron" (pretiosissimus patronus noster), chose

56. Michael Lapidge, Hilduin of Saint-Denis, The Passio S. Dionysii in Prose and Verse (Leiden: Brill, 2017).

57. This history is synthesized in Gabrielle Spiegel, "The Cult of Saint Denis and Capetian King-ship," Journal of Medieval History 1 (1975): 43–69.

58. Laurent Theis, "Dagobert, Saint-Denis et la royauté française au Moyen Âge," in Le métier d'historien au Moyen Âge: Études sur l'historiographie médiévale, ed. Bernard Guenée (Paris: Publications de la Sorbonne, 1977), 19–30; Renee Lynn Goethe, "King Dagobert, the Saint, and Royal Salvation: The Shrine of Saint-Denis and Propaganda Production (850–1319 C.E.)" (PhD diss., University of Iowa, 2016).

59. Crosby, Royal Abbey of Saint-Denis, 13–50.

60. Crosby, Royal Abbey of Saint-Denis, 8.

61. Georgia Sommers Wright, "The Royal Tomb Program in the Reign of St. Louis," Art Bulletin 56 (1974): 224–43; Alain Erlande-Brandenburg, Le roi est mort: Étude sur les funérailles, les sépultures et les tombeaux des rois de France jusqu'à la fin du XIIIᵉ siècle (Geneva: Droz, 1975); Elizabeth A. R. Brown, "Burying and Unburying the Kings of France," in Persons in Groups: Social Behavior as Identity Formation in Medieval and Renaissance Europe: Papers of the Sixteenth Annual Conference of the Center for Medieval and Early Renaissance Studies, ed. Richard Trexler, Medieval and Renaissance Texts and Stud-ies (Binghamton, NY: Center for Medieval and Early Renaissance Studies, 1985), 241–66.

62. Crosby, Royal Abbey of Saint-Denis, 52.

to be buried there.[63] Charles the Bald purportedly gave the monastery a cache of relics, including a portion of the Crown of Thorns, a nail from the crucifixion, a fragment of the True Cross, and the arm of Saint Simeon, which Charlemagne had brought to Aachen from Jerusalem.[64] The monks in turn actively sought to cultivate royal favor, produced writings that indicated a special tie, and elevated their patron saint's role as a protector of the French kings and ultimately the French kingdom. In the ninth century, Hincmar of Reims (d. 882), who was educated at Saint-Denis, wrote a life of King Dagobert, the *Gesta Dagoberti*, that recounted the king's patronage and favor of the monastery and in turn its saint's favor and protection of those who honor him.[65] Hugh Capet, the first king of the Capetian dynasty, elected in 987, and his son Robert the Pious (r. 987–1031) both regularly showed favor to the monastery.[66] Louis VI spoke of the saint as the *dux et protector* of France.[67]

By the time of Philip Augustus, Saint-Denis was considered a royal abbey and enjoyed an increasingly important, even unique, relationship to the Crown.[68] The monks of Saint-Denis were the custodians of the regalia, which each new king would need for his coronation.[69] The monastery also bore custody of the so-called Oriflamme, purportedly Charlemagne's own battle standard, which the French kings were expected to claim from Denis, the saint, before leaving for battle—battles that Saint Denis would then aid in fighting. This singular relationship was especially evident during the abbacy of Suger (b. ca. 1090, abbot 1122–51), a childhood schoolmate of Louis VI, who later served as co-regent of the kingdom during Louis VII's absence on the Second Crusade between 1147 and 1149.[70] By the middle of the twelfth century, then, the abbey benefited from its special connection to the French

---

63. Rolf Grosse, "Reliques du Christ et foires de Saint-Denis au XIᵉ siècle," *Revue d'histoire de l'église de France* 87 (2001): 357–75, at 358.

64. This is the "Descriptio clavi et corone domini," which has an extremely complicated textual history, with several variants. The information presented here is digested from Grosse, "Reliques du Christ et foires de Saint-Denis," 358–67, and Jerzy Pysiak, *The King and the Crown of Thorns: Kingship and the Cult of Relics in Capetian France*, trans. Sylwia Twardo (Berlin: Peter Lang, 2021).

65. *Gesta domini Dagoberti regis Francorum*, ed. Bruno Krusch, MGH Scriptores rerum Merovingicarum (Hannover, 1888), 2:396–425.

66. Thomas G. Waldman, "Saint-Denis et les premiers Capétiens," in *Religion et culture autour de l'an Mil: Royaume capétien et Lotharingie*, ed. Dominique Iogna-Prat and Jean-Charles Picard (Paris: Picard, 1990), 191–97.

67. Crosby, *Royal Abbey of Saint-Denis*, 8.

68. For the development of the status and meaning of "royal abbey," see discussion in Crosby, *Royal Abbey of Saint-Denis*, 9–12.

69. Richard Cusimano and Erid Whitmore, eds., *Selected Works of Abbot Suger* (Washington DC: Catholic University of America Press, 2018), 223–26; Crosby, *Royal Abbey of Saint-Denis*, 10–11.

70. Suger's co-regent was Ralph I of Vermandois (d. 1152). Suger was appointed to represent the clergy while Ralph, Louis VI's cousin, was appointed to represent the nobility.

kings, who were settling the center of royal government ever more in Paris. In turn, the kings of France benefited from the variety of ways in which the monks of Saint-Denis, and the particular patronage of the saint himself, could legitimize, augment, and memorialize their deeds and growing authority.[71]

The monks of Saint-Denis took up the work of writing history in the middle of the twelfth century.[72] Certainly, like any self-respecting Benedictine monastery, they had long had a scriptorium and had produced authentic, original works before Rigord's time.[73] An important example is found in Hilduin's composition, in the ninth century, of the hagiographic life of Saint Denis, the monastery's patron, mentioned above.[74] The monks had also maintained the practice of recording brief annals since about the same time.[75] But at the start of the twelfth century, it was the monks at Saint-Benoit-de-Fleury, at Jumièges and Mont-Saint-Michel, at Saint-Germain-des-Prés, and in Rome, rather than those of Saint-Denis, who were producing the most original, informed, and up-to-date works of history.[76] Examples that would ultimately feed into the Dionysian historiographical tradition include the *Historia Francorum* (*History of the Franks*) of Aimon of Fleury (d. ca. 1010), written in the tenth century, and a continuation of that history written at Saint-Germain-des-Prés by a monk called Gislemar in the years around 1100.[77] Sometime around 1120 a number of these works were gathered together in a manuscript (now Bibliothèque Mazarine MS 2013) made at Saint-Denis.[78] Many of the works so gathered related to French royal history going back to the Carolingians and before, demonstrating early interest in collecting the materials pertaining to the history of the French kings. As noted above, Rigord himself seems later to have consulted and annotated the manuscript when working on his own material.[79]

---

71. Spiegel, "Saint Denis and Capetian Kingship."

72. For an overview of the historiography at Saint-Denis, see Spiegel, *Chronicle Tradition*, 39–72. Elizabeth A. R. Brown is revisiting the early stage of historiographical compilation and writing at Saint-Denis, particularly around the composition and history of Mazarine 2013. Some of her conclusions are included in Brown, "Children of Louis VI of France and Adelaïde de Maurienne."

73. Spiegel, *Chronicle Tradition*, 12n1.

74. Lapidge, *Hilduin of Saint-Denis*.

75. Élie Berger, "Annales de Saint-Denis, généralement connues sous le titre de Chronicon Sancti Dionysii ad cyclos paschales," *Bibliothèque de l'École des chartes* 40 (1879): 261–95.

76. Brown, "Children of Louis VI of France and Adelaïde de Maurienne."

77. Jean Dérens, "Gislemar, historien de Saint-Germain-des-Prés," *Journal des savants* (1972): 228–32.

78. This is the collection represented by Mazarine 2013, and its companion volume BnF MS lat. 12701 (which was probably copied from it at the abbey but not made for the monks of Saint-Denis).

79. *HPA*, 87. On Rigord's interest in this manuscript see Brown, "Children of Louis VI of France and Adelaïde de Maurienne," citing an unpublished thesis by Marc du Pouget.

It was probably the work and vision of the irrepressible abbot Suger that transformed Saint-Denis into a center of historiographical production in the middle years of the twelfth century. Suger, a major figure in the history of the abbey, undertook transformative building projects on the abbey church and has traditionally been associated with the development of the early Gothic style. He may have had a hand in the abbey's first attempt to compose a single, unified history of the Franks and its kings, the so-called *Abbreviatio*.[80] He was, in any event, the first at Saint-Denis to write an account of the life and reign of a single king. The *Life of Louis the Fat* (*Vita Ludovici Grossi*) recounted the deeds of his friend Louis VI. Suger also produced numerous writings on his own administration of the abbey and the building of the new basilica.[81] Finally, Suger started an account of Louis VI's son, Louis VII, but died before he had made much progress, and the unfinished account was eventually completed by an anonymous monk at Saint-Germain-des-Prés.[82] Shortly after Suger's death, one of his confreres, Odo of Deuil, authored an account of Louis VII's adventures on the Second Crusade, which he composed as a letter to Suger.[83] And another monk, William, wrote an account of Suger's own abbacy and regency shortly after the abbot's death in 1151.[84]

Rigord joined the abbey at the point where the monks were becoming increasingly interested in history writing. It was in this climate that his abbot encouraged him to continue work on the *Deeds*, which, as we saw, he took up through 1206. At Rigord's death around 1207, Philip Augustus was only forty-two years old, and still had sixteen years of his rule ahead of him. In fact, the most mature phase of his reign, and his most impressive accomplishment, the victory at Bouvines (1214), were still to come. It is for this reason that William le Breton (d. after 1226), a Breton cleric and scholar (*doctorus*) who had come to Paris and joined the royal court as tutor and sometimes envoy, undertook to complete the story of Philip's reign. William had been part of the king's inner circle (he was instructor to Philip's illegitimate son Pierre Charlot) and had accompanied the king on the campaign that culminated at

---

80. Also known as *Anthenor et alii*, edited as "Historia regum Francorum monasterii sancti Dionysii," ed. George Waitz, MGH Scriptores (Hannover, 1851) 9:395–406. Elizabeth A. R. Brown argues for Suger's involvement in this compilation.

81. Suger, *The Deeds of Louis the Fat*, ed. Richard Cusimano and John Moorhead (Washington, DC: Catholic University of America Press, 1992); Suger, *Abbot Suger on the Abbey Church of St.-Denis and Its Art Treasures*, ed. Erwin Panofsky, 2nd ed. by Gerda Panofsky-Soergel (Princeton: Princeton University Press, 1979); Cusimano and Whitmore, *Selected Works of Abbot Suger*.

82. Cusimano and Whitmore, *Selected Works of Abbot Suger*, 22.

83. Odo of Deuil, *De Profectione Ludovici VII in Orientem; The Journey of Louis VII to the East*, ed. and trans. Virginia Gingerick Berry (New York: Columbia University Press, 1948).

84. Cusimano and Whitmore, *Selected Works of Abbot Suger*, 24–29, 84–216.

Bouvines, which stood for him as the central glory of Philip's achievements and the centerpiece of his own account. William found a copy of Rigord's *Deeds* in the Saint-Denis archives, suggesting Rigord's text had not, in the end, found a permanent place in Philip's library.[85] William then composed in several stages his own *Gesta Philippi Augusti*, building on Rigord's account, and going so far as to include at the beginning of his own history a summary of Rigord's material. Although William was not associated with Saint-Denis, he apparently turned to its library, and perhaps to some intermediary writings or records the monks had made in the meantime, to fill in the years between the end of Rigord's account in 1206 and the start of his own in 1209.[86] The complete version of William's continuation was copied at Saint-Denis, integrated seamlessly with Rigord's account in one manuscript (BnF MS latin 5925), and incorporated as a core piece in the growing trove of historiographical sources that was forming the source base for the Dionysian historiographical tradition.

Rigord's and William le Breton's works were thus part of the foundation for the thirteenth-century Dionysian integration of royal history and ultimately the composition of the vernacular *Grandes chroniques de France* that sought to provide a definitive, synthetic account of the kings of France and of French history more generally.[87] Rigord's and William's texts, we saw, were copied, as if a single work, into a manuscript (BnF MS latin 5925) in the middle of the thirteenth century.[88] This manuscript, which also included Aimon of Fleury's *Historia Francorum* and Suger's *Life of Louis the Fat* (among others), was in turn critical for the work of the abbey's two most important historians in the second part of the thirteenth century: William of Nangis (d. 1300) and Primat (d. after 1277). William of Nangis, monk of Saint-Denis, archivist, and historian, authored accounts of the life and reigns of Philip Augustus's grandson Louis IX (*Vita Ludovici*, largely a compilation from earlier material) and great-grandson, Philip III (the *Gesta Philippi III*, largely a new work), along with two royal chronicles (the *Chronicon* and the *Chronique*

---

85. *Œuvres*, 1:169; *HPA*, 63.

86. Spiegel, *Chronicle Tradition*, 66–67. William's account went through four redactions.

87. Good English-language introductions to the *Grandes chroniques* tradition include Spiegel, *Chronicle Tradition*, 72–89, 117–28; and Anne D. Hedeman, *The Royal Image: Illustrations of the Grandes Chroniques de France, 1274–1422*, California Studies in the History of Art 28 (Berkeley: University of California Press, 1991), 1–6.

88. Pascale Bourgain, "La protohistoire des chroniques latines de Saint-Denis (BNF, lat. 5925)," in *Saint-Denis et la royauté: Études offertes à Bernard Guenée*, ed. Françoise Autrand, Claude Gauvard, and Jean-Marie Moeglin (Paris: Éditions de la Sorbonne, 1999), 375–94. At a later date, the lives of Louis VII, Louis VIII, Louis IX, and Philip III were added. For a review of the contents of MS 5925, see Spiegel, *Chronicle Tradition*, 68–71.

abrégée) that extended the Latin histories of the kings of France to the end of the thirteenth century.[89] William's regnal histories followed in the footsteps of Rigord's and Suger's before him, solidifying the practice begun by them in the twelfth century and turning it into an enduring tradition at the abbey.

William of Nangis and his predecessors had all written in Latin, but about the same time, a tradition of vernacular historiography began to take root at Saint-Denis. Sometime after 1254, King Louis IX (r. 1226–70) invited Primat, a monk at Saint-Denis, to compose a synthetic vernacular history of the kings of France. Other than Rigord's brief *Cronica*, Primat's *Roman des roys* was the first attempt to knit together and reconcile earlier sources in order to present a single unified narrative of the history of the French. In doing so, Primat consulted the manuscript (BnF MS latin 5925) containing the only complete account of Rigord's *Deeds of Philip Augustus*. When the *Roman des roys* was ready, Primat presented the earliest version to Louis's heir and successor, Philip III, in 1274. Beginning with the Trojan origins, and covering the Merovingians, Carolingians, and Capetians, the first version of Primat's history went up through 1214. Rigord's *Deeds of Philip Augustus* was Primat's principal source for the years between 1180 and 1206, having been translated into the vernacular for this purpose.[90] In due course, Primat's continuators added material bringing the history up to date and ultimately following royal history through the end of the fifteenth century. In its extended form, Primat's *Roman des roys* came to be called the *Grandes chroniques de France*.[91]

The abbey's commitment to writing history, and in particular royal history, continued, with some interruptions, through the fifteenth century. Richard Lescot drafted materials that covered the years 1328 to 1344.[92] In the fifteenth century Saint-Denis's principal historians were Michel Pintoin (often called simply "le Religieux de Saint-Denis," d. ca. 1421) and Jean Chartier (d. 1450), contributing to the Latin chronicles and the French *Grandes chroniques* respectively.[93] It would be a mistake to call these histories "official," in that the histories, with the exception of Primat's, were rarely commissioned

---

89. On William of Nangis, see Isabelle Guyot-Bachy, "La Chronique abrégée des rois de France de Guillaume de Nangis: Trois étapes de l'histoire d'un texte," in *Religion et mentalités au Moyen Âge: Mélanges en l'honneur d'Hervé Martin*, ed. Lionel Rousselot et al. (Rennes: Presses universitaires de Rennes, 2003), 39–46; and Spiegel, *Chronicle Tradition*, 98–108.

90. Jules Marie Édouard Viard, *Les grandes chroniques de France* (Paris: Société de l'histoire de France, 1920), 6:89–283.

91. Bernard Guenée, *Comment on écrit l'histoire au XIIIe siècle: Primat et le Roman des roys*, ed. Jean-Marie Moeglin (Paris: CNRS Éditions, 2016).

92. Spiegel, *Chronicle Tradition*, 108–12.

93. Spiegel, *Chronicle Tradition*, 117–26.

or authorized by the Crown. For the most part, it was the monks who took it upon themselves to become the custodians of the quasi-official history of the French crown. But these histories, and especially the *Grandes chroniques* with the increasingly broad readership enabled by its vernacular form, became in time the essential and definitive account of French history. At each stage, these historians knew and drew on the work of their predecessors, including Rigord. In this way Rigord's *Deeds*, as adopted in both Latin and French, and integrated into subsequent histories—both medieval and modern—constitutes our most important narrative evidence for the early part of Philip's consequential reign.

The Importance and Major Themes of the Text

Rigord is a keen, if not unbiased, observer, who often gives us unique insights into twelfth-century events and mentalities, including the rapid development of Paris, the importance of popular religious practice and the power of sanctity, the persecution of the Jews, the myth of Trojan origins, the circulation of prophetic hopes and fears, the importance of the Crusades, and the public and private lives of the French and English kings.

The Development of Paris

The *Deeds of Philip Augustus* spans the years in which Paris emerged as the true capital of the kingdom of France. Although never defined by a royal act or official declaration, Philip's bureaucratic and archival innovations, along with developments in court procedures and practices, meant that Paris increasingly became the center of government, even in the king's absence. Rigord's account, particularly his details of Philip's initiatives and capital improvements to the city, offers anecdotal color to this process. The narrative itself assumes the king's home base was Paris, and at one point Rigord even calls Paris "the head of the kingdom of the Franks" (ch. 10). Thus a royal delegation from Jerusalem was sent to find Philip in Paris (chs. 30–31), the king greeted Geoffrey Plantagenet and later King John there (chs. 48, 142), and it was at Paris that the king convened a number of general councils (chs. 2, 31, 63, 99). Tellingly, the testament-ordinance he drew up before departing for the Holy Land (ch. 77) assumes Paris as the administrative center.

Several famous stories of Paris's urban development come from Rigord, as when Philip promoted the open markets of Champeaux on the Right

FIGURE 4. Surviving portion of Philip II's wall, rue Clovis on the Left Bank, Paris. Photograph by Bernard Myers, used by permission.

Bank, building covered structures (Les Halles) and safeguarding the vendors' security through guards and walls (ch. 19). Because the Champeaux neighborhood was taking off as the city's commercial center, the story reveals a king who sought to promote and secure Paris's economic vitality. Philip also built walls around the nearby cemetery of the Holy Innocents (ch. 51) and walled in the forest of Vincennes, a favorite royal hunting ground (ch. 20). And he ordered all the streets and squares of Paris to be paved with stone, famously because the stench of the dirt roads on which horse-drawn carts were conducted was unbearable to him as it wafted through the windows of his palace on the Île-de-la-Cité (ch. 38). Most important, before leaving on crusade Philip ordered "that the city of Paris, which the king greatly loved, be enclosed with the very best wall, with towers and gates properly and carefully arranged" (ch. 78). We know from other sources that Philip began with a wall on the Right Bank (as protection from a Plantagenet threat from the north), and followed up later with a wall on the Left Bank (to the south), effectively encircling the palace and the cathedral and enclosing the heart of Paris. But it is from Rigord that we get a picture of Philip's personal concern and motivations regarding urban development in the capital.[94]

Christian Practice, the Power of Relics, and Saint Denis

Rigord offers a series of anecdotes that testify to something of the religious culture of the period. For instance, several episodes illustrate the flowering of devotion to the Virgin Mary in the twelfth century,[95] including the story of a poor man named Durand, to whom the Lord appeared holding a scroll on which the Virgin sat enthroned holding the Christ child (ch. 25). Durand preached a message of peace among dueling political factions around Le Puy in the south, enticing men in the region to vow nonviolence. Ultimately the image of the Virgin was impressed upon pieces of tin and worn upon their bodies as a sign of their promise to one another and to God. Another story recounted the miracles that followed when a blasphemous mercenary threw a stone at a statue of the Virgin holding the Christ child (ch. 58). Elsewhere (ch. 16), Rigord says that after expelling the Jews, the king had their synagogues reconsecrated as churches in honor of Christ and the Virgin Mary. We also observe with Rigord a number of common religious practices of the period: the performance of penitential processions in times of crisis or need (chs. 84, 119, 146), the veneration of relics (chs. 76, 84, 87, 153), and the belief in holy men (chs. 11, 92) and miracles (chs. 5, 11, 29, 55, 58, 68, 132).

Among holy figures, Saint Denis is preeminent as saintly protector and intercessor. Denis is, in one sense, the shadowy second protagonist of the *Deeds of Philip Augustus*. Rigord introduces him early on, at chapter 3. Philip,

---

94. Denis Hayot, *Paris en 1200: Histoire et archéologie d'une capitale fortifiée par Philippe Auguste* (Paris: CNRS Éditions, 2018); Baldwin, *Paris, 1200*.

95. Miri Rubin, *Mother of God: A History of the Virgin Mary* (New Haven: Yale University Press, 2010).

aged fourteen and not yet crowned, gets lost in the woods when on a boar hunt, and, frightened, commends himself to God, the Virgin, and "the most Blessed Denis, patron and defender of the kings of the Franks," after which he is rescued by a local woodsman. The episode singles out Denis among all possible saints, and identifies him specifically as the king's particular patron and defender. In turn, Rigord recounts Philip's particular devotion to Saint Denis, often rendered by ritual supplication at the abbey of Saint-Denis, or before the altar containing the relics of Denis and his companions. In 1189 Philip prostrated himself before the martyrs before he left for crusade (ch. 76), and the first thing he did upon his return from Outremer was go to Saint-Denis to offer thanks for his safe journey and return (ch. 90). Philip also rendered prayers and thanks to "his patron and protector" in 1195 after Richard offered him homage (ch. 117), emphasizing the notion of hierarchical faith and loyalty. And again, after a series of victories over the Plantagenets in 1199, following which Eleanor of Aquitaine did homage to Philip, Philip returned to Saint-Denis to pledge his devotion, give thanks for his victories, and make offerings (ch. 136).

Because of Denis's power and his role as protector of the king of France, his relics, along with those of Rusticus and Eleutherius, were in turn deployed when needed to beseech God for Philip and his efforts. While Philip was in the East, the two regents (Queen Adele and William of the White Hands) arranged for the relics to be placed upon the high altar in a special ceremony to ask God for the king's success in the crusade (ch. 87). Elsewhere, Rigord records Denis's particular power in rendering miracles (chs. 98, 101, 104). That said, the relics of Saint Denis were too precious ever to leave the monastery. And so, on several occasions some of the monastery's other relics—most notably the holy nail, the piece of the Crown of Thorns, and the arm of Saint Simeon the Elder that were believed to have been given to Saint-Denis by Charles the Bald—were borne in procession to beseech divine aid. In July 1191, when Philip was still in the East, Prince Louis fell seriously ill and the relics were carried in a solemn intercessory procession into Paris, first to the church of Saint-Lazare and then on to Notre-Dame (ch. 84). In 1196 and in 1206, Saint Denis's relics were again processed to beseech God's help in combatting the devastation of massive flooding (chs. 119, 156). Rigord recalls that Philip himself participated in the 1196 procession "as though but one of the people" (ch. 119). In turn, Philip's devotion to both Saint Denis and his monastery meant that when, in 1205, the king received new relics from Baldwin I, the new emperor of Constantinople installed as a result of the Fourth Crusade, the king gave those relics to the abbey (ch. 153).

The Persecution of the Jews

Philip II's actions from 1180 to 1182 constitute the first mass expulsion of a Jewish community from a medieval kingdom.[96] As such they are a crucial turning point in the history of anti-Jewish persecutions, foreshadowing later, larger expulsions from England (1290), France (1306, 1394), and Spain (1492). Rigord's record of Philip II's persecution of the Jews is among the most important elements of the *Deeds*, and his own anti-Jewish attitudes are one of its defining traits. Rigord provides the only substantial account of these events (chs. 5, 11–18) from early in Philip's reign, and so his record takes on particular significance for anyone seeking to understand this pivotal moment in Christian/Jewish relations. Moreover, Rigord frames the whole first part of the *Deeds* as a larger battle between the righteous king and those enemies, Christians and Jews alike, who would undermine the power and liberties of the Church. For Rigord, Philip's attacks on the Jews are the first and best proof of his status as a warrior for God. Conversely, in Rigord's eyes, Philip's decision to readmit the Jews to his realm in 1198 (ch. 133) is the strongest evidence that the king had momentarily lost his way. Although Rigord's anti-Judaism offends twenty-first-century readers, his overt expression of prejudice makes this text central to understanding how ritual murder accusations were weaponized in late twelfth-century France, how some churchmen portrayed Jewish "threats" to Christian society at this pivotal moment, and how intolerance toward Jews became linked to the status of the "most Christian kings" of France.[97]

The Myth of Trojan Origins

Rigord in fact concludes the most intensely anti-Jewish section of his text with a brief foray into the distant past, asserting that in the seventh century the Byzantine emperor Heraclius had urged the Merovingian king Dagobert to "drive all of the Jews from his kingdom" (ch. 18). According to Rigord, Dagobert complied because astrological signs had predicted that the Roman Empire "was to be destroyed by a circumcised people." Only a few chapters later (chs. 38–43), Rigord returns to this strategy of legitimization through highly mythologized historical claims, interrupting his accounts of the years 1184/85 and 1185/86 with a potted history of the origins and lineages of

---

96. Jordan, *French Monarchy and the Jews*; Juliette Sibon, *Chasser les juifs pour régner* (Paris: Perron, 2016).

97. For the long history of anti-Jewish thought, see David Nirenberg, *Anti-Judaism: The Western Tradition* (New York: Norton, 2013).

French kingship, beginning with the mythic Pharamond, Marcomer, and Francion, and running through the Merovingian, Carolingian, and then Capetian dynasties to get the reader all the way to Philip II himself. In this sense, Rigord's historical detour was in keeping with Saint-Denis's developing tradition as guardian of royal history, and partner with the Crown in using that history for institutional and dynastic legitimation.[98] Rigord explained that in modernizing the city, the king sought to do away with its former name, Lutetia (which Rigord said derived from *lutum*—or "mud"), and instead call the city Paris, "after Paris Alexander, the son of the king of Troy" (ch. 38).

This reference to the king of Troy derived from the long-established myth of the Trojan origins of the Franks.[99] The French were not the only ones that claimed that their nation (*natio,* meaning "people of the same origin") stemmed from an exiled offshoot of the Trojans, the noble people who left Troy in the wake of its fall to the Greeks in the Trojan War. Romans, Britons, and Germans all claimed Trojan origins. As told by Rigord, King Priam of Troy's grandson Francion led a group and settled in Sicambria, on the Danube River. (Note that other authors elaborated that it was from this Francion that the Franks, and ultimately France, would derive its name.) One group from Sicambria, under the leadership of a certain Ibor, named themselves the Parisians, after Paris Alexander, the son of Priam; and these traveled to Gaul. Here, Rigord insists not only on the origins of the French people, but also on the foundation of Paris.[100] Another group, Rigord explained, remained in Sicambria for over a millennium and a half before moving, under the leadership of Marcomer, into the Rhine valley. These were the Franks, who conquered all of Germany and Gaul, and when they arrived among the Parisians, they were greeted as fellows of Trojan descent. Marcomer's son Pharamond was

---

98. Kordula Wolf, *Troja—Metamorphosen eines Mythos: Französische, englische und italienische Überlieferungen des 12. Jahrhunderts im Vergleich* (Berlin: Akademie Verlag, 2009); Marc-René Jung, *La légende de Troie en France au Moyen Âge: Analyse des versions françaises et bibliographie raisonnée des manuscrits,* Romanica Helvetica 114 (Basel: Franke, 1996); Wolfgang Brückle, "Noblesse oblige: Trojasage und legitime Herrschaft in der französischen Staatstheorie des späten Mittelalters," in *Genealogie als Denkform im Mittelalter und Früher Neuzeit,* ed. Kilian Heck and Bernhard Jahn (Tübingen: De Gruyter, 2000), 39–65. Rigord's *Cronica* also sought to reconcile the conflicting and confusing histories provided in earlier accounts, such as Pseudo-Fredegar, *Book of the History of the Franks,* and Aimon of Fleury, *History of the Franks.* The chronological relationship between the composition of his two texts remains less than clear.

99. It appears in Latin sources at least as early as a continuation of Fredegar's *Liber historiae Francorum* from the 660s.

100. For this point, see Jerzy Pysiak, "De la Lutèce des Troyens au Paris des Capétiens: Philippe Auguste et l'origine troyenne du Royaume de France," in *Le sacre d'une capitale: Paris vu par les écrivains, les historiens et les voyageurs,* ed. Zbigniew Naliwajek and Joanna Żurowska (Warsaw: Institut d'Études romanes de l'Université de Varsovie, 2005), 11–22.

made king, and is considered "the first king of the Franks" (ch. 40). In turn, Pharamond's grandson Merovic gave his name to the Merovingian dynasty. Merovic's own grandson Clovis converted to Catholic (Nicaean) Christianity, becoming the first Christian king of the Franks. His great-grandson King Dagobert employed a man named Pepin as major of the palace. The mayors of the palace constituted their own dynasty, and ultimately one of his descendants would usurp the kingship from the Merovingians. Rigord simply lists the succession of mayors, neglecting to say that King Pepin, "who fathered Charlemagne the emperor" (ch. 41), was crowned as the first Carolingian king, replacing a Merovingian successor; rather he states merely that Pepin reigned after Louis. On the other hand, when recording the advent of Hugh Capet, the first Capetian, he notes that his immediate predecessor, Louis [V], was "the very last of this [Carolingian] royal bloodline" (ch. 41). From there, Rigord quickly gets the reader to Philip Augustus.

The idea of Trojan descent played several roles in the historical and ideological imagination of Capetian kingship at the time Rigord was writing. The point was both to offer Philip and the Capetians the prestige of antique origins, and to present a kind of legitimizing lineage that papered over dynastic breaks that might call Capetian claims into question. For one, the myth furnished a foundation story for France and the French that was independent from the Roman world and Roman inheritance. Moreover, the notion of lineage, and in particular patrilineal descent, was becoming increasingly important in the twelfth century both legally and culturally. The Capetian fortune in producing an unbroken succession of male heirs since 987 was a key to its stability and the growing strength and legitimacy of its claim to the crown. But the ideal of lineage was also coming in this period to define nobility itself as a legal and social category. Even Jesus Christ (whose Father had no father, of course) needed a lineage, one that was in this period provided for him in visual iconography. A generation before Rigord wrote, Suger had overseen a broad iconographical program on Saint-Denis's west facade that showed Old Testament kings and queens, both as "royal ancestors of Christ" and as mythic ancestors of the French kings; and the popular Tree of Jesse image, found at Saint-Denis and elsewhere, also traced Christ's lineage back to King David and his father, Jesse.[101]

---

101. Stephen G. Nichols, *Romanesque Signs: Early Medieval Narrative and Iconography* (New Haven: Yale University Press, 1983), 91–92; R. Howard Bloch, *Etymologies and Genealogies: A Literary Anthropology of the French Middle Ages* (Chicago: University of Chicago Press, 1986).

Finally, Rigord's evocation here of Trojan origins may have further been a pointed response to the so-called Valerian Prophecy.[102] The prophecy, which claimed that seven generations following the coronation of Hugh Capet the French crown would revert to the Carolingians, was itself a provocation to Capetian legitimacy precisely on the grounds that the Capetians were not direct descendants of the Carolingians. In the specific instance, Philip's court answered this challenge by trumpeting Isabelle of Hainaut's descent from Charlemagne, and claimed that Louis VIII, Philip's son and heir, duly returned the crown to the line of Charlemagne (without, notably, its Capetian surrender). But the myth of Trojan origins—which was in some ways more about the origins of the French people (*gens*) than its king—enveloped both people and kings in a mythic, unifying, and notionally lineal haze; it was a foundation story that preceded the Carolingians and even the Merovingians and insisted that legitimacy was rooted as much in the leadership of a shared people as in a singular lineage.

The Prophetic Future

Rigord's interest in returning to the beginnings (however mythical) of Frankish history can be paired with his own treatment of the prophetic future. The *Deeds of Philip Augustus* places Philip II within the full sweep of secular and sacred history, as a king at the end of a long Frankish genealogy, perched on the edge of the end-time.[103] Indeed, in retelling his highly dubious story of Heraclius, Dagobert, and the Jews, he notes that ultimately it was not the Jews who plundered the Roman (or Byzantine) Empire, but the Saracens (the term often deployed in referring to Muslims or Arabs). And this, he

---

102. Gabrielle Spiegel, "The *Reditus regni ad stirpem Karoli Magni*: A New Look," *French Historical Studies* 7 (1971): 145–74; Elizabeth A. R. Brown, "Vincent de Beauvais and the *Reditus Regni Francorum ad Stirpem Caroli Imperatoris*," in *Vincent de Beauvais: Intentions et réceptions d'une œuvre encyclopédique au Moyen-Age. Actes du XIVᵉ Colloque de l'Institut d'études médiévales, organisé conjointement par l'Atelier Vincent de Beauvais (A.R.Te.M., Université de Nancy II) et l'Institute d'études médiévales (Université de Montréal) 27–30 avril 1988*, ed. Serge Lusignan, Monique Paulmier-Foucart, and Alain Nadeau, Cahiers d'études médiévales, Cahier spécial 4 (Paris: Vrin, 1990), 167–96; Elizabeth A. R. Brown, "La généalogie capétienne dans l'historiographie du Moyen Âge: Philippe le Bel, le reniement du *reditus* et la création d'une ascendance carolingienne pour Hugues Capet," in *Religion et culture autour de l'an Mil*, 199–214. The myth of Trojan origins was later specifically paired with the Valerian Prophecy in the *Grandes chroniques*.

103. For an overview, see Bernard McGinn, *Visions of the End: Apocalyptic Traditions in the Middle Ages* (New York: Columbia University Press, 1998); for the context of prophecy and twelfth-century crusading, see Jay Rubenstein, *Nebuchadnezzar's Dream: The Crusades, Apocalyptic Prophecy, and the End of History* (Oxford: Oxford University Press, 2019).

asserts, will happen again "in the end of times" (ch. 18), when the Ishmaelites, or Saracens, join Antichrist in inflicting "trials and tribulations" upon
good Christians. Rigord explicitly cites his authority for this prediction, the
Apocalypse of Pseudo-Methodius, a widely read text originally written in sev-
enth-century Syriac but subsequently translated into Latin and well known
in twelfth-century Europe.[104] Rigord's tendency to see events such as earthquakes and storms as divine portents is hardly unusual for authors of his era,
yet he shows a particularly keen interest in prophecy. He carefully copies
out not one but two letters predicting upheavals and the emergence of a
false prophet in the East in the year 1186 (chs. 53–55); he similarly includes
a "certain poet's" prophetic verses about Philip II (ch. 72), which place the
French king in the role of Last World Emperor.[105] More subtly, in referring
to the striking events of the Fourth Crusade (ch. 147), Rigord imagines a
future in which he hopes for "greater and better things in the Holy Land,
when one will pursue a thousand, and two will drive away ten thousand."
Suger and Odo of Deuil had shown some interest in prophecies in writing
about Louis VI and Louis VII, and the monks of Saint-Denis had long been
invested in tracing the deep history of the Franks. But Rigord was the first to
place the deeds of his royal hero within this long trajectory from Troy to the
end-time. In this sense it was his breadth of vision that came to characterize
the *Grandes chroniques de France*.

The Crusades

The Crusades occupy a pivotal position within Rigord's grand narrative. The
years covered by his chronicle encompassed both the Third Crusade (1189–92)
and the Fourth (1202–4). Rigord participated in neither, and so his accounts
were based on the experiences and testimony of others. Nevertheless, beginning at chapter 62 and continuing intermittently through chapter 97, Rigord
recounts Philip Augustus's participation in the Third Crusade. He also devotes two long chapters (chs. 146–47) to the Fourth Crusade, even though
Philip did not participate in it, because, as he says explicitly, these events seem
noteworthy enough to require inclusion.

---

104. Pseudo-Methodius, *Apocalypse: An Alexandrian World Chronicle*, ed. and trans. Benjamin
Garstad (Cambridge, MA: Harvard University Press, 2012). MS *V* (one of the two extant manuscript
of the *Deeds*) in fact begins with a copy of this text.

105. Jerzy Pysiak, "Philippe Auguste: Un roi de la fin des temps?," *Annales: Histoire, sciences sociales* 57, no. 5 (2002): 1165–90; Elizabeth A. R. Brown, "La notion de légitimité et la prophétie à la cour
de Philippe Auguste," in Bautier, *La France de Philippe Auguste*, 78–110.

The Crusades had begun at the end of the eleventh century with Pope Urban II's call for Christian soldiers to take up arms to aid their Christian brethren against Muslims in the East, and resulted in the capture of the Holy City of Jerusalem in 1099 from Muslim (Fatamid) control.[106] By 1109, the crusaders had established four new states, ruled by Latin Christians, with the most important being the Kingdom of Jerusalem. Philip Augustus's father, Louis VII, took part in the Second Crusade (1147–49), mounted after substantial losses were incurred by crusader forces in the northern principality of Edessa. The Second Crusade itself failed to make any gains. When, a generation later, in the summer and fall of 1187 under Saladin's leadership, Muslim forces slaughtered the Christian army at the Battle of Hattin and then retook Jerusalem, the pope called another crusade. Both Philip Augustus and Henry II of England took the cross (ch. 62), although Henry died before being able to fulfill his vow. In the end, it was his son, the new king of England, Richard the Lionheart, who went East, joining Philip and the rest of the crusaders in the siege of Acre, the port city whose control would be necessary to take and hold the inland city of Jerusalem.[107] Given the tensions between the kings of England and France over control of Angevin lands in France, fully narrated in Rigord's account, neither Philip nor Richard would agree to go on crusade unless the other did. They patched up a temporary peace at home in order for both to go fight the infidel (ch. 74). But clashes were inevitable and disputes emerged quickly in the East.

Rigord's account provides both a French perspective on the Third Crusade and something of a whitewashing of Philip's contributions, which were nugatory and somewhat embarrassing in an age that prized the exploits of Christian knighthood and in which military leadership was a hallmark of good kingship.[108] In 1189, Philip was only in his midtwenties and still comparatively inexperienced. All in all he paled in comparison to the

---

106. Good English-language overviews of the Crusades include Thomas F. Madden, *A Concise History of the Crusades*, 3rd ed., Critical Issues in History (Lanham, MD: Rowman & Littlefield, 2014); and Christopher Tyerman, *God's War: A New History of the Crusades* (Cambridge, MA: Harvard University Press, 2006).

107. Kings obviously did not crusade alone. A king's participation in a crusade involved recruiting a substantial army, which accompanied the king, who served as general. And crusaders from all over Christendom, not just from England and France, participated in the Third Crusade.

108. On the Third Crusade, in addition to the general histories above, see Hosler, *Siege of Acre*. Still useful is Sidney Painter, "The Third Crusade: Richard the Lionheart and Philip Augustus," in *A History of the Crusades*, ed. Kenneth Setton (Madison: University of Wisconsin Press, 1962), 2:45–86. Rigord's narrative is treated in Catherine Croizy-Naquet, "Rigord, Philippe Auguste et la croisade," in *De la pensée de l'histoire au jeu littéraire: Études médiévales en l'honneur de Dominique Boutet*, ed. Sébastien Douchet, Marie-Pascale Halary, and Sylvie Lefèvre, Nouvelle bibliothèque du Moyen Âge 127 (Paris: Champion, 2019), 148–60.

military prowess of Richard the Lionheart, who, thirteen years older and a natural military leader, came to be hailed as the hero of the Third Crusade. Philip and Richard departed in July 1190, but relations between the two kings soured quickly at a stop in Messina (Sicily) when Richard repudiated a marriage promise to Philip's sister Alix in favor of Berengaria of Navarre (ch. 80). Philip arrived in the Holy Land first, in April 1192, joining the siege of Acre, already underway. When Richard arrived in June, having accrued a series of military victories along the way, he effectively took command of the operation. Both Philip and Richard fell ill, Richard probably more seriously and with a longer recovery time. Ultimately, Acre was delivered to the crusaders on 12 June, not through conquest, but through negotiations with Saladin (ch. 88).

Immediately after Acre was in crusader hands, Philip returned to France, in part out of concern that the English might well invade in his absence. Philip was widely criticized for abandoning the crusade. Richard stayed on to solidify crusader gains in the East, won several important victories against Saladin, and, although he did not manage to retake Jerusalem itself, was able to get the Kingdom of Jerusalem (now in exile in Acre) back on its feet. He concluded a three-year truce with Saladin in September 1192 before himself leaving the Holy Land, only to be captured by the duke of Austria on his return home and imprisoned for a year and a half.

If the only account we possessed was Rigord's we would be forgiven for concluding that Philip was primarily responsible for the success of the siege of Acre and its capture by the crusader forces, and that Richard arrived only when all the hard work was done (ch. 80).[109] Rigord further suggests underhanded motives in Richard's negotiations with Saladin (ch. 88) and neglects entirely to mention that Richard too was ill, while using Philip's illness to explain his abrupt departure. (Anglo-Norman and Arabic sources reveal a fuller story far more favorable to Richard's leadership on crusade.) Beyond the narrative imperative for a *Gesta* (*Deeds*) of the king, Philip's participation in the Third Crusade was a vehicle to demonstrate that the king fulfilled the duties of Christian knighthood. It also permitted Rigord to highlight Saint Denis and his abbey's role in fighting "the enemies of the cross of Christ," since upon his departure Philip took up the ceremonial scrip and staff and the royal battle standard from the altar at Saint-Denis (ch. 76), the relics of Saint Denis and his companions were ritually deployed in offering prayers to the Lord "for the liberation of the Holy Land, and for the king of the Franks

---

109. Croizy-Naquet, "Rigord, Philippe Auguste et la croisade," 154–55.

and all his host" (ch. 87), and Philip made a pilgrimage to Saint-Denis immediately upon his return to France (ch. 90).

Monarchies and Monarchs

Beyond the Crusades, Rigord also affords us a biased but powerful view of the
wider European political landscape. Philip II's battles with first Henry II and
then his sons Richard and John are the connecting thread that runs through
the *Deeds*. Rigord depicts Philip working to oppose each new English king
through alliances with disgruntled members of the Plantagenet clan; first
Richard and Geoffrey against Henry, then John against Richard, finally Arthur (Geoffrey's son) against John. Although Rigord does let his admiration
for Richard's martial prowess peek through at times, generally his narrative
makes the English always dastardly, the French forces almost always favored
by God.[110] If it is difficult to arrive at a balanced sense of Philip's military
fortunes in the 1180s and 1190s by reading Rigord, the turning point against
John in the crucial years of 1200–1204 fits more comfortably into the *Deeds*,
making Rigord an important source for French understanding of the king's
sudden victories. Similarly, Rigord is not shy about criticizing the German
emperors, particularly Henry VI (r. 1191–97), whom Rigord portrays as a
tyrant (ch. 128). By contrast Pope Innocent III receives approving, though
hardly laudatory, language from Rigord's pen.

Rigord also affords his readers glimpses of the rapidly developing ma-
chinery of royal government, in part because he was careful to copy several
original documents into the *Deeds*. Rigord evidently had access to numerous royal acts, such as the so-called Saladin tithe (chs. 64–66) issued in 1188,
and the Treaty of Le Goulet between Philip and King John in 1200 (referred
to but not included in the text). Most important in this regard, however, is
the testament-ordinance executed by King Philip just before departing on
crusade in 1190.[111] This act, the first ever to lay out a system of centralized
justice and finance for the French kingdom, survives only because it was
incorporated into Rigord's text (ch. 77). It was certainly issued as a solemn
act confirmed by the royal seal and monogram and witnessed by Philip's
seneschal, butler, chamberlain, and constable. The sealed original, however,
does not survive, nor do any of the official copies that presumably must

---

110. On Rigord's view of Richard, see José Ricardo Sánchez Rodríguez, "El enemigo de mi
señor, la imagen de Ricardo Corazón de León en la *Gesta Philippi Augusti* de Rigord de Saint-Denis,"
Ab initio 13 (2019): 145–61.

111. See Baldwin, *GPA*, 102–4.

FIGURE 5. Seal of Philip II. Text reads: Philippus dei gratia Francorum rex. Wikimedia Commons, image placed in the public domain by the Archives nationales de France.

have been made (for the regents, for Philip to take with him to the Holy Land, perhaps for deposit at Saint-Denis). Such originals and official copies may have seemed superfluous once the king returned from crusade, and in any case the loss of the royal baggage train in 1194 might account for the destruction of any copies preserved by the court to that point. Rigord's decision to copy the testament-ordinance makes the *Deeds* an indispensable text for the history of French government; all printed editions and translations of this crucial document depend directly on Rigord.[112] We are lucky in this. Rigord's decision to include the testament-ordinance seems to have been almost an afterthought; his narrative proceeds all the way up through the moment when Philip and Richard sailed from Genoa and Marseille, and only then backtracks in time to record that "before King Philip departed" he assembled his close associates in Paris to execute "his testament and set in order the whole kingdom" (ch. 76). If Rigord completed his first version of the text in 1190 and wrote his first dedicatory letter at that point, he probably added the testament-ordinance a few years later, when he decided to continue the work.

112. See below for printed editions of Rigord, all of which contain the testament-ordinance, as well as Henri-François Delaborde, ed., *Recueil des actes de Philippe Auguste, roi de France*, vol. 1 (Paris: Imprimerie nationale, 1916), 416–20, no. 345.

On a more intimate level, although Rigord does not detail the domestic affairs of the king, he does give his own perspective on Philip II's controversial marital life.[113] He mentions Isabelle of Hainaut, Philip's first wife, only a few times, but includes a vivid description of the king and queen drenched with lamp oil, following a mishap involving an unruly crowd and an overzealous guard at the time of the queen's coronation at Saint-Denis (ch. 9). Rigord takes a more critical stance on the king's second marriage. When Philip rejected Ingeborg of Denmark in 1193 the day after their wedding, Rigord's sympathies evidently lay with the queen. Rigord does not attempt to explain the source of the king's sudden change of heart, except to remark that "it is said" that he was "snared . . . by the spells of sorceresses (*maleficiis per sorciarias*)" (ch. 99).[114] But Rigord is openly scornful of the French churchmen who were unwilling or unable to enforce Pope Celestine III's insistence on the marriage's validity. Referring to Ingeborg as "the holy queen" (ch. 138), Rigord leaves little doubt that he sees her as a woman wronged, and Philip as turning his back on God's will. Later, Rigord still seems as mystified as anyone when Philip, pressured by Pope Innocent III, unexpectedly takes Ingeborg back "as his wife," after the death of Agnes of Méran, with whom he had produced several children. Innocent III eventually legitimized these children, which Rigord reports as having "dissatisfied very many people" (ch. 143). Thus if Rigord's text does not provide the secret to Philip's marital affairs, it does offer contemporary commentary and judgment on the rapidly changing social and legal expectations around royal marriage.[115]

Rigord's account of Philip Augustus's reign constitutes an enormously important historical source for the political, cultural, intellectual, and religious history of the years around 1200. It should also be understood in the context of the long history of Christian rulership and political biography, heir not only to Aimon of Fleury and Suger, but to Einhard's *Life of Charlemagne*, Eusebius's *Life of Constantine*, and even Suetonius's *Lives of the Twelve Caesars*. Read in this context, Rigord's portrait of Philip's reign lies in a broader history of writing about kingship, monarchy, and state and royal power. Rigord built on this tradition while transforming the nature of political writing to suit the changing circumstances of his day. He balanced anecdote and

---

113. John W. Baldwin, "La vie sexuelle de Philippe Auguste," in *Mariage et sexualité au Moyen Âge: Accord ou crise?* ed. Michel Rouche (Paris: Presses de l'Université de Paris-Sorbonne, 2000), 217–29.

114. See Constance Rousseau, "Neither Bewitched nor Beguiled: Philip Augustus's Alleged Impotence and Innocent III's Response," *Speculum* 89 (2014): 410–36.

115. Still valuable is George Duby's classic *The Knight, the Lady, and the Priest: The Making of Modern Marriage in Medieval France*, trans. Barbara Bray, intro. Natalie Zemon Davis (Chicago: University of Chicago Press, 1983), esp. 189–209.

specificity with the ideals of kingship within a French and Frankish context. Inheriting a local tradition of royal biography, Rigord placed his protagonist, Philip Augustus, between his subjects on the ground and his saint (Denis) in heaven. He also sought to locate the king's reign within a broad sweep of history, looking backward to Troy and forward to the Last Judgment. Written at a crucially important moment in the transformation of political culture and royal power, Rigord's *Deeds of Philip Augustus* stands as a singular witness to his time while marking an important point in the long trajectory of political authority and state formation in the West.

Note on Manuscripts, Editions, and Translations

Rigord's *Deeds of Philip Augustus* survives in two medieval manuscripts and two later copies.[116] The first medieval manuscript, BnF MS lat. 5925 (= *P*), has been mentioned several times above as one of the most important compilations of royal history created at Saint-Denis. It preserves the only full copy of Rigord's *Deeds*.[117] The first half of the manuscript, which includes Rigord's text, was copied near the middle of the thirteenth century. It also contains Aimon of Fleury's *History of the Franks*, Einhard's *Life of Charlemagne*, Pseudo-Turpin's *Deeds of Charlemagne in Spain*, the *Deeds of Emperor Louis the Pious*, Suger's *Life of Louis [VI] the Fat*, and then (fols. 248rb-286ra) Rigord's *Deeds of Philip Augustus*, followed (fols. 286ra-301vb) by William le Breton's continuation. Later in the thirteenth century, perhaps around 1285 (before Rigord's text), scribes at Saint-Denis added (by inserting two new quires that are now fols. 232–247) Suger's *Deeds of King Louis [VII], Son of Louis the Fat*, and then (following William le Breton's continuation) the *Deeds of Louis VIII*, William of Nangis's *Deeds of King Louis [IX] of Holy Memory*, and the same author's *Deeds of Philip [III]*.

The second medieval manuscript is BAV, Reg. lat. 88 (= *V*).[118] It contains only the dedicatory letter to Prince Louis, the prologue, and the first seventy-six chapters of the *Deeds of Philip Augustus*. It was made in France, perhaps in Bourges. The section of the manuscript that contains the incomplete copy of Rigord (fols. 176–189) was copied in the last third of the thirteenth century.

---

116. Detailed descriptions and examinations of these four manuscripts can be found in *HPA*, 20–51; shorter treatment in *Œuvres*, 1:iii-vi. See also Pascale Bourgain, "La protohistoire des chroniques latines de Saint-Denis (BNF, lat. 5925)"; and Léopold Delisle, "Notes sur quelques manuscrits du Musée Britannique," *Memoire de la société de l'histoire de Paris et de l'Ile-de-France* 4 (1877): 203–10.

117. Digitized (black and white, from microfilm) at https://gallica.bnf.fr/ark:/12148/btv1b9076644b.

118. Digitized (color, high resolution) at https://digi.vatlib.it/view/MSS_Reg.lat.88.

The two more modern copies are BAV, Reg. lat. 1758 (made directly from *P* in 1587), and Reg. lat. 930 (which mixes pages of Pithou's printed 1596 edition with passages copied from both *P* and *V*). Since these two copies depend directly on *P* and *V* (and on Pithou's printed edition, which depends on *P*), they add nothing as independent witnesses to the text.[119]

Pierre Pithou used *P* to prepare the first printed edition of Rigord in 1596,[120] which was the basis for that by François Duchesne (completing the work of his more famous father, André) in 1649.[121] The edition by Michel-Jean-Joseph Brial in 1818 continued to take *P* as its base, compared against Duchesne,[122] while in 1882 Henri-François Delaborde offered an advance by comparing readings from *V* to those in *P*.[123] The same two manuscripts continue to serve as the basis for the most recent edition, published by Élisabeth Carpentier, Georges Pon, and Yves Chauvin in 2006.

The 2006 edition also has a convenient facing-page French translation, the first since François Guizot's in 1825 (itself done from the 1818 *RHGF* edition).[124] No previous full English translation has appeared, but several twentieth- and twenty-first-century scholars have translated Rigord's sections on the Jews,[125] and William North has also translated portions concerning King Philip's preparations for the crusade and his relationship to Queen

119. Reg. lat. 1758 is digitized (black and white, from microfilm) at https://digi.vatlib.it/view/MSS_Reg.lat.1758; Reg. lat. 930 is not currently available in digitized form.

120. *Historiae Francorum ab anno Christi DCCCC ad ann. M.CC. LXXXV, scriptores veteres XI, in qvibvs Glaber, Helgaudus, Sugerius Abbas, M. Rigordus, Guillermus Brito, Guillermus de Nangis & anonymi alij., extrema stirpis Carolinae et Capetiorvm regvm res gestas vsque ad Philippum, D. Ludouici filium Regem, explicantes. Ex bibliotheca P. Pithoei V. CL. nvnc primum in lucem dati* (Frankfurt: Apud Andreae Wecheli heredes Claudium Marnium & Ioannem Aubrium, 1596), 158–207.

121. *Historiae Francorvm scriptores, a Philippo Avgvsto rege vsqve ad r. Philippi IV. dicti pvlchri tempora. Quorum plurimi nunc primum ex variis Codicibus MSS. in lucem prodeunt: alij vero auctiores & emendatiores. Cvm epistolis regvm, pontificvm, dvcvm, abbatum, & aliis veteribus rerum Francicarum monumentis. Opera ac studio Filij post Patrem Francisci Dvchesne, in Suprema Parisiensium Curia, & Sacro Consistorio Patroni, necnon Geographi, & Historiographi Regij,* tomvs V (Paris: Sebastian et Gabriel Cramoisy, 1649), 1–49.

122. *RHGF*, vol. 17 (1818), 1–62.

123. *Œuvres*, 1:1–167. See also August Molinier, ed., "Ex Rigordi Gestis Philippi II. Augusti," MGH Scriptores 26 (Hannover, 1882), 288–94.

124. François Pierre Guillaume Guizot, "Vie de Philippe-Auguste, par Rigord," in *Collection des Mémoires relatifs à l'histoire de France*, vol. 11 (Paris: Brière, 1825), 1–179. This translation has been reprinted several times, including in a reedited version by F. Fougère in 2003.

125. Jacob Rader Marcus and Marc Saperstein, *The Jews in Christian Europe: A Sourcebook, 315–1791* (Pittsburgh: Hebrew Union College Press, 2015), 98–102 (this translation, as printed in Marcus's original 1938 edition, can also be read at https://sourcebooks.fordham.edu/jewish/1182-jewsfrance1.asp); Alex J. Novikoff, ed., *The Twelfth-Century Renaissance: A Reader* (Toronto: University of Toronto Press, 2017), 172–77.

Ingeborg.[126] In the 1990s Paul Hyams made available his "fast and free" translation of chapters 1–76, which may still be found online.[127]

These partial English translations were all prepared from Delaborde's venerable nineteenth-century edition. We are now fortunate to be able to base this first full translation on the 2006 Latin edition by Carpentier, Pon, and Chauvin, and grateful to benefit from the meticulous scholarship that went into the introduction and notes to that publication. Although the high quality of the new edition renders a word-by-word verification of the manuscripts unnecessary, we have nevertheless checked reproductions of the two thirteenth-century sources in order to verify unexpected readings and correct a small number of typographical errors.

Our translation follows the new chapter numbering established by Carpentier, Pon, and Chauvin, but occasionally introduces additional paragraph breaks for clarity. Direct biblical quotations, which we print in italics, are based on the Douay-Reims translation of the Vulgate. Psalm numbering follows the Vulgate. Although we have been able to identify a few biblical quotations that were missed by Carpentier, Pon, and Chauvin, we have benefited greatly from their editorial efforts in this regard. We generally employ English forms of personal names.

Any translation has to balance fidelity to the original language with flow in the resulting prose, and any collaboration between a translator and editors necessarily involves a certain amount of negotiation around such issues. We hope to have managed this balancing act in such a manner as to provide a clear but not entirely inelegant translation of Rigord's Latin prose to a wide anglophone readership. The translator's own perspective can be found in the postscript to the volume.

---

126. See https://thehaskinssociety.wildapricot.org/Translated-Documents.

127. As he indicates in the foreword, Paul Hyams's translation began its life in the early 1990s as source material for a course on medieval France at Cornell University. It remains accessible at http://prh3.arts.cornell.edu/408/texts/Rigindex.html. The section pertaining to the persecution of the Jews is printed in Kenneth Stow, *Jewish Dogs: An Image and Its Interpreters* (Stanford: Stanford University Press, 2006), 183–87.

The Deeds of Philip Augustus, by Rigord

To his most fair and beloved lord Louis,[1] illustrious son of Philip [II] by the grace of God ever Augustus king of the Franks, a youth of royal lineage destined for *honor and glory*,[2] master Rigord, a Goth in origin,[3] a doctor by calling, historian of the king of the Franks, the least of the clergy of the Blessed Denis the Areopagite,[4] wishes life and salvation from Him *through* whom *kings reign*.[5]

Holy mother church *is glad and rejoices*[6] in the Lord, because the Lord *visiting will visit*[7] his people *and will have mercy on his servants*.[8] *The voice of rejoicing and salvation* resounds everywhere *in the tabernacles*[9] of the Franks, for they see that their king, the son of the king Augustus, raised from the cradle

---

1. The future Louis VIII, born September 1187. This dedicatory letter was probably added about 1206.

2. Psalms 8:6.

3. Rigord is using self-consciously antiquated terminology to refer to his origins in Languedoc.

4. The monks of Saint-Denis believed that the third-century martyr-bishop Denis, apostle to Gaul and first bishop of Paris, was the same as Denis the Areopagite, in whose name in turn important works of apophatic theology were written (referred to under the name Pseudo-Dionysius). For a summary of Rigord's perspective on this, see Baldwin, *GPA*, 376–77.

5. Cf. Proverbs 8:15.

6. Psalms 9:3; Canticles 1:3. Biblical quotations are placed in italics throughout the text.

7. Cf. Exodus 3:16.

8. Deuteronomy 32:36.

9. Psalms 117:15.

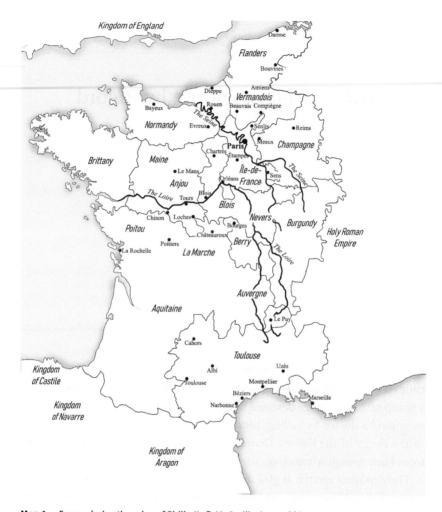

Map 1. France during the reign of Philip II. © M. Cecilia Gaposchkin

in the dwelling of wisdom, ascends to the royal throne of full-grown wisdom, and with divine grace smiling upon his efforts, drawing upon heaven, *prepares* for himself *a throne* of judgment and justice.[10] Oh, what a solemn and royal wedding of our Solomon! Oh, what a union, than which there is no happier on earth, when a king cleaves to himself the cohort of wisdom, and wisdom in return undertakes the office of king, in accordance with the divine oracle of Plato who foretold that the whole world would be blessed

---

10. Cf. Isaiah 16:5.

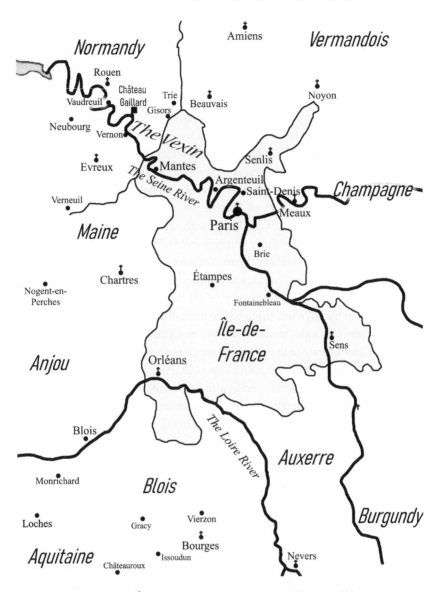

MAP 2. Enlargement of the Île-de-France and the Vexin. © M. Cecilia Gaposchkin

either when wise men began to rule or when kings began to be wise![11] And how admirable the maturity of this royal youth who, though still young in years, is now in some sense older than himself and ready for honor, for he has

---

11. From Plato's *Republic*, but Rigord would have known this saying through its citation by later authors, such as Boethius in his *Consolation of Philosophy*.

matured into virtue. His understanding outpaces his years, and his mind embraces vigorous reasoning. Indeed, with regal magnificence, impatient with the waste of ill-borne, ignoble delay, he does not wait for great accomplishments slowly born of the years, since to the Caesars virtue comes early. Now I seem to see in the days of this most wise and gentle prince the restoration both of peace to the poor and of the respect formerly shown to churches, when power will have been vested in him for the judgment of wickedness,[12] and his ways will have been honed by knowledge to a model of uprightness, when, that is, he will understand and be able to *render to Caesar the things that are Caesar's, and to God the things that are God's*.[13] Then indeed he, the foundation of morals and the glory of knights, will show himself the example of the former and the sword of the latter, with no less praise for the one as for the other, for he will gloriously triumph over other foes when, through the armor of wisdom, he will have triumphed over sin; that is, preserving on one hand the freedom of his mind, and on the other the safe condition of the kingdom. Whatever is praiseworthy of the mind, the hand, or the tongue, his wisdom in his days will bring to the peak of praise.

Therefore, O youth "descended from royal lineage,"[14] it is because you study and love literature that I have made so bold as to submit my writing to your most fair good judgment, and I have determined that you must first see and read, just as I have fashioned it, a certain modest product of my nightly study, concerning the deeds of your most glorious father, Philip, ever Augustus. And I have done this with two goals in mind; that you may comprehend absolutely my devotion to the kingdom of the Franks and to your glorious father, and that you may have always before your eyes, as though in a mirror, the laudable deeds of such a prince as *an example of virtue*.[15] For although the offspring of a brave man may come to know the aspect of warfare while still in his mother's arms, and in obedience to nature learn to love the inspiration of fear, still he may be inspired to virtue no less by means of examples.

Therefore, famous youth, I ask that you take joyfully from the hands of your cleric this little work announcing your father's virtue. For though I may have written it in a rough, inelegant fashion, and with a vocabulary unequal

---

12. Rigord is articulating the ideal of the king as the guarantor of peace, protector of the poor and the church, with an obligation to promote good and restrain evil. The idea echoes the oath that a new king took upon his coronation. See, for example, the *promissio* from the Ordo of 1200, which is the promise the king takes before God, the clergy, and the people. Richard A. Jackson, ed., *Ordines Coronationis Franciae: Texts and Ordines for the Coronation of Frankish and French Kings and Queens in the Middle Ages* (Philadelphia: University of Pennsylvania Press, 1995–2000), 1:262.

13. Matthew 22:21; Mark 12:17; Luke 20:25.

14. Horace, *Odes* 1.1.1 (Loeb Classical Library [hereafter LCL], 33:22–23).

15. Cf. Ruth 4:11; 2 Maccabees 6:31.

to the subject, still in this humble speech you will be able to behold truth, and in truth, virtue. Let royal youth not reject royal courses raised to him as a toast, even if they are in vessels of common ware, but clean. Therefore, royal offspring, keep in mind and keep cultivating "the glories of heroes and your father's deeds, so you can know what virtue is."[16] And we may rejoice to engender in you the virtue of your august family, so that

Now when the strength of years has made you a man[17]
A world by your father's virtues pacified you can[18]
rule gloriously in the kiss of justice and peace.

At the close of this letter let us beseech the mercy of the Savior, so that "He in whose hand are all powers and rights of kingdoms, may look kindly on the empire of the Franks,"[19] and through the intervention of his glorious martyr and our blessed patron Denis and his companions, with the same grace with which He has happily raised you into boyhood, may He more happily move you through young manhood and by the pull of time through progressive accomplishments, according to your prayers, may He most happily perfect you into consummate adulthood to *the praise and glory*[20] of his name and the defense of his holy Church.

Here begins the prologue to the book of the deeds of King Philip Augustus "Given by God."[21]

As I was undertaking the task of writing a book about the deeds of Philip Augustus, the most Christian king of the Franks, many obstacles converged upon me: a general need or lack of resources, obtaining food, the press of business, a plain writing style, and a mind less tuned to such a thing. And especially because "when something novel is recited to numerous listeners, they often divide into different camps. One person applauds and says what he

---

16. Virgil, *Eclogues* 4.26–27 (LCL 63:50–51).

17. Virgil, *Eclogues* 4.37 (LCL 63:50–51).

18. Virgil, *Eclogues* 4.17 (LCL 63:50–51).

19. Rigord is quoting from a common prayer written originally for Good Friday but ultimately adapted for a variety of purposes. Eugene Moeller and Jean-Marie Clément, eds., *Corpus Orationum*, CCSL 160 (Turnhout: Brepols, 1992–), 6:67, no. 3846. The prayer originally asked the Lord to protect the empire of the Romans from heathen people, but was adapted in Frankish lands to read sometimes "the empire of Christians" and "the empire of the Franks." Rigord quotes only the middle part of the prayer.

20. Cf. Philippians 1:11.

21. This prologue was probably written after Rigord's first redaction (up through ch. 76) was completed in 1190, perhaps when it was given to Philip II upon his return from crusade at the end of 1191.

hears is worthy of praise, while another, led either by ignorance or the prick of envy or wicked with burning hate, maligns even what is well said. And it is a wonder that human kind has been so corrupted from its original state—insofar as God made good all created things—that it is more ready to condemn than to foster, and finds it easier to take something unclear and misconstrue it to its detriment than to place it in a better light."[22] Rumor wildly swings to both sides, and the tongues of deceit speak evil about good things and good about evil. For virtue always endures envy and is subjected to the venomous howls of rivals. If, in setting out to write the deeds of the most Christian King Philip, I strictly relate each and every fact about his virtues, I will be thought to flatter. But if I leave some things out because they might seem unbelievable, my modesty will stifle his due praise. Dreading just this, "I decided to suppress this work," the product of ten years' labor, "or destroy it altogether, to bury it in darkness, at least while I lived."

"At last," responding to the prayers of the venerable father Hugh, blessed abbot of Saint-Denis,[23] to whom I had shown these things in confidence, and at his encouragement, "I have brought this work to light" and have humbly offered it to our most Christian king, so that through the king's hand "it might enter the public records of history."[24] In all truth, however, "I willingly beseech the readers of this work that, if they should find here something worthy of mockery,"[25] they may take into account the depth of the subject matter, the simple nature of my learning, and the fact that my strength was unequal to the steep task. "Considering things in this light, may they at least learn that many things ought to be accepted which, if one were to examine them more closely, could be condemned out of strict severity."[26] I have written down some things which I saw with my own eyes, and some things which were inquired into diligently by others and which I may have learned less fully. What was not known to me I skipped entirely.

But perhaps you wonder that in the title of this work I call the king "Augustus." Writers were accustomed to call those Caesars "Augustus" who

---

22. As Marvin Colker and then the *HPA* editors have shown, Rigord is quoting from the beginning of Walter of Châtillon's prologue to his *Alexandreis*, written between 1171 and 1181 for Philip II's uncle William of the White Hands, archbishop of Sens and then of Reims. See Marvin L. Colker, ed., *Galteri de Castellione Alexandreis* (Padua: Antenore, 1978), 3–4, verses 1–13; compare the translation in Walter of Châtillon, *The Alexandreis: A Twelfth-Century Epic; A Verse Translation by David Townsend* (Toronto: Broadview, 2007), 29.

23. Abbots of Saint-Denis were Hugh Foucaud (r. 1186–97) and Hugh of Milan (r. 1197–1204).

24. Modified from the *Alexandreis*, ed. Colker, 4–5, verses 15–19; trans. Townsend, 29.

25. Modified from the *Alexandreis*, ed. Colker, 5, verses 30–33; trans. Townsend, 29.

26. Modified from the *Alexandreis*, ed. Colker, 5, verses 36–39; trans. Townsend, 30.

FIGURE 6. Birth of Philip II. London, British Library, Royal MS 16 G VI, fol. 329v. Reproduced by permission of the British Library.

"augmented" the *res publica*, from the Latin *augeo, auges*.[27] Thus he is indeed rightly called Augustus, from the increase of the *res publica*. He added all the Vermandois to his kingdom, which his predecessors had lost long ago, as well as many other lands. He most greatly augmented the royal revenue. For he was born in the month of August, in which month, the barns and presses are filled and all seasonal goods abound.

And first, as God wills, let us begin with the miraculous birth of this king, with the help of God, *who is the* prince and *beginning* of all.[28]

[1] The deeds of Philip Augustus, the most Christian king of the Franks.

In the year of our Lord's incarnation 1165, Philip, king of the Franks, was born in the month of August, eleven before the Kalends of September, on the feast day of Timothy and Symphorian.[29] He ought to be called "Given by God" due to the circumstances of his birth, because although his most religious father, King Louis [VII], had conceived a number of daughters by

---

27. *Augeo* means "I increase" in Latin.
28. Cf. Colossians 1:18.
29. 22 August 1165.

his three wives,[30] he was unable to have a male heir to the kingdom.[31] At last, along with his wife, the illustrious queen Adele,[32] and all the clergy and people of the entire kingdom, he turned to alms and prayer and asked God for a son, not asserting that he was worthy of this but trusting only in God's mercy, and saying, *"I beseech you, O Lord, remember me*[33] and *enter not into judgment with your servant, for in your sight no man living is justified,*[34] but *be merciful to me, a sinner,*[35] and *if I have sinned*[36] as other men, yet Lord, be sparing lest all that I have done before you perish. *Have mercy on me, O Lord, according to your great mercy*[37] and give to me a son, an heir to the kingdom of the Franks and a strong leader lest my enemies say, *'Your hope has come to nothing, and your alms* and prayers are naught.'[38] But you, *O Lord, do with me according to your will* and *at the end of* my *days*[39] and *command my spirit to be received in peace."*[40] Thus did he pray with all the clergy and people of the entire kingdom, and their *prayers were heard in the sight of the Lord.*[41] And so *was given* to him by God a son[42] named Philip, whom he caused to be raised most religiously and to be instructed fully in the faith of our Lord Jesus Christ. He had him most solemnly crowned at Reims. And living himself

---

30. Louis VII married Eleanor of Aquitaine in 1137. Their daughter Marie married Henry I of Champagne, and their daughter Alix married Henry's brother Thibaut V of Blois. After his first marriage was annulled in 1152, Louis married Constance of Castile in 1154. Their daughter Marguerite married Henry the Younger of England; after his death (1183) she married Bela III of Hungary. Their second daughter Alix was betrothed to Richard I of England, but the marriage never occurred and she eventually married William of Ponthieu. Constance died giving birth to Alix in September 1160, and Louis married Adele of Champagne in November. In addition to Philip II, this union produced a daughter, Agnes, who married the Byzantine emperor Alexius II Comnenas. For further details, see Cast of Characters.

31. For Louis VII, see the essays in Michael L. Bardot and Laurence W. Marvin, eds., *Louis VII and His World* (Leiden: Brill, 2018).

32. Louis VII's third wife, Adele of Champagne. See Jean Dufour, "Adèle de Champagne, troisième femme de Louis VII, une reine méconnue," in *Reines et princesses au Moyen Âge,* ed. Marcel Faure (Montpellier: Université de Paul-Valéry, 2001), 1:35–41; Maria Carriere, "Adele of Champagne: Politics, Government, and Patronage in Capetian France, 1180–1206" (master's thesis, University of Vermont, 2021); and Cast of Characters.

33. Isaiah 38:3; Luke 23:42.

34. Psalms 142:2.

35. Luke 18:13.

36. Job 10:14.

37. Psalms 50:3.

38. Tobias 2:22.

39. Cf. Daniel 12:13.

40. Tobias 3:6.

41. Cf. Judith 4:11; Jeremias 36:7; Tobias 3:25.

42. Cf. Isaiah 9:6; the Christ-like element is shown by the fact that this passage is used in the introit to Christmas Mass.

for hardly a year thereafter, he saw him ruling most gloriously *on the throne of the kingdom* of the Franks.[43]

King Louis had a vision about him like this, in a dream, even before his birth. It seemed to him that Philip, his son, was holding a golden goblet in his hand, full of human blood, and from it he was toasting all his leading men *and they all drank of it.*[44] At the very end of his life he recounted this vision to Bishop Henry of Albano, legate of the Apostolic See to France,[45] making him swear in God's name[46] that he would not reveal this to anyone before the king's death. When King Louis died, Bishop Henry made the vision widely known among the clergy.[47]

Thus Philip's father, the most Christian King Louis, happily went to the Lord in the first year of his son's reign, in the city once known as Lutetia and now called Paris. We will speak further of this later on. Now let us turn our pen to the deeds of the first year of the reign of Philip Augustus, the illustrious king of the Franks.

[2] The deeds of the first year of the reign of Philip Augustus, king of the Franks.[48]

In the year of our Lord's incarnation 1179, Louis [VII], the most Christian king of the Franks, now almost sixty years old,[49] mindful of the shortness of human life and feeling himself in ill health and suffering from partial paralysis, convened a general council of all the archbishops, bishops, abbots, as well as barons of the entire kingdom of the Franks, in Paris at the palace of our venerable father Maurice, the bishop of Paris.[50] When everyone had taken their places, King Louis entered the chapel alone, and after praying

---

43. Deuteronomy 17:18.

44. Cf. Mark 14:23.

45. Henry of Marcy (d. 1189) was a Cistercian monk and abbot of Clairvaux before being created cardinal in 1179.

46. I Corinthians 1:10.

47. This story of Louis VII's vision is lacking in the Vatican manuscript (*V*). It may perhaps have been added to Rigord's text when the Paris manuscript (*P*) was copied at Saint-Denis in the mid-thirteenth century.

48. Rigord begins by counting Philip's regnal years from the time of his initial coronation, while Louis VII was still alive. According to this reckoning, his first regnal year is 1 November 1179 to 31 October 1180.

49. The Paris manuscript (*P*) indicates "almost seventy years old," but since Louis VII was born in 1120, the reading in the Vatican manuscript (*V*) "almost sixty" is clearly correct.

50. Maurice of Sully was bishop of Paris from 1160 to 1196. The episcopal palace, which was begun around 1160, stood on the south flank of the cathedral, Notre-Dame of Paris, thus quite near the royal palace on the Île-de-la-Cité. See Victor Mortet, *Étude historique et archéologique sur la cathédrale et le palais épiscopal de Paris du VIe au XIIe s.* (Paris: Picard, 1888), 73–79; and more broadly Dany

to the Lord, as was his custom in all matters, he summoned one by one the archbishops, bishops, abbots, and all the leading men of the kingdom, and informed them that he planned, with their advice and consent, to raise his most beloved son Philip "Given by God" to be king at the coming feast of the Assumption of the Blessed Virgin Mary.[51] The prelates and leading men of the kingdom, hearing the will of the king, being of one mind, exclaimed one and all, "So be it!" Thus ended the council.

As this feast of the most Blessed Virgin Mary approached, the most Christian King Louis came to Compiègne[52] with his most beloved son Philip. There, as God would have it, matters turned out differently than he had hoped. For while the king delayed, as we have learned from many people, the renowned Philip went into the woods, with his father's permission, to hunt with the royal huntsmen. Just as he entered [the woods], he encountered a boar. At this sight the hunters quickly released the dogs and set off after the boar through the wilds of the woods *and of the vast wilderness*,[53] sounding their horns in pursuit down the woodland trails.

[3] Meanwhile Philip, astride the fastest horse, had outdistanced all the others and followed the boar alone for some time along another hidden path. After a little while he looked about and realized, as darkness came on, that no other hunter was around. Seeing that he was indeed left all alone in the wide empty woods, he quite reasonably began to worry as he wandered here and there, wherever his horse carried him. At last, now very anxious, looking high and low but seeing no one, with a groan and sighs he crossed himself and with great feeling commended himself to God, to the Blessed Virgin Mary, and to the most Blessed Denis, the patron and defender of the kings of the Franks. When he finished his prayer he looked to his right and suddenly saw in the distance a woodsman, a really quite large man, fanning coals in a fire. He was terrible to behold, all covered with black soot, with an ugly face and a huge ax slung over his shoulder. When Philip first saw him, he was afraid for a moment, like a boy. But his great heart soon overcame his fear, and he went up to the man and greeted him kindly. When the woodsman learned who he was and whence he came and why he was there, understanding that he was

Bull Shit

Sandron and Andrew Tallon, *Notre Dame Cathedral: Nine Centuries of History*, trans. Lindsay Cook and Andrew Tallon (University Park: The Pennsylvania State University Press, 2020).

51. 15 August 1179.

52. Compiègne is about eighty-eight kilometers (fifty-five miles) northeast of Paris, and about equidistant from Reims.

53. Deuteronomy 32:10.

his lord, he put aside what he was doing and immediately led him back to Compiègne by the most direct route. — K·u ɣ ɣ p̃wɛ̃r

As a result of this frightening experience Philip "Given by God" fell seriously ill. For this reason his royal elevation to the throne was put off until All Saints' Day.[54] But our Lord Jesus Christ, who never abandons *those hoping in Him*,[55] *restored* him *to* his former good *health* after a few days,[56] on account of the prayers and worthiness of his most holy father, Louis, who was praying continuously to the Lord on his behalf both night and day,[57] and because of the prayers of the entire Church. So, upon the arrival of All Saints' Day, with all the archbishops, bishops, and barons of his land gathered together, Philip was crowned at Reims by the reverend William, archbishop of Reims, cardinal-priest of Saint Sabina, legate of the Apostolic See, the king's own uncle.[58] Also present was Henry, king of England,[59] who out of due submission humbly held one side of the crown on the French king's head,[60] as all the archbishops, bishops, and other leading men of the kingdom and all the clergy and people shouted and proclaimed, "Long live the king, long live the king!"

Philip had just turned fourteen on the feast of Timothy and Symphonian, so that his fifteenth year had begun to roll by.[61] Thus he was anointed in the fifteenth year of his life, on the feast of All Saints, while his father, the most Christian King Louis, was still living but sorely weighed down by bad health; that is, by paralysis which prevented his getting about.

---

54. 1 November 1179.

55. Judith 13:17.

56. Cf. Matthew 12:13.

57. Rigord does not mention that Louis VII undertook a pilgrimage to Canterbury at this time to pray at the tomb of the recently canonized Thomas Becket, making Louis the first king of France to set foot in England.

58. William of the White Hands, archbishop of Reims from 1175 to 1202, was the brother of Philip Augustus's mother, Adele of Champagne (see Cast of Characters).

59. This is not King Henry II of England but his son Henry "the Young King" (1155–83), married by papal dispensation (due to their young age) to Marguerite, the daughter of Louis VII and Constance of Castile, in 1160, crowned in 1170 (Marguerite crowned 1172). See Matthew Strickland, *Henry the Young King, 1155–1183* (New Haven: Yale University Press, 2016) and Cast of Characters.

60. See Baldwin, *GPA*, 6–7. According to the liturgical rite, after the archbishop crowned the new king, the "peers" of France symbolized their support for the new king by ceremonially "holding up" or "touching" the crown upon the new king. This element of the rite is most clearly indicated in a manuscript of the mid-thirteenth century, BnF MS lat. 1246, fol. 25r; Jackson, *Ordines Coronationis Franciae*, 2:357. The young Henry carried the crown in the procession; although he was already crowned co-king of England, he was probably regarded as representing the house of Anjou. Though Rigord does not say so, the future Richard I and his brother Geoffrey were present as well (Louis VII had supported their rebellion against Henry II in 1173–74). By contrast, the absence of most members of the house of Champagne was notable.

61. That is, the fifteenth year of Philip's life began on 22 August 1179.

FIGURE 7.   Coronation of Philip II. London, British Library, Royal MS 16 G VI, fol. 331r. Reproduced by permission of the British Library.

[4] About his decree on gamblers.

We have decided, however, to write only briefly about the things which he did at the start of his reign, so that the chatter of our book and the exceeding plainness of our speech may not offend the refined ears of our audience.

From his earliest youth Philip had the fear of the Lord as his guide in schooling, because *the fear of the Lord is the beginning of wisdom,*[62] and he requested in prayer and humbly beseeched the Lord to guide his every deed and step. He loved justice as though it were his own mother. He sought to *exalt mercy above judgment.*[63] He never allowed truth to leave his side. More than all other kings, his home was a scene of marital fidelity.[64] Now in all truth, since it pleased him from his earliest youth to develop these renowned virtues in himself, it came to pass as time went on that just as the king

---

62. Psalms 110:10; Ecclesiasticus 1:16.

63. Cf. James 2:13.

64. Rigord could write this in all sincerity around 1190. His judgment would later change.

himself *feared and revered God*,[65] so he insisted that these virtues be adopted by everyone residing at his court. And what is even more marvelous, he so detested the mighty curses that gamblers at courts and in gambling dens often produce that if by chance a knight or some other person was playing in the king's presence and suddenly let out a curse, straightaway at the king's order he would be tossed in the river or some lake. And he ordered that such a rule should be most vigorously observed by everyone from then on. Well done, what virtue![66] From such beginnings, similar ends will result. *And thus the hand of the Lord was with* him.[67]

Jews welcomed → thrive → Collect debts in Christians

[5] On the king's hatred for the Jews.   *Christians are red*

A few days after the new king returned to Paris following his holy anointing,[68] he undertook a project which he had long considered but feared to carry out due to an excess of respect shown to his most Christian father. For he had quite often heard from boys reared with him in the palace, and had stored firmly in his memory, that each year the Jews of Paris would cut the throat of a Christian.[69] They would do this out of disdain for the Christian religion, as though in sacrifice,[70] hiding in underground crypts, on Maundy Thursday or during that holy week.[71] And continuing to perpetrate this sort of diabolical deception, many times in his father's day they had been caught and burned alive.[72] Saint Richard, whose body rests in the church of Saint-Innocent-des-Champeaux,[73] was slain and crucified in this way at Paris by the Jews, and

---

65. Cf. Luke 18:4.

66. Virgil, *Aeneid* 9.641.

67. Acts 11:21.

68. Since Philip II was anointed and crowned as king at Reims on 1 November 1179, Rigord implies that this episode begins before 1180.

69. The first ritual murder accusation against Jews arose in Norwich, England, following the 1144 death of a boy named William. See Thomas of Monmouth, *The Life and Passion of William of Norwich*, trans. Miri Rubin (London: Penguin, 2014).

70. The phrase *quasi pro sacrificio* seems to invoke the Eucharist.

71. Maundy Thursday is the Thursday before Easter, commemorating the day of the Last Supper.

72. The reference is presumably to events in Blois, where more than thirty Jews were burned in 1171, at the command of Count Thibaut V of Blois. See E. M. Rose, *The Murder of William of Norwich: The Origins of the Blood Libel in Medieval Europe* (Oxford: Oxford University Press, 2015), ch. 6; Jacob Rader Marcus and Marc Saperstein, *The Jews in Christian Europe: A Sourcebook, 315–1791* (Pittsburgh: Hebrew Union College Press, 2015), 92–97; and William Chester Jordan, *The French Monarchy and the Jews: From Philip Augustus to the Last Capetians* (Philadelphia: University of Pennsylvania Press, 1989), 18–19.

73. The church and adjacent cemetery of Les Saints Innocents (the Holy Innocents) is here referred to by its earlier name of Le Saint Innocent (Saint Innocent, that is, Pope Innocent I). It stood near the market area of "les Champeaux" in the heart of the Right Bank.

went happily to the Lord in martyrdom.[74] We have heard that many miracles have occurred there, brought about by the Lord through prayer and through the intercession of Saint Richard, to the honor of the Lord. And because, after careful inquiry, the most Christian King Philip learned more fully from his elders these and countless other unspeakable things about the Jews, such was his burning zeal for God that at his command the Jews throughout all of France were seized in their synagogues, sixteen before the Kalends of March, which was a Saturday, in the very year in which he took the holy reins of the kingdom of the Franks by his consecration at Reims.[75] And they were then stripped of their gold and silver and their clothes just as the Jews had themselves stripped the Egyptians when leaving Egypt.[76] This foreshadowed their own exile which followed afterward in the course of time as God so arranged.

[6] On King Philip's first war for the defense and liberty of churches.

About a month after Philip Augustus had received holy unction,[77] it happened that Ebbe [VI] of Charenton, in the region of Bourges, began to tyrannize churches of God and to crush with oppressive exactions the clergy who were serving God there. The clergy, unable to withstand his rage, sent envoys to the most Christian King Philip Augustus, protesting the violence done to them by this Ebbe and humbly seeking justice from the king. After the king heard the complaint of these religious men, burning with zeal for God in defense of churches and the freedom of the clergy, he marched forth with a strong force and devastated [Ebbe's] lands and plundered them; and [the king] so suppressed [Ebbe's] audacity that [Ebbe], driven by necessity, seeing that it was *impossible to escape* the *hand* of the king,[78] *fell down at the king's feet*,[79] begging his forgiveness and promising upon his solemn oath that he would most fully recompense all churches and clergy serving God to the wish and satisfaction of the king and would behave himself in such matters.

---

74. This Richard of Pontoise (or of Paris) was supposedly abducted by Jews and crucified. On this episode, see Rose, *Murder of William of Norwich*, 209–32; Kenneth Stow, *Jewish Dogs: An Image and Its Interpreters* (Stanford: Stanford University Press, 2006), ch. 3; and Jordan, *French Monarchy and the Jews*, 18–19.

75. According to the logic of Rigord's text, this date should be 14 February 1180. But that date did not fall on a Saturday in 1180. The date 14 February 1181, however, was indeed a Saturday, and William Chester Jordan has thus argued for the latter as the correct date (*French Monarchy and the Jews*, 30–31).

76. Exodus 12:35.

77. Thus December 1179.

78. Cf. Wisdom 16:15.

79. Esther 8:3.

Philip "Given by God" waged this first war at the start of his reign in his fifteenth year, and *consecrated* it *to the Lord.*[80] He is called "Given by God" because as king he was given by God for the liberty of churches and clergy and for the protection of the entire Christian people.[81]

[7] On the second war for the defense and liberty of churches.

Thereafter, in the same, that is to say the first, year of his reign, *the children of iniquity*[82]—that is, Humbert of Beaujeu[83] and the count of Chalon,[84] along with their accomplices—rose up against the churches of God, prompted by *the old serpent,*[85] the enemy of the human race. Since these men dared to impose grievously upon churches, contrary to royal exemptions, the clergy and religious men who ceaselessly serve God there reported all these evil deeds to their lord, the most Christian king of the Franks. Then, for the defense of churches and the liberty of the clergy, the king assembled an army and entered their lands and seized great amounts of property, and he so smashed their arrogance and their tyranny that by God's arrangement, although against their will, he returned everything and made full restitution to the churches. He reestablished a period of peace for the clergy and those serving the Lord there while humbly commending himself to their prayers.

Indeed, it is right that the universal Church should pray for the most Christian King Philip, for it is he who tirelessly stands for this Church, protecting her from enemies and defending her by expelling the Jews, who are the enemies of the Christian faith, and driving out heretics, who misunderstand the catholic faith. Indeed his *good* works are *established in the Lord, and so all the church of the saints shall declare his* words and deeds.[86]

[8] On the conspiracy of certain leading men against the king.

Later in the first year of the reign of Philip Augustus, the fifteenth year of his life, certain conflicts arose; that is, hatreds that developed among the leading

---

80. Cf. 1 Paralipomenon 18:11.

81. Again Rigord draws on classic tropes of good kingship. This passage mirrors the coronation oath in the rite of 1200, where the king promises to "uphold the justice and holy peace of the church of God and the people subject to me." Jackson, *Ordines Coronationis Franciae*, 1:262.

82. 1 Paralipomenon 17:9.

83. Humbert III of Beaujeu (1137–93).

84. William II of Chalon-sur-Saône (1168–1204).

85. Apocalypse 12:9.

86. Cf. Ecclesiasticus 31:11.

men of the realm. Certain of his leading men (*principes*),[87] at the instigation of the devil, the enemy of the Church's peace, dared to form a conspiracy against their lord King Philip Augustus. These men assembled an army and began to plunder the king's lands. Seeing these things, the most Christian King Philip, *inflamed with a very great fury*,[88] led an army of vast extent against these men. And after a few days he routed them and so bravely and powerfully chased them out that, as God miraculously arranged it, he brought them all to heel and most powerfully forced them to obey his will.[89]

Truly the Lord, who gives and restores all good things, leaves no good deed unrewarded. For the most Christian King Philip Augustus fiercely waged his first two battles at the start of his reign to defend churches and the liberty of the clergy, in honor of our Lord Jesus Christ and the Blessed Virgin and Mother of God Mary. And so our Lord Jesus Christ, who does not abandon *them that hope in Him*,[90] stood by him in the deceit of them that overreached him, and kept him safe from his enemies, and defended him from seducers.[91] And He turned the struggle in his favor so that he conquered all his foes, and He gave him might against those who unjustly connived to overthrow him. For *the Lord* is the One who *brings to nothing the counsels of nations, rejects the devices of peoples, and casts away the counsels of princes*.[92] This man is not abandoned by God *in the day of battle*,[93] for the angel of the Lord, *standing on his right side*,[94]

---

87. We generally translate *principes* as "leading men" rather than "princes," to avoid giving the impression that it refers to the king's sons, and also because Rigord uses it in contexts that include churchmen as well secular figures. In ch. 14 Rigord defines the term as "counts, barons, archbishops, and bishops."

88. Esther 1:12.

89. In the months after his coronation (November 1179) Philip reversed his father's long-standing alliance with the family of Count Henry I of Champagne, on which see Theodore Evergates, *Henry the Liberal, Count of Champagne, 1127–1181* (Philadelphia: University of Pennsylvania Press, 2016); and Cast of Characters. Philip II confiscated the dower lands of his own mother, Adele of Champagne (Henry's sister), dismissed Thibaut V of Blois (Henry's brother) as seneschal of France, and instead turned to the family of Count Philip of Flanders. Philip II's marriage to Isabelle of Hainaut (Count Philip's niece) in April 1180 was a blow to the Champenois contingent, since Isabelle had long been promised to the future Henry II of Champagne, son of Henry I and Marie of France (Philip II's own half sister). If this revolt by "leading men" was really in early 1180, as Rigord seems to suggest, then it would have been led by the Champenois faction (Count Henry I himself was not a factor, since he was absent on crusade between May 1179 and early 1181, and died in March 1181). But Rigord's chronology is not very precise, and more likely he is referring to the summer of 1181, when the Flemish and Champenois factions briefly joined against Philip in a wider revolt. See Theodore Evergates, *Marie of France, Countess of Champagne, 1145–1198* (Philadelphia: University of Pennsylvania Press, 2019), esp. 30–33, 42.

90. Cf. Judith 13:17.

91. Wisdom 10:11–12.

92. Psalms 32:10.

93. Zacharias 14:2.

94. Luke 1:11.

breaks the heads of his enemies.[95] *And why is this?*[96] Because he *continues always in the commands of the Lord.*[97]

[9] The deeds of the second year of the reign of Philip Augustus, king of the Franks.[98]

In the year of our Lord's incarnation 1180, four before the Kalends of June,[99] on that day on which our Lord Jesus Christ ascended *to heaven* on swelling *clouds,*[100] in the church of Saint-Denis, on the advice and counsel of a certain good man[101] who was observed to have *the zeal of God,*[102] this King Philip *put on the crown* for the second time.[103] And then was anointed his wife Isabelle,[104] the venerable queen, the daughter of Baldwin [V] the illustrious count of Hainaut,[105] the niece of Philip the great count of Flanders,[106] who respectfully brought the sword before the lord king on that day, as is the custom.[107] While these things were solemnly happening in the church of the most Blessed Denis, and while the king and queen, on bent knees and with heads bowed before the great altar were humbly receiving the nuptial blessing from the venerable Guy, archbishop of Sens,[108] in the presence of bishops and barons, there occurred an event worthy of recall which we believe should be mentioned here.

As these things were going on, a great throng of people had gathered from the surrounding cities, suburbs, towns, and villages. Greatly rejoicing to see

---

95. Psalms 67:22.

96. Genesis 3:13.

97. Cf. Ecclesiasticus 22:23.

98. Philip's second regnal year, counting from his coronation, should have run from 1 November 1180 to 31 October 1181, which would put these events in his first regnal year. Rigord, however, seems to treat 1180 (counting from 25 March, when he considered the new year to commence) as the second year of the reign.

99. 29 May 1180.

100. Cf. Matthew 24:30.

101. This may be a reference to Brother Bernard of Vincennes; see ch. 11 below.

102. 1 Maccabees 2:54.

103. 1 Maccabees 13:32.

104. Philip II and Isabelle of Hainaut were married 28 April 1180. The ceremony referred to here is not the marriage itself but the subsequent crowning of the queen and recrowning of the king. On Isabelle, see Aline G. Hornaday, "A Capetian Queen as Street Demonstrator: Isabelle of Hainaut," in *Capetian Women,* ed. Kathleen Nolan (New York: Palgrave, 2003), 77–97.

105. Baldwin V of Hainaut (r. 1171–95).

106. Philip of Flanders (r. 1168–91) was the brother of Isabelle of Hainaut's mother, Marguerite, the wife of Baldwin V of Hainaut.

107. The liturgical rites of coronation and unction included the ceremonial bestowing of the emblems of royal authority, including a sword, rod, and scepter.

108. Guy of Noyes, archbishop of Sens from 1176 to 1193.

FIGURE 8. Philip of Flanders leading King Philip; coronation of Isabelle of Hainaut with King Philip. London, British Library, Royal MS 16 G VI, fol. 332v. Reproduced by permission of the British Library.

such a solemn occasion and to behold the king and queen distinguished with the crown, the crowd got out of hand. A knight, one of the royal officials, with his staff in hand, tried to restore order by lashing about with the staff to the right and the left. With one blow he suddenly smashed the three lamps which were hanging above their heads, before the great altar. And the oil of these lamps, which dripped down upon the heads of the king and queen, was a sign, we believe, of the fullness of the gifts of the Holy Spirit miraculously sent from heaven to increase the fame of [the king's] name and to spread his glory far and wide across the earth.[109] For Solomon in the Song of Love seems to have said prophetically, *Your name is as oil poured out*,[110] as though he were saying *the fame* and glory and wisdom of your name will be *spread*[111] *from sea to sea and from the river to the ends of the earth.*[112] *And kings* will bow their heads before him and many *nations will serve him.*[113] From these and other things of this sort, we can see that these deeds, which happened around the king at God's direction, should be interpreted in this way.

---

109. Rigord implicitly evokes the myth of the Holy Ampulla and the miraculous consecration of Clovis, wanting to link Philip's second coronation to this sacralizing tradition established by Hincmar of Reims in his "Legend of the Holy Ampulla," which recounted the miraculous provision of holy oil from heaven at the coronation by Saint Remegius, of Clovis, the putative first Christian king of the Franks.

110. Canticles 1:2.

111. Cf. 2 Maccabees 8:7.

112. Psalms 71:8.

113. Cf. Psalms 71:11.

[10] On the death of the most pious King Louis [VII].

In this same year, fourteen before the Kalends of October, on a Thursday,[114] Louis, the most pious king of the Franks, died in the city which is now called Paris and is now the head of the kingdom of the Franks. Thus it came to pass, perhaps as God so arranged it, that the person who was king and head of the whole kingdom of the Franks happily went to the Lord in his palace in the city which is the head of the kingdom of the Franks. And thus it would become clear to everyone that he was passing in glory from a palace to the Palace, from a kingdom to the Kingdom, from an earthly palace to the expanse of the celestial paradise, from a realm that passes away to the eternal Realm *that eye has not seen, nor ear heard, neither has the* human mind been able to grasp, *what things God has prepared* from eternity *for them that love Him* in truth.[115] His body was entombed in the church of Sainte-Marie-de-Barbeau, which he himself had founded.[116] There, in honor of our Lord Jesus Christ and the Blessed Mother of God, the Virgin Mary, and of all the saints, saintly and religious men celebrate the divine office day and night for his soul, for that of all his predecessors, and for the state of the kingdom of the Franks. In this same church over the king's burial place, Adele, the aforesaid and renowned queen of the Franks, the mother of Philip Augustus, king of the Franks, had constructed a tomb made with marvelous skill from stones that were most delicately decorated with gold, silver, bronze, and precious gems. *Such a work of such delicacy has not been found in any kingdom* since the time of Solomon.[117]

But, enough of such matters. Let us turn to those things the king did, inspired by the Lord, concerning the treacherous Jews.

[11] The reasons why the most Christian King Philip, ever Augustus, expelled the Jews from the whole of France. Here the first reason is specified.

At that time a great multitude of Jews was living in France. Because of the lengthy peace and the generosity of the French people, they had gathered there long ago from various parts of the world. For the Jews had heard of the French kings' might against their foes and their great goodness toward their subjects. Therefore, their elders and those more learned in the law of Moses,

---

114. 18 September 1180. As he proceeds, Rigord becomes inconsistent in dating Philip's reign either from his coronation (1 November 1179) or from Louis VII's death (18 September 1180).

115. Cf. 1 Corinthians 2:9.

116. A Cistercian abbey founded by Louis VII. It was unusual that Louis chose not to be buried at Saint-Denis.

117. Cf. 3 Kings 10:20.

whom the Jews call *didascali*,[118] decided to come to Paris. There, by long association and usage, they grew so wealthy that they claimed nearly half the whole city for themselves. Moreover, against the decree of God and the established Church, they employed in their homes Christian servants and maids who thus were falling away from the faith of Jesus Christ and becoming Judaized with these Jews. And because the Lord, through Moses in Deuteronomy, had said, *You shall not lend to your brother, but to the stranger*,[119] the Jews, wickedly interpreting *stranger* to mean all Christians, loaned their money to these Christians in usury. And they oppressed the citizens, knights, and peasants from the suburbs, towns, and villages so much that most of them were forced to give up their property. Others in Paris, constrained by their bond, were kept in the homes of the Jews as though held captive in prison. Upon hearing of this, the most Christian King Philip, moved by piety, went to a certain hermit named Bernard,[120] a holy religious man who at that time lived in the woods of Vincennes, and asked him what to do. On his advice, [the king] absolved all the Christians of his kingdom from their debts to the Jews, retaining one-fifth of the entire amount for himself.[121]

[12] Here the second reason is specified.

The height of [the Jews'] damnation was their use of ecclesiastical implements consecrated to God, such as gold and silver crosses bearing the image of our crucified Lord Jesus Christ, and vessels which, because of the churches' pressing need, had been left as security with them. In great insult and affront to the Christian religion, their children drank their wine and ate sopped bread from the vessels in which the body and blood of our Lord Jesus Christ had been prepared.

They did not recall the story which can be read in the Book of Kings, wherein Nebuchadnezzar, the king of Babylon, in the eleventh year of the reign of Sedecias, the king of Jerusalem, captured the holy city of Jerusalem through his military commander Nabuzardan, because of the sins of the Jews. He plundered the Temple and carried away with him the valuable vessels

---

118. Rigord chooses a learned term of Greek origin to refer to rabbis. See Gilbert Nahon, "*Didascali*, rabbins et écoles du Paris médiéval, 1130–1161," in *Rashi et la culture juive en France du Nord au Moyen Âge*, ed. Gilbert Dahan, Gérard Nahon, and Elie Nicolas (Paris: Peeters,1997), 15–31, at 19–23. At this time the main area of Jewish settlement in Paris was on the Île-de-la-Cité. Out of perhaps some five thousand total inhabitants on the Île, as many as one thousand may have been Jewish (Nahon, 16–17).

119. Deuteronomy 23:19–20.

120. Bernard had been prior of Grandmont and then a hermit in the Bois de Vincennes. Baldwin, *GPA*, 34.

121. Thus Christians owing debts to Jews now only had to pay back 20 percent of the principal, which went not to the Jewish lenders but to the king's coffers.

dedicated to God which the most wise Solomon had made.[122] But Nebuchad-nezzar, although a gentile and an idolater himself, nevertheless feared the God of the Jews and did not wish to drink from these vessels or turn them to personal use. Indeed he saw that they were kept like a holy treasure in his temple right next to his idol. But Balthazar came along, who was the sixth to rule after him, and he *made a great feast for his nobles; he commanded that they should bring the vessels which his grandfather Nebuchadnezzar had brought away out of the Temple* of the Lord, *and the king and his nobles, his wives and his concubines, drank in them. In that same hour* did our Lord, angry with Balthazar, show to him the sign of his doom, that is, the *hand writing on the wall*[123] before him *Mane, Techel, Phares*, which, when interpreted, means, *number, weight, division. That same night* Babylon was captured by Cyrus and Darius, and *Balthazar was slain* amid his feast,[124] just as Isaiah had long before predicted: *Prepare the table. Behold in the mirror*, that is, on the wall, *them that eat and drink* from vessels of the Lord: *Arise, princes*,[125] take arms, for the state has been captured! And at once, as the *Medes and Persians* overran them all unawares,[126] Balthazar *was slain* amid his feast. Who then would dare to cloud over what God chooses to reveal?

[13] Here the third reason for the expulsion of the Jews is specified.

At this time therefore, as the Jews were afraid that their homes would be searched by the king's agents, it happened that a certain Jew then staying in Paris was holding some items as security for church loans. Specifically, he had a golden, gem-encrusted cross and a book of the Gospels marvelously adorned with gold and precious stones. He put these in a bag, together with silver cups and vessels, and—oh, for shame!—most wickedly threw it into the deep latrine where he usually relieved his bowels. Shortly thereafter, by the Lord's revelation, the Christians found all these items and returned them to the church which owned them, with the greatest joy and respect, after a fifth part of the whole had been paid to the lord king.

This year can by all rights be called a jubilee year, since according to the old law all property in a jubilee year was returned unencumbered to the original owners and all debts were forgiven.[127] And thus, by this release of obligations, brought about by the most Christian king, the Christians living in the kingdom of France enjoyed lasting freedom from the debts of the Jews.

---

122. Cf. 4 Kings 25:8 and following.
123. Daniel 5:1–5.
124. Daniel 5:25–30.
125. Isaiah 21:5.
126. Daniel 5:28.
127. Cf. Leviticus 25:10.

FIGURE 9. Philip II expelling the Jews. London, British Library, Royal MS 16 G VI, fol. 333v. Reproduced by permission of the British Library.

[14] Deeds of the third year of the reign of Philip Augustus, king of the Franks.[128]

In the year of our Lord's incarnation 1182, in the month of April, which is called Nisan by the Jews,[129] *there went out a decree*[130] from the most serene king Philip Augustus that all Jews should be prepared to leave his kingdom before the next feast of St. John the Baptist.[131] And he then granted them permission to sell all their household goods *unto the time appointed*[132]—that is, the feast

128. 1 November 1181 to 31 October 1182, dating from Philip's coronation.
129. First month of the Jewish lunar calendar.
130. Luke 2:1. No text of such a decree from Philip II survives.
131. 24 June 1182. On the expulsion, see Jordan, *French Monarchy and the Jews*, 30–34.
132. Galatians 4:2.

day of St. John—reserving their properties for himself and the kings of the Franks who would succeed him; specifically their houses, fields, vineyards, barns, presses, and the like. When the perfidious Jews heard this, some of them, born anew *of water and the Holy Spirit,*[133] turned to the Lord and carried on in the faith of our Lord Jesus Christ. To them, the king, because of his devotion to the Christian religion, restored entirely all of their property and gave them their freedom forevermore.[134] Others, imbued with their ancient error, and persisting in their perfidy, began to entice the leading men of the land—that is, the counts, barons, archbishops, and bishops—with gifts and large promises, trying to determine if, by their counsel and the promise and offer of great sums of money, they might somehow make the king turn away from his fixed decision. But the *merciful and compassionate God,*[135] *who does not forsake them that hope in Him*[136] *and humbles those who presume their own strength,*[137] by a flood of grace sent down from heaven, so fortified the king's mind, which was alight with the fiery force of the Holy Spirit, that he could not be softened by entreaties or promises of worldly wealth. And truly, we can adapt something said about the blessed Agatha, "Sooner will rocks soften and iron turn to lead than will the mind"[138] of the most Christian king abandon its purpose *inspired by God.*[139]

[15] On the defeat of the leading men.

Therefore the infidel Jews marveled at the fortitude of King Philip and his immovable *constancy* in the Lord,[140] when they perceived the defeat of the leading men through whom they had easily bent the king's predecessors to do as they wished. Thunderstruck and nearly dumbstruck, subject to no little wonderment, they went about crying out *"Scema Israhel!"* that is, "Hear, O Israel!"[141] and ran off to sell all their household goods. *For the time* now was approaching[142] when by the king's decree they were bound to leave all of France, for it could not be put off for any reason. Then the Jews, rushing to do as the king ordered, sold off their movable possessions in wondrous haste.

---

133. John 3:5. That is, they accepted baptism.

134. Jews were regarded as serfs of the crown. Thus, according to Rigord, Philip II was acknowledging that conversion to Christianity brought with it a change in this status.

135. Cf. James 5:11.

136. Judith 13:17.

137. Cf. Judith 6:15.

138. Cf. *Vita s. Agathae* (*Acta sanctorum* 5, 1 Feb., 624–25).

139. 2 Timothy 3:16.

140. Cf. Acts 4:13.

141. The phrase appears numerous times in Deuteronomy and elsewhere in the Old Testament.

142. Apocalypse 1:3.

All interests in immovable property were assigned to the royal treasury.[143] Therefore, because their possessions had been sold, the Jews had money for their travels. And they left with their wives and children and their entire households in the abovementioned year of our Lord 1182 in the month of July, which is called Tamuz by the Jews,[144] in the third year of the reign of King Philip Augustus and in the seventeenth year of his life, which had begun in the previous month of August, that is, on the feast of St. Symphorian, eleven before the Kalends of September.[145] And thus the seventeenth year of the king's life came to an end the following month, after the expulsion of the Jews, that is, in August. They had departed, as we said, in the month of July, and thus only three weeks or fifteen days were left until the end of his seventeenth year.

[16] How King Philip, ever Augustus, had the synagogues of the Jews consecrated as churches to God.

When the expulsion of the perfidious Jews and their dispersal throughout the world had been accomplished, King Philip, ever Augustus, mindful of what they had done, in the year of the Lord's incarnation 1183 and at the start of his eighteenth year, more gloriously completed, thanks to God, the work he had gloriously begun. For he ordered that all the Jews' synagogues—which is what they called these supposed schools where the Jews gathered daily for duplicitous sermons ostensibly about their concocted religion—be made clean. And then, against the will of all the leading men, he had these same synagogues consecrated as churches to God, and he directed that altars there be consecrated in honor of our Lord Jesus Christ and of the Blessed Mother of God, the Virgin Mary. For, indeed, it was his upright and considered opinion that where the name of Jesus Christ of Nazareth had been maligned from day to day, as we are told by Jerome in his introduction to the Book of Isaiah,[146] that in that same place the clergy and all the Christian people should praise God, *who alone does great wonders.*[147]

---

143. The distinction is that the Jews were allowed to sell personal property, but "real" property (interest in real estate and buildings) would revert to the royal fisc and could be sold off or donated to churches.

144. Fourth month of the Jewish lunar calendar.

145. 22 August 1182.

146. The reference is to the prologue to Isaiah provided by Saint Jerome, the translator of the Vulgate Bible.

147. Psalms 135:4.

[17] On the founding of the prebends at Orléans.

When all the knights of France and the citizens and other townspeople observed the miraculous works of the king, which were coming to pass in their own time, as God ordered, and when they considered their king, *an ingenious young man*,[148] and marveled at his deeds, *they blessed the Lord*,[149] *who gave such power to men*.[150] And, if you wish to *consider diligently* the matter,[151] you will find in him those same four glorious virtues that Moses said were to be foremost in choosing a leader—that is, power, fear of God, love of truth, hatred of greed.[152] With offense to no one, I say that this man is careful in speech, just in judgments, sharp in answers, prudent in counsel, true in promises, energetic in deeds, fierce to his foes, dutiful to his subjects, famous in generosity, renowned in all honest things.

Led by his example and desiring to emulate their head, that is, the king, the citizens of Orléans founded perpetual prebends in a church which had once been the synagogue in Orléans.[153] Designated clergy perform divine offices there day and night on behalf of the king, all Christian people, and the state of the kingdom of the Franks. We have seen that this same thing has been done in a church in Étampes, which had been a synagogue.

We have learned from the deeds of the kings of the Franks that on another occasion, but many, many years earlier, another such exile or expulsion of the Jews was brought about.

[18] The first exile of the Jews, which is placed last in our story.

In the *Deeds of the Franks*,[154] we read that at the time of Dagobert, the most eloquent king of the Franks,[155] the emperor Heraclius ruled the empire of the Romans.[156] He was a man most wise in the liberal arts and especially in

---

148. Cf. 3 Kings 11:28.

149. 2 Maccabees 15:34.

150. Matthew 9:8.

151. Proverbs 23:1.

152. Cf. Exodus 18:21.

153. A prebend is church revenue designated to support a canon or chapter member of a collegiate church. In other words, not only was the synagogue of Orléans made into a church, but financial measures were put in place to guarantee that clerics would perform the divine office there.

154. Rigord was able to drawn on previous historical writing at Saint-Denis, and directly on the monastery's library. As Carpentier, Pon, and Chauvin show (*HPA*, 88–89), his direct source was the *De Gestis Francorum*, which is today Paris, Bibliothèque Mazarine MS 2013, fols. 136 and following, augmented by Aimon of Fleury and other writings which he cites directly.

155. Dagobert I, king of the Franks (r. 629–38).

156. Heraclius, Byzantine (or Eastern Roman) emperor (r. 610–41).

astronomy, which flourished widely at that time. But as the number of the faithful grew, the study of astronomy fell away from common use and was eliminated by congregations of the faithful as idolatrous. Heraclius wrote to Dagobert, the most outstanding king of the Franks, that he should drive all of the Jews from his kingdom. And this was done, because that same emperor had foreseen through astronomical indications, to which he gave constant attention, that the Roman Empire was to be destroyed by a circumcised people.

He had thought this was going to be done by the Jews, but it is now clearly discernible that it was done by the people of Hagar, whom we call the Saracens,[157] since it is known that his empire was seized and violently plundered by these people, and Methodius says it will happen once again *in the end of times.*[158] These people are the Ishmaelites, who are descended from Ishmael. They are all circumcised, because, as it is written, their father, Ishmael, son of Abraham, was circumcised.[159] The martyr Methodius has even left us writing about them. For it will come to pass *in the end of times*—that is, around the time of Antichrist—that they will come out *yet once more*[160] and they will have the earth through eight weeks of years, that is, for fifty-six years. And because of the trials and tribulations which Christians will endure at that time, their path will be called "the way of hardship."[161] "They will slay priests in holy places, and sleep with women there as well."[162] "They will tie their mounts to the tombs of the saints"[163]—that is, in churches—and make their stables by the bodies of the martyr saints. And this will be because of the wickedness of the Christians who will then be there. Josephus even says that the whole earth will be their abode, and he is witness that they will even hold the islands of the sea.[164]

---

157. In Genesis 16, Hagar (Sarah's maid) gives birth to Abraham's firstborn son, Ishmael. Well before the rise of Islam, Christians already considered Arabs descendants of Ishmael; eventually the terms Agarenes, Saracens, and Ishmaelites were used interchangeably by medieval Christian authors. See John V. Tolan, *Saracens: Islam in the Medieval European Imagination* (New York: Columbia University Press, 2002), 10–11.

158. Daniel 11:13. The *Apocalypse* of Pseudo-Methodius was written in Syria in the seventh century (subsequently translated into Latin). Pseudo-Methodius was the first author to incorporate Islam into the prophesized history of the Second Coming based on the Book of the Apocalypse (also known as the Book of Revelation). See Pseudo-Methodius, *Apocalypse: An Alexandrian World Chronicle*, ed. and trans. Benjamin Garstad (Cambridge, MA: Harvard University Press, 2012).

159. Genesis 17.

160. Hebrews 12:26, 27.

161. Pseudo-Methodius, *Apocalypse*, trans. Garstad, 116.

162. Cf. Pseudo-Methodius, *Apocalypse*, trans. Garstad, 118.

163. Pseudo-Methodius, *Apocalypse*, trans. Garstad, 120.

164. Flavius Josephus (37–100), *Jewish Antiquities*. HPA points out that a copy of this work was made at Saint-Denis in the ninth century.

Having briefly touched on these things, God willing, let us return to the examination of the deeds of the fourth year of the reign of Philip Augustus, king of the Franks.

[19] The deeds of the fourth year of the reign of Philip Augustus, king of the Franks.[165]

So in that same year, which was the year of our Lord's incarnation 1183 and the fourth year of the reign of the most Christian King Philip, it came to pass that that king, in response to the entreaties of many people, and especially to the proposal of a particular official who at that time seemed to be very devoted to advancing the king's interests in Paris, bought for himself and his successors the markets possessed by lepers who lived outside the city,[166] and moved [these markets] into the city, that is, within the open market space known as the Champeaux.[167] He had two large structures built there, which the people call Les Halles, for the convenience and the greatest advantage of occupants. This was done through the management of the abovementioned official, who was truly outstanding at this kind of business, so that when it rained the merchants could sell their wares good and dry, and at night they could keep them safe from attack by robbers. As a greater safeguard for these *halles*, [the king] ordered that a wall be built around them, directing that there be a sufficient number of gates which would always be shut at night. And between this outer wall and the merchants' *halles* he erected covered booths so that the merchants would not have to halt their commerce and thus suffer losses when it rained.

[20] On the circuit of the wall around the forest of Vincennes.

At this same time Philip Augustus, king of the Franks, desiring the expansion and development of the kingdom, built an excellent wall around the forest of Vincennes, which during all the time of his predecessors had not been fenced off and remained wide open to all passersby. Upon learning of this,

---

165. If Rigord had continued dating from Philip's coronation, he would have treated 1 November 1182 to 31 October 1183 as Philip's fourth regnal year. Instead, he seems now to switch to counting from the death of Louis VII, which would make Philip's fourth regnal year 18 September 1183 to 17 September 1184.

166. The fairs of Saint-Lazare, north of Paris on the road to Saint-Denis.

167. A market had been established on the Right Bank during the reign of Louis VI, at "les Champeaux" (see ch. 5 above). This area has continued to serve commerce since then. Today a large mall (after several rounds of urban redevelopment), the Forum des Halles, occupies the same spot.

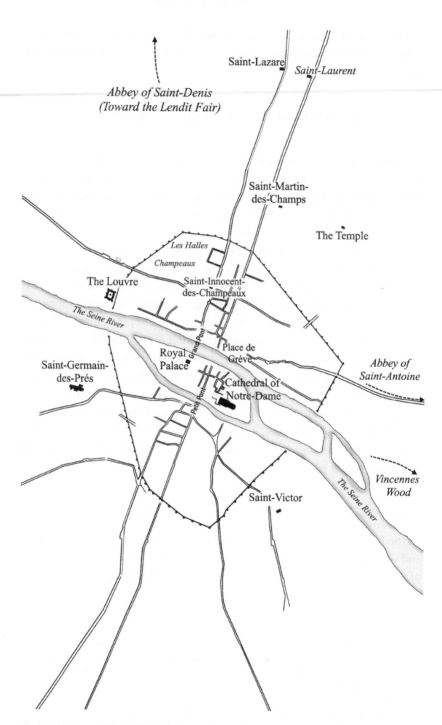

Saint-Lazare

Saint-Laurent

Abbey of Saint-Denis
(Toward the Lendit Fair)

Saint-Martin-
des-Champs

The Temple

Les Halles

Champeaux

The Louvre

Saint-Innocent-
des-Champeaux

The Seine River

Grand Pont

Royal
Palace

Place de
Grève

Saint-Germain-
des-Prés

Petit Pont

Cathedral of
Notre-Dame

Abbey of
Saint-Antoine

Saint-Victor

The Seine River

Vincennes
Wood

MAP 3. Paris, ca. 1200. © M. Cecilia Gaposchkin

Henry [II], king of the English, who had succeeded King Stephen on the throne of England,[168] arranged to have wild animals gathered from throughout Normandy and Aquitaine; that is, fawns and does and woodland goats. With great care he had them loaded onto a large boat, cleverly sheltered there and provided with forage, and he sent them down the Seine, a long trip by water, to his lord King Philip in Paris. The most Christian king *courteously entertained*[169] this present and had them enclosed in the forest of Vincennes beside the aforesaid city, with *garrisons* constantly *there to keep it.*[170]

[21] Events.

At this time many heretics were burned alive in Flanders by William, reverend archbishop of Reims, cardinal-priest of Saint Sabina, legate of the Apostolic See, and by Philip the worthy count of Flanders.[171]

[22] Another event.

In that same year, in the province of Quercy, in the castle called in the vernacular Martel, thirteen before the Kalends of June, Henry the Young King of England died. His body was taken to the city of Rouen in the province once known as Neustria but which is now called Normandy.[172]

---

168. Henry II reigned from 1154 to 1189, following a period of civil war between his mother, Mathilda, and her cousin Stephen from 1135 to 1154. See Wilfred L. Warren's classic study, *Henry II* (Berkeley: University of California Press, 1973).

169. Cf. Acts 28:7.

170. Cf. 1 Maccabees 12:34.

171. This campaign against heresy by the archbishop of Reims and the count of Flanders led to burnings at Arras around Christmas 1183. Briefly discussed in Evergates, *Marie of France*, 48; and more fully in Bernard Delmaire, *Le diocèse d'Arras de 1093 au milieu du XIVe siècle: Recherches sur la vie religieuse dans le nord de la France au Moyen Âge* (Arras: Conseil Général du Pas-de-Calais, 1994), 1:385–89.

172. The date would be 20 May, but Henry the Young actually died 11 June 1183. On his death and burial, see Strickland, *Henry the Young King*, 306–13. Martel is near Limoges. At the time of his death Henry the Younger and his brother Geoffrey were attacking their brother Richard (who was supported by their father, Henry II) in Aquitaine. The Young King's death also reopened the question of his wife's inheritance; Marguerite (daughter of Louis VII and Constance of Castile) had married the younger Henry in 1160, bringing with her the Norman Vexin and Gisors. Henry II refused to give back these lands, but the two kings agreed that when Philip's other half sister Alix married Richard (they had long been betrothed) she would bring Gisors as a dowry. Henry II, however, was forced for the first time to do homage to Philip II, in December 1183. For legal context, see Paul R. Hyams, "The Common Law and the French Connection," in *Proceedings of the Battle Conference on Anglo-Norman Studies IV, 1981*, ed. R. Allen Brown (Woodbridge: Boydell, 1982), 77–92.

[23] On the death of mercenaries near the city of Bourges.

In that same year, seven thousand mercenaries or more were slain in the province of Berry by the inhabitants of the region who had joined together as one against the enemies of God.[173] These [mercenaries] were villainously leading away prisoners and plundering the king's land, hauling away spoils and—for shame!—sleeping with the wives of the captives as they watched. And, *what is worse*,[174] they were burning down churches consecrated to God. They led away captured priests and religious men, and in mockery, while torturing them, they scornfully called them their chorus, saying, "*Sing to us*, chorus, sing!"[175] And straightaway *they gave* them *blows*[176] or vilely beat them down with huge clubs. Some were so badly thrashed that they gave up their blessed souls to God. Others, redeemed out of long imprisonment, ransomed for money, returned half-dead to their own. How will we ever be able to relate what follows without weeping and sighing?

[24] On the same.

Therefore at this time, as a result of our sins, these mercenaries attacked and plundered the churches. With dreadful daring and at the devil's bidding, and with hands defiled by human blood, they took out from the vessels the body of Our Lord which, serving the pressing need of the sick, was set aside there in vessels of gold and silver as was befitting, and—for sorrow!—they vilely flung it down, and *stamped upon it with their feet*.[177] And from the sacred linen cloth called the *corporal*[178] their concubines made scarves for their heads. With no respect, they carried off the gold and silver vessels in which [the body of Our Lord] was kept and prepared, and hacked them to pieces with hammers and stones.

Seeing all this, the local inhabitants sent letters to their lord Philip, the most Christian king of the Franks, informing him of these evils. *When he heard this*,[179] burning with God's zeal, he dispatched his army to aid them.

---

173. As Rigord's positioning of this episode immediately following the death of Henry the Young hints, these "mercenaries" were involved in fighting between Henry II's sons in southern France, a region notorious for the problems created by the use of such soldiers-for-hire in the battles between Angevins, Capetians, the king of Aragon, and the count of Toulouse.

174. John 2:10.

175. Cf. Psalms 136:3.

176. John 19:3.

177. Cf. Daniel 7:19.

178. The *corporal* is a linen cloth placed on the altar during Mass.

179. Matthew 15:121.

At the arrival of the king's army, together they attacked the enemy and slew them all, *from the least to the greatest,*[180] and from the spoils many were enriched. The people, *seeing what was done,*[181] came back glorifying and praising God *for all the things they had heard and seen.*[182]

[25] On the miraculous restoration of peace between Count Raymond of Saint-Gilles and the king of Aragon.

There had arisen, however, *a great dissension,*[183] developed now from years long past, between the king of Aragon and Count Raymond of Saint-Gilles,[184] which by the prompting of the devil, the enemy of the human race, could not in any way be laid to rest. But *the Lord, hearing his poor* people crying out in such oppression and long suffering,[185] *sent them a savior;*[186] not an emperor, not a king, not a prince of the church, but a certain poor man named Durand.[187] It is said that the Lord appeared to him in the city of Anicius, which is now commonly called Le Puy, and gave him a scroll on which there was a picture of the Blessed Virgin Mary sitting upon a throne and holding an image of our Lord Jesus Christ depicted as a boy and encircled by this inscription: *Lamb of God, you who takes away the sins of the world,*[188] *give us peace.*[189] Now, when all the leading men, great and small, with all the people, heard of these things that had come to pass by the Lord's instigation, they gathered together at Le Puy on the feast of the Assumption of the Blessed Mary *as is wont to be done* every year.[190] Then the bishop of that city,[191] together with the clergy and the people *and the whole multitude*[192] gathered for the feast, took Durand, a poor and common carpenter, and put him in a prominent spot in the midst of all the people and listened intently to him. As he most bravely

---

180. Genesis 19:11, etc.

181. Matthew 18:31.

182. Luke 2:20.

183. Cf. Acts 23:10.

184. Alfonso II of Aragon (r. 1162–96) and Raymond V of Toulouse (1148–94). Raymond's wife was Louis VII's sister Constance.

185. Cf. Psalms 68:34.

186. Isaiah 19:20.

187. Durand ("of Orlo") is described in a number of other sources, discussed in George Duby, *The Three Orders: Feudal Society Imagined,* trans Arthur Goldhammer (Chicago: University of Chicago Press, 1980), 327–36; and more recently in several articles by John France, including "People against Mercenaries: The Capuchins in Southern Gaul," *Journal of Medieval Military History* 8 (2010): 1–22.

188. John 1:29.

189. The entire phrase is used in the *Agnus Dei* section of Mass.

190. Cf. Ezekiel 46:12.

191. Peter IV of Solignac (1159–89).

192. 2 Paralipomenon 29:23.

related to them the Lord's command to make peace among themselves, and while he showed as a sign to all the scroll with the picture of the Blessed Virgin Mary, *lifting up their voice with weeping*,[193] shouting out their astonished response to the holiness and mercy of God, and laying their hands upon the sacrosanct Gospels, *with a most ready mind*[194] they solemnly swore to the Lord their promise that they would maintain the peace in every way possible. And, to indicate that the peace was to be maintained, the abovementioned image of the Blessed Virgin was stamped in tin and placed on their chests, with white linen hoods like the scapulars of the white monks, as a sign of their confederation. And, what is even more wondrous, all those wearing this kind of hood with this sign were so secure that if someone had killed the brother of another member in some fashion or other, and if the surviving brother, wearing the sign just mentioned, had observed his brother's murderer, he would instantly put his brother's death out of his mind and welcome that man with the kiss of peace, and *with lamentations and tears*[195] would lead him into his own home and *provide necessary* sustenance.[196]

Can it not be said in this instance that in some sense the prophecy of Isaiah [11:6] has again been fulfilled: *The wolf will dwell with the lamb and the leopard will lie down with the kid. The calf and the lion and the sheep and the bear will feed together, and a little child will lead them?* Surely by these beasts who live by prey and by flesh we understand wicked men; that is, killers and plunderers. By the remaining flocks [we understand] plain and gentle folk. And of these the prophet said that Christ tells them to live together and to keep the peace. And why is this? Because *the earth is filled with the knowledge of the Lord.*[197] This reconciliation of peace, accomplished through the man of God, was most strongly maintained for some time throughout Languedoc.[198]

[26] The deeds of the fifth year of the reign of Philip Augustus, king of the Franks.[199]

In the year of our Lord's incarnation 1184, in the fifth year of the reign of Philip Augustus, when he was twenty years old, a dispute arose, such as often

193. Genesis 49:2.

194. Exodus 35:21.

195. Cf. 2 Maccabees 11:6.

196. 3 Kings 4:7.

197. Isaiah 11:9.

198. Rigord writes *per totam Gothiam*, just as he referred to himself as a "Goth."

199. Philip began the twentieth year of his life 22 August 1184, and so at this point Rigord is clearly dating regnal years from the death of Louis VII. The fifth year would thus be 18 September 1184 to 17 September 1185.

happens in changing times, between the most Christian Philip, king of the Franks, and Philip, count of Flanders, over a certain land which is commonly called the Vermandois.[200] For the king was claiming that all of the Vermandois, with its forts, towns, and villages, belonged legally to the kings of the Franks by valid right of succession. Further, he was asserting that he would show this by the clergy and the laity; that is, the archbishops, bishops, counts, viscounts, and other leading men. In answer, the count of Flanders replied that he had long held this land during the lifetime of the most Christian King Louis [VII] of blessed memory, and that he had held it for a very long time without disturbance, in peace; and he was firmly asserting that as long as he lived he would never give it up. It seemed to the count that he would easily be able to reverse the king's view of the matter with many promises and blandishments, *for he was yet a boy*.[201] Indeed the hand of the leading men, as it was said, was on his side. But, as the proverb goes, "they conceived the wind, and *wove the webs of spiders*."[202] Finally, upon the advice of the leading men and the barons, Philip Augustus summoned *all the leading men of his land*[203] to gather at Karnopolis, the most beautiful castle called in the vernacular Compiègne. After holding counsel with them, he assembled a vast army near the city called Amiens. When the count of Flanders learned of the arrival of the king, *his heart lifted up*.[204] And gathering an army against the king, he advanced in arms against the king his lord, and swore *that he would defend himself from all*,[205] *with the strength of his arm*.[206]

[27] On the same.

Therefore, in the fifth year of the reign of Philip Augustus and in the twentieth year of his life, *the king went forth*[207] with his army over all that land and *covered the face of the earth like locusts*.[208] When the count of Flanders beheld

---

200. Philip, count of Flanders, controlled the county of Vermandois (in northern France, around Péronne and Saint-Quentin) through his marriage to Elizabeth of Vermandois, but his claims were in dispute after her death (without children) on 26 March 1182. Elizabeth's sister Eleanor claimed the Vermandois and sought Philip II's support. See Baldwin, *KLL*, 30–31, and *GPA*, 24–26. At about this time (March 1184) King Philip briefly announced that he intended to repudiate his marriage to Isabelle of Hainaut, who was to this point still childless. But Isabelle's public demonstration of grief brought this plan to an end. See Hornaday, "Capetian Queen as Street Demonstrator."

201. Cf. Judges 8:20.

202. Isaiah 59:5.

203. Isaiah 14:9.

204. Cf. 2 Paralipomenon 32:26.

205. Judith 1:12.

206. Isaiah 44:12.

207. 1 Kings 26:20, etc.

208. Judith 2:11.

the *exceedingly strong and mighty army* of the king,[209] *his spirit was terrified*[210] and *the heart of his people melted away* and they sought refuge in flight.[211] Then the count took counsel with his men and summoned by messengers Thibaut, count of Blois, the seneschal of France and leader of the king's army, and also William, archbishop of Reims, both uncles of the king.[212] Since both were loyal men of the king, the management of affairs was put in their hands at that time. Through these intermediaries, the count of Flanders addressed the king in this fashion: "Lord, may your scorn for us fade away. Come to us in peace and employ our services as best you please. The land which you claim, that is, the Vermandois, I restore to you in whole, my lord, freely and without any reservation, with all the forts and villages belonging to it. However, if it pleases your royal majesty, I ask that the castle of Saint-Quentin and the castle called Péronne be released to me, by royal gift, for my lifetime. And after I am gone may they revert to you or to your heirs and successors, that is, of the kingdom of the Franks, without reservation."

[28] On the restoration of peace between the king and the count.

Upon hearing this, Philip, the most Christian king of the Franks, called together all the archbishops, bishops, abbots, counts, viscounts, and all the barons who had come together with the sole intention of conquering this man's savagery and bringing down his pride. Turning to them for counsel, they all answered, as if with one voice, by praising what the count of Flanders was suggesting the king should do. After that, the count of Flanders was led in. And in the presence of all the nobility and the whole crowd there assembled, he justly returned to King Philip the land in question; that is, the Vermandois, which he had unjustly occupied for so long. And straightaway, in the presence of all, when the land was returned, he was placed in possession of [the two castles]. Moreover, he swore before the king that, in accordance with the king's will and command, he would make good, in whole and without delay, all the losses which he had caused to Count Baldwin of Hainaut and the king's other friends.[213]

---

209. 1 Maccabees 5:45.
210. Daniel 2:1.
211. Cf. Joshua 7:5.
212. Thibaut V of Blois (r. 1151–91) and William "of the White Hands" were the brothers of Queen Adele of Champagne. Thibaut was also married to Philip II's half sister Alix (daughter of Louis VII and Eleanor of Aquitaine). See Cast of Characters.
213. This peace was reached in July 1185.

And thus peace was restored between the king and the count [of Flanders], as though by a miracle, for it was concluded without shedding human blood. One and all who witnessed this, filled with excessive joy, *praised and blessed God*[214] who preserves all those *that hope in Him.*[215]

[29] Of the miracle done by the Lord for Philip, king of the Franks.

Among the other wondrous things which the Lord deigned to show to men on earth on behalf of his servant King Philip, we believe this one, worthy of greater wonder, is worthy to relate. Some good churchmen of Amiens have told us that while the most Christian king was encamped with his army near the castle which is called Boves, the horses that were hauling wagons all over the fields, and men as well as horses from the whole army, trampled down the harvest. And they harvested most of it by sickle and fed it as fodder to their horses, such that for that year almost no crops were left growing above ground. It was the season when the harvest produces ears of grain and flowers forth, that is, around the feast of St. John the Baptist.[216] But when peace was reestablished, certain canons of Amiens, who were accustomed to gather the crops of their prebends in the spot where the army of the king had been,[217] saw that the harvest was flattened and trampled to destruction under the horses' hooves. Grieving over the loss of their crops, they began to complain to their dean and chapter, humbly seeking and insisting that according to law the following should be done; namely, that for that year they deserved, in the name of fraternity, that the crops of the prebends lost to them from their allotted lands should be supplied from all the others that were held in common. Finally, the dean, upon the advice of the assembled chapter, asked that they patiently wait until the gathering of the harvest and the flaying of the grain, until they could carefully gather what was left of the harvest that had been trampled down by the army of the king of the Franks. And if it did not amount to the usual crop, the chapter would make it up to them in full. Well, marvel of marvels and beyond belief! As the days went by and through the miraculous work of the Lord, it came to pass that, contrary to what everyone thought, the harvest that had been trampled by the king's army was fully and abundantly restored that year, so that, after the flaying of

---

214. Cf. Luke 24:53.

215. Cf. Judith 13:17.

216. 24 June.

217. That is, these canons gained their allotted income by harvesting and selling the crops from designated plots of land.

the grain and the winnowing floor, they found a hundred times the estimate not only of the ears which been trampled down, but also of what had been cut with the sickle and fed to the horses of the whole army! Where, however, the army of the count of Flanders had been gathered, all the plants were withered, and not a blade of grass was found there that year.

Are not these and other things which the Lord accomplishes for his servant, the most Christian King Philip, worthy to be recorded in the book of his deeds? Beholding such a miracle, the canons of Amiens, with all the people, were in fear of the king, *seeing that the wisdom of God was in him*[218] *which instructed and teaches him*[219] what it wishes done with the help of Him who is the leader and origin of all.

[30] On the messengers from Jerusalem sent to Philip, king of France.

In that same year, seventeen before the Kalends of February,[220] a Wednesday, there came to Paris the patriarch of Jerusalem, Heraclius,[221] who had been sent to Philip Augustus, the most Christian king of the Franks, with the prior of Outremer for the Hospital[222] and the grand master of the Temple.[223] At that time the Saracens had entered the lands of the Christians of Outremer with a great army, and had slain many of them and had led many more away as captives. They had captured Jacob's Ford, a very powerful settlement of the Christians.[224] There they had killed most woefully many of the brothers of the Hospital and knights of the Temple and had led others away with them in captivity. For this reason, all of the Christians of Outremer, fearing lest the Saracens in their growing boldness seize the holy city of Jerusalem and outrage with pollution the Temple of the Lord's Sepulcher, sent the patriarch with the abovementioned two masters to France. They carried the keys of the city of Jerusalem and the Holy Sepulcher of the Lord to the most Christian king of the Franks, asking and humbly beseeching that he, by the inspiration of God and for the love of the Christian religion, might deign to

---

218. 3 Kings 3:28.

219. Isaiah 40:14.

220. 16 January 1185. Rigord has stepped backward in time to before the treaty with Philip of Flanders.

221. Patriarch of Jerusalem from 1180 to 1191.

222. Roger of Moulins held this position from 1177 to 1187. "The Hospital" refers to the Order of Knights of the Hospital of Saint John of Jerusalem, otherwise known as the Hospitallers. "Outremer" literally means "over the sea" and refers to the Christian crusader states in the Holy Land.

223. Arnold of Torroja held this title from 1181 to 1184. "The Temple" refers to the Knights of the Temple or the Templars.

224. Jacob's Ford was a crossing point on the Jordan River, near which the Templars built a castle, which was captured by Saladin's forces in August 1179 (on Saladin, see ch. 59 below).

offer help to the city of the forlorn land of Jerusalem. They endured many dangers at sea, repeated pirate attacks, and a long march overland, during which the master of the knights of the Temple succumbed to death.[225] The remaining two men, however, with the Lord leading their way, arrived at Paris. There Maurice, the venerable bishop of Paris, received the patriarch *like an angel of God*,[226] with a solemn procession and by the clergy and the people of the whole city. The next day [Heraclius] celebrated Mass in the church of Notre-Dame and preached before the people.

[31] On the messengers received kindly by the king.

As he learned of this, Philip Augustus, king of the Franks, laying aside all other business, hastened to meet the messengers, and he received them honorably with the kiss of peace. He particularly instructed his *prévôts* and administrators that they should provide funds from his revenues to meet their expenses wherever in his land they might go. He was moved by paternal piety upon learning why they had come, and he ordered that a general council of all archbishops, bishops, and leading men of his land assemble at Paris. A common council was held with them all, and by royal authority he instructed the archbishops, bishops, and all ecclesiastical prelates that they should encourage his subjects through frequent preaching and instruction to go off to fight at Jerusalem and defend the faith of the Christians against the enemies of the cross of Christ. Philip himself was then very busy with governing the kingdom of the Franks by himself, since he and the venerable queen Isabelle, his wife, had not yet produced a much desired child.[227] Therefore, upon the advice of his leading men, he devoutly dispatched to Jerusalem powerful knights with a host of armed foot soldiers, and he provided adequate funds from his own revenues, as I have learned from common report.

[32] On the duke of Burgundy.

Meanwhile Hugh, duke of Burgundy,[228] had gathered an army, laid a most forceful siege to a castle called Vergy *at the ends of* his *land*,[229] and fortified

---

225. Arnold of Torroja died in Verona (Italy) in October 1184.

226. Cf. 2 Kings 14:17.

227. In other words, Philip II was not willing to commit to the crusade at this point. He and Henry II met in May 1185 and decided that neither would go, but both would encourage their vassals to leave for the Holy Land.

228. Hugh III, duke of Burgundy (r. 1162–92).

229. Isaiah 62:11.

four *forts against it roundabout*.[230] He was alleging that this castle was within his jurisdiction and insisting, as though upon a sworn oath, that he would not abandon his siege through any accord until he should bring that castle within his own power and domain. Now, when Guy, the lord of the castle, saw the duke's resolute intention, and saw that the duke was working to deprive him entirely of the castle, he dispatched his messengers to Philip Augustus, the most vigorous king of the Franks. In his letter he laid out his desire that as soon as the king should come, he would convey the castle, that is, Vergy, to the king and to his successors to have forever. Now the ever august king, when he had seen and heard this letter, gathered an army and made haste to come to his aid to *deliver the poor from the hand of them that are stronger*, besieged and hemmed in by plunderers.[231] The king arrived as though from nowhere, lifted the siege, and leveled the four outposts which the duke had built. Having recovered the castle and garrisoned it with guards, he absorbed it into his domain forever and added it to the kingdom of the Franks. Shortly thereafter, Guy of Vergy did homage to the king, and upon public oath he pledged perpetual fealty to the king and his successors.[232] When this was done, the king forthwith restored the castle of Vergy, with all rights pertaining to it preserved in their entirety, to Lord Guy and his heirs. He kept lordship over it, however, for himself and his heirs.

[33] Events.

In this same year there was a partial eclipse of the sun on the first day of May, in the ninth hour, when the sun was in Taurus.[233]

[34] On the campaign of King Philip against the duke of Burgundy for the defense of the churches.

Following these events, after a short time, the bishops and abbots and other churchmen from all of Burgundy sent messengers to the most Christian King Philip Augustus complaining of this same Hugh, duke of Burgundy, on many counts, and seeking justice from the king. For long ago the most pious kings of the Franks, afire with the zeal of the Christian faith, like Charlemagne

---

230. The castle of Vergy was eighteen kilometers (eleven miles) southwest of Dijon.

231. Psalms 34:10.

232. For a discussion of the implications of pledging homage (and liege homage) in Philip's kingdom, see Baldwin, *KLL*, 107–9.

233. 1 May 1185.

and his successors,[234] having driven out the Saracens, the foes of the Christian faith, and after much sweat and hard work, reigning in peace, established with their own hands churches and a host of monasteries in honor of our Lord Jesus Christ and the Blessed Virgin Mary, Mother of God, and all the saints. They allocated to these same churches as a dowry, out of their own revenue, adequate income from which the clergy honestly serving the eternal God there could obtain their basic subsistence. Some of these kings, while they lived, chose burial for themselves in these churches which they had founded, giving them every sort of immunity, such as Clovis, first of all the kings of the Franks to accept the faith of the Christians,[235] who was buried with the venerable queen Clotilda, his wife,[236] in the church of Saint-Pierre at Paris, which he himself had founded and which, by a change of name, is now called the church of Sainte-Geneviève.[237] Childebert was buried in the church which was once founded in honor of Saint Vincent the Martyr,[238] and which is now called the abbey of Saint-Germain-des-Prés.[239] Clothar I was buried in the church of Saint-Médard of Soissons,[240] but this Clothar was not the father of Dagobert.[241] Dagobert is buried at the right side of the great altar in the church of the most Blessed Denis, which he himself founded.[242] Louis [VII] of holy memory, the father of our king Philip Augustus, was buried in the church of Notre-Dame of Barbeau which he himself founded.

[35] On the freedom of churches granted by kings.

Therefore, since the kings of the Franks desired to protect forever these said churches in their freedom, when they handed over lands to various nobles for their management and care they proclaimed that they were keeping the churches under their own power and protection, lest the nobles to whom the care and management of the land was entrusted should presume to load any burdens, taxes, or other exaction on the churches or the clergy there

234. Charles the Great or Charlemagne, king of the Franks (r. 768–814) and emperor (crowned 800).

235. Clovis I, king of the Franks (r. 481–511).

236. Clotilda married Clovis in 492 and is generally credited with convincing him to convert to Catholic (or Nicaean, as opposed to Arian) Christianity.

237. Sainte-Geneviève was on the Left Bank, inside Philip Augustus's wall.

238. Childebert I, king of the Franks (r. 551–58).

239. The Benedictine abbey of Saint-Germain-des-Prés was just outside the Left Bank wall of Philip Augustus.

240. Clothar I, king of the Franks (r. 511–61), founded Saint-Medard of Soissons, one of the great monastic institutions of the Merovingian period, in 557.

241. It was Clothar II (r. 594–629) who was father of Dagobert I (r. 629–39).

242. Dagobert founded the abbey of Saint-Denis, on the site north of Paris to which Saint Denis, after having been decapitated, was said to have miraculously carried his head.

serving the Lord. Now, in all truth, because the duke of Burgundy had sorely oppressed the churches of the lands rendered to him with frequent burdens of this sort, contrary to royal immunities, King Philip, having heard the complaint of the churchmen, gave warning two or three times in the presence of his friends, most kindly, that, out of concern for God and the faith which [the duke] owed to the kingdom of the Franks, he should return what he had taken and henceforth cease such presumption. And if he were unwilling to return the money to the churches, [the king] would punish him most severely.

[36] On the siege of Châtillon.

The duke of Burgundy, observing the intent of the most Christian king and his steadfast conviction in the Lord by word and deed, was much disturbed, and he left the court and returned to Burgundy. The royal majesty directed him to return to the churches immediately a total of thirty thousand Parisian livres which he had forcefully taken from them, and to make satisfaction to the king for the violence he had done. Since the duke was unwilling to do this and was obstructing with delaying tactics, Philip ever Augustus, king of the Franks, marshaled his army and moved against him. This knight of Christ, going to do battle, invaded Burgundy in defense of the churches and the liberty of the clergy, and he laid siege to the castle known as Châtillon,[243] since *the people as with the priest* were being trampled upon.[244] After some two or three weeks, when siege engines surrounded the castle, the king launched a vigorous assault. Many men were killed both inside and outside the castle. Others were wounded but restored to their former health by the blessing of medicine. Finally the victorious king took the aforesaid castle, that is, Châtillon, and had it well fortified and garrisoned with his own men.

[37] On the restoration of peace.

The duke of Burgundy, seeing that he *could not oppose the king,*[245] received some very sound advice and came and *threw himself at the feet* of the king[246] and sought his forgiveness. And he promised that he would make full and

---

243. Châtillon-sur-Seine is about 205 kilometers (130 miles) from Paris, and seventy kilometers (forty-three miles) from Dijon.
244. Isaiah 24:2.
245. 2 Maccabees 14:29.
246. Judith 13:30.

complete satisfaction to all the churches and clergy there serving God, in accordance with the judgment of the king's court. But Philip Augustus, most
wisely understanding that *wickedness of men was great on the earth, and that all
the thought of their heart was bent upon evil at all times,*[247] wished to safeguard
both the churches and himself in the days to come. For the king had indeed
heard from many people who had had long familiarity with his father, Louis
[VII] of good memory, that this very duke of Burgundy had often offended
that king, and had very often been summoned before the court, where he
would give assurance that he would obey royal orders to the best of his
ability and behave himself in matters like this; but as soon as he was back in
Burgundy, he would once again fearlessly offend the most pious king Louis.
Being well instructed by these and similar experiences, King Philip took an
appropriate guarantee as a bond, specifically three excellent castles, on the
understanding that he would hold and keep them until such time as the duke
entirely repaid the thirty thousand livres to the churches. But a short time
later, upon sounder advice from his friends, the king gave the three castles
back to the duke. Moreover, because the duke was not able to pay the said
amount of money from his own property, he granted to the duke by royal
gift a fief pertaining to Vergy. And so peace was restored and Philip, ever
Augustus, returned in glory to his palace in Paris, praising and extolling the
Lord.

[38] That King Philip commands that all roads and squares of Paris be paved.

A few days later it happened that King Philip, ever Augustus, was spending a
little time at Paris. While engaged in the affairs of the kingdom, he was walking about the royal hall. And when he came to the windows of the palace,
where it was his custom to divert himself by gazing out over the river Seine,
the horse-drawn carts crossing the city were churning up the mud and caus-
ing an unbearable stench.[248] The king, walking about the hall, *could not bear
this.*[249] And so he conceived a very difficult but quite necessary project, one
which none of his predecessors had yet dared undertake because of the excessive effort and expense of the endeavor. He summoned together leading
citizens and the *prévôt* of the town, and by royal authority he commanded
that all of the squares and streets of the entire city of Paris be paved with
strong, hard stones. The most Christian king was thus aiming to do away

---

247. Genesis 6:5.
248. This is in the royal palace on the western end of the Île-de-la-Cité.
249. Esther 7:6, 15:6.

with the ancient name of the city, for it had once been called Lutetia from the stench of the mud (*lutum*). But, rejecting such a name based on stench, people had then called the place Paris, after Paris Alexander, the son of the king of Troy.[250]

We read in the *History of the Franks*[251] that the first of all the kings of the Franks who ruled among them in royal fashion was Pharamond, the son of Marcomer, who was the son of Priam the king of Austria.[252] This Priam, king of Austria, was not Priam the great, king of Troy, but he was descended from his son Hector through Francion, the son of Hector,[253] as the chart below reveals:[254]

Priam, king of Troy

Hector	(brothers)	Troilus	
Francion, son of Hector		Turcus, son of Troilus	
Priam, king of Austria			
Marcomer, his son			
Pharamond, a son, first king of Gaul, ruled		11 years	
Clodius, his son		20 years[255]	
Merovic, of his line		17 years[256]	
Childeric, his son		20 years[257]	

---

250. Rigord devotes the rest of this chapter and chs. 39–43 to a mythical history of the Franks, who were supposed to descend from the Trojans. Broadly speaking, tradition had it that as the Greeks sacked Troy, the Trojans fled. Aeneas, son of Priam, king of the Trojans, was the fabled founder of Rome, while Brutus, another son, founded England (Britain). For an overview of this myth in the French context, see Colette Beaune, *The Birth of an Ideology: Myths and Symbols of Nation in Late-Medieval France*, trans. Susan Ross Huston, ed. Fredric L. Cheyette (Berkeley: University of California Press, 1991), 226–44; and more specifically Jerzy Pysiak, "De la Lutèce des Troyens au Paris des Capétiens: Philippe Auguste et l'origine troyenne du Royaume de France," in *Le sacre d'une capitale: Paris vu par les écrivains, les historiens et les voyageurs*, ed. Zbigniew Naliwajek and Joanna Żurowska (Warsaw: Institut d'Études romanes de l'Université de Varsovie, 2005), 11–22 and Baldwin, *GPA*, 372–74. As Pysiak points out, Rigord emphasizes Philip's descent from Priam and the Trojans in order to gloss over the discontinuity between Carolingians and Capetians.

251. That is, Pseudo-Fredegar's *Liber Historiae Francorum* (*Book of the History of the Franks*).

252. The fictional Pharamond and Marcomer are taken from Pseudo-Fredegar's *Liber Historiae Francorum*. Priam "the king of Austria" is Rigord's addition.

253. Priam "the great" and his son Hector are well-known figures from Homer's *Iliad*. Rigord makes "Francion" a son of Hector to create his link between the rulers of ancient Troy and the first Frankish kings.

254. The diagram is found in the bottom margin in *P* (BnF MS. lat. 5925, fol. 259v), but is absent in *V* (BAV Reg. lat. 182v).

255. Taken from Pseudo-Fredegar's *Liber Historiae Francorum*.

256. The semimythical founder of the Merovingian dynasty.

257. The first of these kings to be securely datable, Childeric was king of the Franks from about 456 to 481.

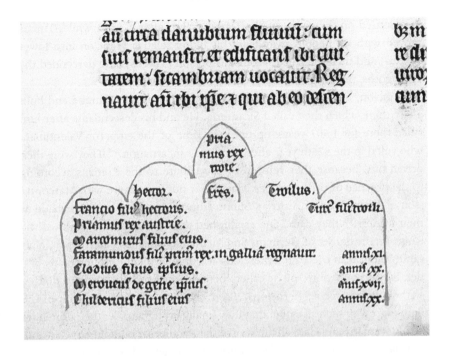

FIGURE 10. Diagram showing Rigord's reconstruction of early Frankish history. Paris, Bibliothèque nationale de France, MS lat. 5925, fol. 259va. Courtesy of the Bibliothèque nationale de France.

Since many often question the origin of the kingdom of the Franks, just how and in what way the kings of the Franks may be said to have descended from the Trojans, we have therefore worked it out rather more carefully with sufficient clarity, in this history of ours, insofar as we have been able to gather it from the *History* of Gregory of Tours, the *Chronicles* of Eusebius and Hydatius, and from the writings of many others.[258]

[39] After the fall of Troy, a whole host fled and then split into two peoples. One of these selected for their king a certain Francion, who was grandson of Priam the king of Troy, and specifically the son of Hector. The other group followed Turcus, the so-named son of Troilus, [another] son of Priam.

And this is how, as the story goes, these two peoples got their names, and why even today they are called Franks and Turks. Traveling out of Thrace

---

258. Gregory of Tours (d. 594) described early Frankish history in his influential *History of the Franks;* Eusebius of Caesarea (d. ca. 340) wrote (among other things) a universal chronicle; Hydatius (d. ca. 470) wrote his chronicle on late Roman history from the perspective of the Iberian Peninsula.

they settled on the banks of the Danube. But, after a short while, Turcus moved with his people away from his blood relative Francion into lower Scythia, and there he ruled. From this person [Turcus] have descended the Ostrogoths, the Visigoths, the Vandals, and the Normans.

Francion, however, remained with his people on the Danube and built a city there which they called Sicambria. He and his descendants after him ruled there for 1,507 years, up until the time of the emperor Valentinian, who ruled in the 376th year after our Lord's incarnation.[259] They were then driven out, because they refused to pay tribute to the Romans according to the practice of other peoples. Having set out from there with Marcomer (son of Priam king of Austria), Sunno (son of Antenor), and Genebaud as their leaders,[260] they came and established their home on the banks of the Rhine on the border of Germany and Alemania, which is called Austria. This same Valentinian tried often thereafter to conquer them, through many battles, but he could not. And he called them Franks from the northern dialect, as though from *feranci* (ferocious). From that point in time the valor of the Franks grew to such an extent that they finally brought under their dominion all of Germany and Gaul all the way to the Pyrenees mountains and beyond. But, later on, when the leaders Sunno and Genebaud remained behind in Austria, Marcomer, the son of Priam the king of Austria, who had descended from Francion, the grandson of Priam the king of Troy (through many successive generations which it would be long to list here), came to Gaul with his followers.

Now others had fled from the fall of Troy, such as the seer Helenus, the son of Priam, who settled with twelve hundred men in the kingdom of Pandras, the king of the Greeks.[261] But afterward Brutus migrated with his followers into England. Indeed Antenor decided to settle around the shores of the Tyrrhenian Sea with twenty-five hundred men. Aeneas, sailing the sea with thirty-four hundred men, was with great effort thrown upon Italy. These and many others of Priam's blood relatives were spread through far-flung places after the fall of Troy. Aeneas, together with his son Ascanius, came to Italy by ship, where Ascanius married Lavinia, the daughter of King Latinus, from whom he begot a son named Silvius. He indulged in a secret love affair and begot of his mother's niece a son, Brutus. He was joined by

---

259. Valentinian I reigned from 364 to 375, but Rigord seems to mean Valentinian II, who reigned from 376 to 392.

260. Figures mentioned by Pseudo-Fredegar's *Liber Historiae Francorum*, who would have fought Valentinian in the early 390s.

261. Rigord now largely moves to drawing from Virgil's *Aeneid* to link the origins of other peoples to this same story of the dispersion of the Trojans.

the offspring of Helenus, the son of Priam, and by Corineus, who was a descendant of Antenor, and then sailed to the island of Albion which he called Britannia after his own name. Appreciating the pleasant climate of the island, he founded the city of London in the likeness of Troy and called it Trinovantum, that is, New Troy. All the kings of England, which was first called Britannia by Brutus himself, are said to descend from him.

And observe that there were kings in Austria all the way until Childeric [III] the son of Clovis [III] the son of Dagobert [III].[262] But then, as the kings declined, leaders called mayors of the palace began to rule, such as Pepin, Charles Martel, and others.[263]

Marcomer, the son of Priam the king of Austria, came to Gaul with his followers. There he found plain-dwelling people who had descended from the fall of Troy and who had come with Francion and lived in Sicambria around the river Tanais by the Meotides swamps *and they grew into a great nation* over many years.[264] But 235 years later some twenty-three thousand of these Trojans left *Sicambria* under the leadership of a man named Ibor, seeking accommodations wherever they could. Crossing through Alemania, Germany, and Austria, they came into Gaul. Settling down there, they established themselves at Lutetia in the 895th year before the incarnation of our Lord. They named themselves after Paris Alexander, son of Priam, calling themselves Parisii. In that spot they carried on a simple existence for a long time. According to others they were called Parisii from a Greek name Parisia, which translates as "boldness." Now from the time these people left Sicambria they were there for 2,070 years until the time of the emperor just mentioned, Valentinian. *In those days there was no king in* Gaul *but everyone did that which seemed right to himself.*[265] They were subject to the Romans, however, and as was their custom they used to appoint a consul every year to govern the populace.

[40] At that time Marcomer came into Gaul with his followers. When the Parisii heard that he was descended from the Trojans, he was welcomed with honor among them. Because he taught them the use of weapons and

---

262. Rigord confuses Austria with Austrasia (the eastern part of the old kingdom of the Franks). Childeric III (r. 743–51) was the last Merovingian king of the Franks, though Rigord is mistaken in the genealogy here of Dagobert III (r. 711–15) and Clovis III (r. 691–95).

263. These two sentences are visually set off as a kind of insert within the text in P (fol. 260ra), and the phrase "called mayors of the palace" is missing from that manuscript. Pepin II, mayor of the palace 687–714, solidified the power of what would eventually be known as the Carolingian family. Charles Martel was mayor of the palace from 714 to 741.

264. Deuteronomy 26:5.

265. Judges 17:6.

because he had built walls around their cities due to the frequent attacks of robbers, they made him the defender of the whole of Gaul. He honored with the diadem his son Pharamond, a vigorous knight, the first king of the Franks. He desired that the city of the Parisii, which was then called Lutetia, be called Parisius from the name of Paris, in order to honor the son of the king of Troy, for whom the people had been named and in order to further please them. For all of the Trojans who had descended from the fall of Troy greatly desired that their name be spread far and wide through the entire world. Pharamond was the father of Clodius. Clodius begot Merovic, and all of the kings of the Franks were called Merovingians after this competent king. Merovic begot Childeric. Childeric begot Clovis, the first Christian king.[266] We will list here the names of the kings of the Franks descending from him according to strict historical sequence.

[41] Clovis begot Clothar [I].[267] Clothar begot Chilperic [I],[268] and he Clothar [II].[269] His son was Dagobert I.[270] This Dagobert had Pepin as mayor of the palace.[271] Dagobert founded the church of the holy martyr Denis and conferred many gifts on this same church. Dagobert begot Clovis [II],[272] and he begot Clothar [III],[273] Childeric,[274] and Theuderic [III].[275] The mayor of the palace to Clothar was Ebroin.[276] These three were brothers, the sons of Saint Baltilda[277] and Clovis [II], who was the son of Dagobert I. Childeric begot Dagobert, and he Theuderic, and he Clothar.[278] Then Ansbert ruled,[279] who begot Arnold, who begot Saint Arnoul who was later the bishop of Metz.[280]

---

266. King of the Franks, 481–511.

267. Co-king from 511, sole king of the Franks 558–61. Because the Merovingians divided the kingdom among sons of each generations, there were usually multiple kings of various parts of the kingdom (Austrasia, Neustria, Burgundy).

268. King of Neustria, 561–84.

269. King of Neustria, 584–613; king of the Franks 613–29.

270. King of the Franks, 629–39.

271. This sentence is written above the line in the Paris manuscript (*P*), absent in the Vatican manuscript (*V*).

272. King of Neustria, 639–57.

273. King of Neustria and Burgundy, 657–73.

274. King of Austrasia, 657–73; king of the Franks 673–75.

275. King of Neustria, 673; king of the Franks 675–90.

276. Again found only as an interlinear addition to the Paris manuscript.

277. Queen Baltilda (d. 680) was wife of Clovis II, and as a widow the powerful foundress of several abbeys including Chelles.

278. The last portion of Rigord's genealogy of the Merovingians is confused.

279. As Rigord moves to the line of the Carolingians, he continues to be on shaky historical ground.

280. Saint Arnoul was bishop of Metz, 614–41. He had been married and fathered children before becoming bishop.

He fathered Anchises or Ansegisel or Ansedun,[281] who fathered Pepin [II], the mayor of the palace, who fathered Charles Martel, who fathered King Pepin [III],[282] who fathered Charlemagne the emperor.[283] He was father to Louis the Pious the emperor.[284] His son was the emperor Charles the Bald.[285] He brought to the church of the thrice-Blessed Denis[286] the nail and the Crown of Thorns, and the arm of the old saint Symeon, and the golden crest of immense value with very costly gems,[287] and a golden cross with precious stones eighty marks in weight, and many other extremely precious gifts, which he gave the aforesaid church [of Saint-Denis] and which it would be long to recite here. Charles the Bald fathered King Louis [II],[288] who fathered Charles the Simple.[289]

In this same period, the Danes sailed over the ocean from Scythia and captured Rouen. They had a leader named Rollo,[290] who brought much grief to the churches of God. He brought under his control the whole of Neustria,[291] calling it Normandy after the name of his people. In the barbarian tongue, northern peoples were called Normanni, since they first came from that part of the world; for *Nort* is north, and then a person is called *man*. Charles the Simple made a pact with them and married his daughter to Rollo and granted to him Normandy along with her. Now this Rollo was baptized in the year of

---

281. D. 679.

282. The first Carolingian king of the Franks, 751–68.

283. Charlemagne, or Charles the Great, king of the Franks from 768, crowned emperor 800, d. 814.

284. Emperor from 814 to 840.

285. King of the western half of the kingdom, or West Francia, from 843; emperor 875–77.

286. "Thrice-blessed" is a common epithet deriving from Greek hagiography, not limited to Denis and not referring to any three particular qualities or events. We thank Christian Förstel for this precision.

287. The Latin word used here is *crista*, which, like its Old French cognate, could mean "crest," "gable," or "roof," and sometimes indicated an ornamental covering. Rigord is here referring to the so-called Escrain de Charlemagne, a ninth-century screen or crest which rested on a later reliquary and was indeed given to Saint-Denis by Charles the Bald. A 1791 watercolor of the gem-encrusted golden grille preserves its appearance before it was melted down at the time of the Revolution (see http://expositions.bnf.fr/carolingiens/grand/063.htm). Only one of the crest's jewels, a stunning aquamarine intaglio with a female face in profile said to represent Julia, the daughter of the emperor Titus, survives today in the Cabinet des Médailles of the Bibliothèque nationale de France. See Suger, *Abbot Suger on the Abbey Church of St.-Denis and Its Art Treasures*, ed. Erwin Panofsky, 2nd ed. by Gerda Panofsky-Soergel (Princeton: Princeton University Press, 1979), 62–63, 190, and plates 24–25; and Josiane Barbier, "Nouvelles remarques sur l'Escrain de Charlemagne'," *Bulletin de la Société nationale des Antiquaires de France* (1995): 254–65.

288. Louis "the Stammerer," king of West Francia, 877–79.

289. King of West Francia, 879–923.

290. Rollo was a Scandinavian (Viking) conqueror who settled in what is now called Normandy in the north of France and came to terms with the West Frankish king. The ruler of the territory was known as the duke of Normandy only several generations later.

291. Neustria was the northwestern part (the "new" part, in relation to Austrasia) of the Frankish kingdom. It included what would later be called Normandy.

the Incarnation 912 and took the name Robert. And from then on the people of Normandy, believing in Christ, have belonged to the Christian faith.

Thereafter, with many years gone by, William, who was called the Bastard, duke of Normandy, conquered England and there ended the line of kings descended from Brutus.[292] After this, Humphrey, the seventh in succession from him, conquered Apulia. Then Robert Guiscard, his son, added Calabria, [and] Bohemond brought in Sicily.[293]

Charles the Simple fathered Louis [IV],[294] and he fathered Lothar,[295] who fathered Louis [V],[296] the very last of this royal bloodline.[297] Upon the death of Louis, the nobles of the Franks made Hugh, duke of Burgundy, king over themselves; [this Hugh] was the son of the great duke Hugh, and was called Capet.[298] He fathered Robert [II],[299] who fathered Hugh, Henry [I], and his brother Eudes.[300]

Now this king Henry heard some rumors that in Germany, in the city of Regensburg, that is, Ramabroc, in the abbey of Saint-Emmeran Martyr, there had been found a certain body which they said was that of Denis the Areopagite.[301] He sent off his envoys bearing a letter to the emperor Henry [III],[302] asking that he delay the excavation of that body until it should most thoroughly be established by means of reliable envoys whether or not the body of the holy martyr Denis the Areopagite, the archbishop of Athens and disciple of the apostle Paul, was in France in the church that King Dagobert had founded. Upon being so informed, the emperor dispatched great and wise

---

292. The Battle of Hastings in 1066, in which William the Conqueror defeated Harold Godwinson and took the throne of England.

293. Rigord's reference to the Normans who forged the kingdom of Sicily is slightly imprecise. Humphry of Hauteville (d. 1057) had made himself count of Apulia by 1051, and his younger half brother (not his son) Robert Guiscard (d. 1085) solidified his power in southern Italy by adding Calabria and Sicily. Bohemond (d. 1111), Robert Guiscard's son, was a leader of the First Crusade and the first prince of Antioch (one of the crusading principalities).

294. Louis "d'Outremer," king of West Francia, 936–54.

295. King of West Francia, 954–86.

296. King of West Francia, 986–87. He died childless.

297. That is, the last Carolingian king of West Francia.

298. The ascension of Hugh Capet (who was not in fact duke of Burgundy) marked the Capetian dynasty's definitive control over the crown, at which point it is traditional to begin referring to "France" rather than "West Francia." Hugh reigned 987–96.

299. Robert "the Pious," r. 996–1031.

300. Hugh died young, Henry I reigned 1031 to 1060; Rigord is confused on the name of the third brother, which was Robert.

301. Rigord's monastery of Saint-Denis near Paris claimed to have the relics of Saint Denis (as Rigord indicates, Denis the Areopagite, Denis the archbishop of Athens, and Denis disciple of the apostle Paul were said to be all the same man as Denis the bishop of Paris), so this rival claim from Regensburg was a serious threat to Rigord's community.

302. King of Germany, then emperor, 1039–56.

men to France so they might learn the truth of this matter. Upon the arrival of these emissaries of the emperor, King Henry called together the archbishops, the bishops, and the barons of the whole realm, and together with his most dear brother Eudes sent them to the church of the most blessed martyr Denis. After a prayer had been said, the three silver reliquaries which had been most carefully sealed—those of Denis, Rusticus, and Eleutherius—were brought before all the assembled people.[303] The reliquary of the blessed martyr Denis was then opened and his entire body was found therein, along with his head;[304] that is, excepting the two bones of his shoulder that are in the church of Vergy, and a certain bone from his arm which Pope Stephen III[305] carried with him to the church in Rome and placed in the church which is today called the School of the Greeks.[306] All the assembled people beheld this, amid tears and sighs, *lifting up pure hands* unto the Lord,[307] commending themselves to God and the Blessed Virgin and the holy martyrs, and they departed in joy. Then the emissaries who had been sent returned with all speed to the emperor and assured him most fully as to what they had seen and heard. This was all done in the time of Pope Leo IX in the year of our Lord 1050.[308]

Philip [I][309] reigned after King Henry. He was the father of Louis [VI] the Fat,[310] who was the father of Philip who was killed by a pig.[311] He was succeeded by [Philip's] brother King Louis [VII] the Pious, who was the father of Philip Augustus.

[42] Now, in all truth, since we have briefly delineated the family succession of the kings, let us establish the period of time in which the Christian kings began to rule in France, according to the chronicles of Hydatius and Gregory of Tours, through the years of our Lord's incarnation. It is to be known that

---

303. The two companions of Denis.

304. Denis's head would have been separate, because according to legend he had been beheaded on the hill north of Paris (today's Montmartre), but then picked up his head and walked north to the site of the future monastery of Saint-Denis.

305. R. 768–72, but it was actually Stephen II, r. 752–57, who came north over the Alps to anoint Pepin III, the first Carolingian king of the Franks.

306. Actually San Silvestro in Capite, on the later history of which see Larry F. Field, trans., *Visions of Sanctity in Medieval Rome: The Lives of Margherita Colonna by Giovanni Colonna and Stefania*, ed. Lezlie Knox and Sean L. Field (Notre Dame: University of Notre Dame Press, 2017).

307. Timothy 2:8.

308. R. 1049–54.

309. R. 1060–1108.

310. R. 1108–37.

311. Louis VI's oldest son (1116–31), co-crowned with his father in 1129. He died after his horse tripped over a pig while galloping through Paris. His death left the future Louis VII as heir to the throne.

Saint Martin, bishop of Tours, departed from this world to the Lord in the eleventh year of the reign of the emperor Arcadius,[312] which is the 407th year from the incarnation of our Lord.[313] And from the passing of Saint Martin up until the death of Clovis, the first Christian king of the Franks, there flowed 112 years. Therefore, from the incarnation of our Lord up until the death of Clovis there flowed 518 years.[314] From the passing of Clovis up until the seventh year of the reign of Philip Augustus there flowed 667 years. It results, therefore, that the seventh year of the reign of Philip Augustus is the 1186th year of our Lord's incarnation.[315]

[43] Again, another demonstration of the same.

In the time of Aod,[316] the fourth judge of Israel, Troy was built and stood 185 years. In the thirteenth year of Abdon,[317] who was the twelfth judge of Israel from Joshua, Troy was captured. From the fall of Troy up until the incarnation of our Lord Jesus Christ there flowed 1,176 years. And from the incarnation of our Lord up until the passing of Saint Martin there flowed 445 years.[318] And from the passing of Saint Martin up until the passing of Clovis there flowed 112 years. And from the fall of Troy up until the start of the reign of Clovis there flowed 1,660. And observe that Marcomer began to rule in Gaul in the year of our Lord 376. Therefore, from that time there flowed 810 years of the incarnation of the Lord, until the sixth year of the reign of Philip Augustus, king of the Franks. We have judged that these matters should be inserted into our history without prejudice to the rest, because we believe that all the kings of the Franks have descended from these ancient roots.

[44] The deeds of the sixth year of Philip, king of the Franks.

In the year of our Lord's incarnation 1185, the sixth year of the reign of Philip Augustus, the twenty-first year of his age, in the middle of Lent,[319]

---

312. Reigned as emperor in the eastern half of the empire, 395–408.

313. Martin of Tours actually died in 397.

314. Since Clovis died in 511, neither of these calculations is quite correct.

315. The seventh year of Philip II's reign began on 1 November 1185 counting from his coronation, or 18 September 1186 counting from the death of his father. The *HPA* editors suggest that Rigord may have written chs. 1–42 by 1186, and then would have continued his first redaction up through ch. 76 by 1190.

316. See Judges 3:15–30.

317. See Judges 12:13–15.

318. Note the discrepancy with the previous chapter.

319. 20 March 1186 (this was still 1185 to Rigord, since he considered the new year to begin on 25 March). This date falls within Philip's sixth regnal year calculated from the death of Louis VII, which would be 18 September 1185 to 17 September 1186.

an earthquake occurred in Languedoc (*Gothia*), in the city which is called Uzès.[320] And in the following month of April, on the fifth of that month, there was a partial eclipse of the moon during the vigils of the Sunday of the Passion.[321] On the following Easter, Gerard, *prévôt* of Poissy, deposited eleven thousand marks of silver of his own property in the king's treasury and then left the court. Walter the Chamberlain replaced him.[322]

[45] Of the abbot of the Blessed Denis.

At that time, William of Gap was governing the church of the Blessed Denis in a lukewarm fashion.[323] The most Christian king, *being greatly displeased*,[324] was looking about to find another leader for that church. One day, however, while on the business of the kingdom, the king was passing through the town of the Blessed Denis,[325] and he stopped at the abbey of the Blessed Denis just as though at his own chamber. The abovementioned abbot, learning of the arrival of the king, was terrified, for at that time the king was seeking from him one thousand marks of silver. Gathering together all the brothers of the chapter, six before the Ides of May, after Nones, on a Saturday,[326] he abdicated his position as abbot. After this, while the monks remained there with the venerable prior Hugh, some of the brothers chosen by the chapter meeting told the lord king what had occurred, and asked him for the right to freely choose another [abbot]. With his usual kindness, the king at once granted them the right of free election, asking and kindly beseeching them that, giving thought to God and the honor of the king, they should choose without rancor or discord a competent and upright person of proven morals for such an illustrious church, which is the crown of the kingdom of the Franks and the burial place of kings or emperors. These brothers returned to the chapter and related the king's commands. And straightaway, by the hand of the Lord, it came to pass that Hugh, the venerable prior of that same church, was elected abbot by all the brothers speaking as one.[327] And right away, his election was confirmed by the most Christian king at that same chapter meeting, in the presence of the clergy and the people. One condition

---

320. It has been suggested that this reference indicates that Rigord was originally from the area near Uzès, since there seems no logical reason to insert this information otherwise.

321. 5 April 1186 (though Easter was in fact on 13 April in 1186).

322. On this event, and on Walter, see Baldwin, *GPA*, 34–37, 107; also Baldwin, *KLL*, 45–47.

323. William of Gap, abbot of Saint-Denis, 1173–86.

324. 2 Maccabees 11:1.

325. That is, the town of Saint-Denis, just north of Paris on the Seine.

326. 10 May 1186.

327. Hugh Foucaud, abbot of Saint-Denis, 1186–97.

and royal prohibition was added; namely, that in this change or advancement no gift whatsoever was to be given or promised to anyone of the royal family or the clergy or the laity or to any other person from the court.

[46] On the blessing of the abbot of the Blessed Denis.

Then the venerable Hugh, elected for the church of the Blessed Denis, understanding that his advancement was done by God alone and not by man, and desiring to maintain wholly intact the ancient worthiness of the church of the most Blessed Denis, most kindly called upon two bishops, that is, of Meaux and Senlis,[328] to celebrate the ceremony of his benediction in that same church. These two, and especially the bishop of Meaux, were bound by turns to attend upon the church of the Blessed Denis in the consecration of altars or the ordination of monks, according to the constitution of the ancient Roman Church. And so the benediction was solemnized by the said bishops in the church of the Blessed Denis, while seven abbots stood in attendance with a vast host of clergy and the people, fifteen before the Kalends of June, a Sunday.[329]

[47] On the king of Hungary's messengers sent to the king.

But while these matters were occurring in France, envoys were dispatched from Bela [III], the king of Hungary, Pannonia, Croatia, Avaria, Dalmatia, and Rama,[330] to Philip Augustus, the most Christian king of the Franks. For the king of Hungary had heard that Henry the Younger, king of England, the son of King Henry [II], under whom the glorious martyr Thomas, bishop of Canterbury, had suffered,[331] had been taken from our midst by the call of the Lord.[332] The king of Hungary passionately desired to marry [Henry the Younger's] widow, whose name was Marguerite—that is, the sister of Philip, king of France—both because of the ancient worthiness of the kings of the Franks and because of the wisdom and faith of the queen, of which he had come to know by her far-flung reputation.[333] Meanwhile, the emissaries of

---

328. Simon, bishop of Meaux, 1177–94; Geoffrey, bishop of Senlis, 1185–1213.

329. 18 May 1186.

330. King Bela III of Hungary (r. 1172–96).

331. Thomas Becket, archbishop of Canterbury from 1162 to his assassination in 1170. After fleeing England following a dispute with Henry II in 1164, Thomas enjoyed Louis VII's protection in Sens until his return to England in December 1170. Hence any mention of the martyred archbishop emphasized the French king's protection of the Church.

332. As noted above, Henry the Younger died in June 1183. In his youth he had been entrusted to Thomas Becket (then Henry II's chancellor) to be raised.

333. On Marguerite, see Cast of Characters.

the king of Hungary arrived at Paris and humbly laid his request before King Philip. He kindly accepted their request and called an assembly of archbishops, bishops, and the greater men of the realm, whose counsel and wisdom he often employed in transacting affairs. After consultation with them, in the presence of the bishops and abbots of his land, the king honorably handed over his most beloved sister Marguerite, the former queen of England, to the emissaries. And he granted her to Bela, king of Hungary, in lawful wedlock, and he amply bestowed royal gifts upon the emissaries. With the king's permission, the emissaries together with the queen then returned happily to Hungary.[334]

[48] On the death of Geoffrey, count of Brittany.

It came to pass at this time that Geoffrey, the famous count of Brittany, son of King Henry [II] of England, fell sick upon his arrival in Paris.[335] Upon learning this, King Philip, who was extremely fond of him, summoned all the physicians who were then in Paris and instructed them to exercise such care and effort as they were able upon the count. For several days the doctors worked away, but in vain. Fourteen before the Kalends of September he went the way of all flesh.[336] The citizens and knights of Paris watched over his body with honor and reverence in the church of Notre-Dame until the king's arrival, while the canons and clergy of the church celebrated the necessary funeral rites with solemn devotion. The next day the king, with Count Thibaut, seneschal of France,[337] arrived at Paris and arranged that [Geoffrey's] body, *embalmed with aromatic scents* and placed in a lead sarcophagus,[338] be buried in the same church before the great altar by the most reverend Maurice, bishop of Paris,[339] amid the assembled abbots, religious men, and clergy of the whole city.

---

334. In August 1186.

335. Geoffrey was the fourth son (after the short-lived William, Henry the Younger, and Richard) of Henry II and Eleanor of Aquitaine, born 1158. He was engaged to Constance, heir to the duchy of Brittany from 1169; they married in 1181. At the time of his death, he was trying to wrest Anjou away from his brother Richard (who was supported by their father). English chroniclers report that he died after injuries at a tournament; if this was the case, Rigord chooses to say nothing about it. Geoffrey and Constance's only son, Arthur, was born after Geoffrey's death; at his birth he was Henry II's only grandson.

336. 19 August 1186.

337. Thibaut V of Blois (see Cast of Characters).

338. Genesis 50:25.

339. Maurice of Sully. See ch. 2 above. In 1186 the cathedral of Notre-Dame was in the process of being rebuilt under Maurice of Sully's stewardship. Geoffrey was buried before the high altar in the choir.

[49] On the establishment of four prebends.

When the burial service had been most solemnly completed, the most Christian King Philip returned to the palace, accompanied by Count Thibaut [of Blois], Count Henry [of Champagne], his mother [Marie] the countess of Champagne,[340] and the former queen of England, Marguerite, sister of the said king, since she had not yet left with the Hungarians.[341] The death of such a prince weighed heavily upon the king, and the nobles just mentioned and many others followed so that they might console him. Being consoled by his friends, and bringing to mind the last deeds of the deceased, he turned his mind to consideration of works of charity and mercy in the fashion of his father's kindness. And he established in perpetuity four priests in the church of Notre-Dame where the count had been buried, so that they might pray for himself, for the soul of his most holy father, Louis [VII], and for the soul of his beloved count of Brittany. Out of his own income he dedicated funds adequate to support two priests, while the countess of Champagne pledged for the third, and the chapter of Notre-Dame promised to allot [funds] for the fourth.

[50] Happenings.

At the start of the year of our Lord's incarnation 1187, the sixth year of Philip's reign, eight before the Kalends of March,[342] in the eleventh hour of the following night, there was an almost complete eclipse of the moon, which was then in the eleventh degree of Libra, while the sun was then in the eleventh degree of Aries, with the head of the Dragon in the fourth degree of Aries. Truly, part of the moon was darkened; it was a sort of red color, and misshapen. This eclipse lasted for two hours.

[51] On the erection of a wall around the cemetery in the Champeaux.

Among the most Christian King Philip's many fine works, we have deemed it worthwhile to record here some that are worthy of remembrance. One day, while King Philip was staying at Paris, word came to his ears concerning

---

340. Henry II, count of Champagne, 1181–97 (not to be confused with Henry II of England), and his mother, Marie of France, half sister of Philip II (through their father, Louis VII) as well as half sister of Geoffrey of Brittany (through their mother, Eleanor of Aquitaine). See Cast of Characters and Genealogy.

341. Marguerite left Paris about a week later. On these events, see Evergates, *Marie de France*, 56–57.

342. 25 March 1187. Rigord is again confused on Philip's regnal year. This date should have fallen within Philip's seventh regnal year.

repairs to the cemetery which is in the Champeaux, next to the church of Saint-Innocent.[343] Since ancient times the cemetery had been a large area open to all foot traffic and full of goods for sale, where the citizens of Paris would bring their dead for burial. But now the bodies of the deceased could hardly be buried there decently, because of storm waters and the excessive overflow of stinking mud. Philip, the most Christian king, ever intent upon good works, seeing therefore that this project was right, decent, and necessary, ordered that the cemetery be entirely enclosed with a stone wall, and that adequate gates be built into the wall which were to be closed at night because of the machinations of passersby. It was his admired and pious opinion that a cemetery in which so many thousands of people lay buried should be most splendidly cared for by God-fearing posterity.

[52] On the king's garments given to the poor.

Throngs of entertainers often gather in the courts of kings or other nobles, where they are accustomed to compete in the production of merriment laced with fawning praise, in order to obtain from these nobles gold, silver, horses, or the garments which nobles are accustomed to change frequently. And to better please them, they do not blush to perform openly whatever they think might be appealing to the nobles, such as all kinds of pleasures, pleasantries, laughter-provoking witticisms, and other such inflated follies. We have seen, once upon a time, that certain nobles, as soon as they were asked, gave to minstrels—that is, minions of the devil—garments of deep design and most skillful workmanship, in various floral patterns, for which they had paid twenty or thirty marks of silver and had hardly used for even seven days. For shame! Surely for the price of these garments twenty or thirty poor people could have been fed for the whole year. But the most Christian King Philip Augustus, seeing that all such things are vain and harmful to the salvation of the soul, remembered what he had once learned from holy and religious men; that to give to entertainers is to make sacrifice to devils. With most zealous thought for our Lord God, he promised that as long as he lived, inspired by God, he would bestow his own garments upon the poor, since alms *deliver from all sin*[344] and display great faith before God in all who give them. "I was *naked*," says the Lord, "*and you covered me*."[345] It is better to clothe the naked Christ than to fall into sin by giving garments to flatterers.

---

343. See ch. 5 above.
344. Tobias 4:11.
345. Matthew 25:36.

If the nobles would consider these things daily, fewer flatterers would run through the world. Therefore, let the lesser nobility behold the merciful and pious king, and by observing his deeds let them learn from him piety and mercy, since they should know for certain that merciless judgment will come to one who has done no mercy.

[53] On astrologers' false prophecy about winds.

In that same year, eastern and western astrologers—that is, Jews as well as Saracens and even Christians—sent letters throughout various parts of the world, predicting and insisting without doubt that in September there would be a storm of mighty winds, an earthquake, the death of men, and plots and strife, warning of upheaval to kingdoms and many other things of this sort. But later the course of subsequent events demonstrated quite clearly otherwise than they foretold by divination. The tenor of these letters was as follows.[346]

[54] Their letters.

"God has known, and the science of mathematics has shown, that in the year of our Lord 1186, the year 582 of the Arabs, the superior and inferior planets will meet in the sign of Libra in the month of September.[347] In this same year, however, before this conjunction, there will be a partial eclipse of the sun, all fire-colored; that is, in the first hour of the twenty-first day of the month of April. Before this a total eclipse of the moon will occur, in the same month of April on the fifth day; that is, in the first hour of the night which will come before the Wednesday. Therefore in this said year, with the planets assembling in Libra, that is, in a windy and atmospheric sign also containing the tale of the Dragon, a marvelous earthquake will occur in areas especially prone to them, and it will destroy places used to earthquakes and liable to outbreaks of destruction. For from the areas of the West there will arise a strong and *violent wind*,[348] blackening the air and befouling it with fetid poison. Then death and sickness will seize many, and thundering will be heard, and voices in the air striking terror in the hearts of those who hear them.

---

346. The fact that various versions of this letter really did circulate is attested by other contemporary chroniclers. For an overview of medieval astrological ideas, see Hilary Carey, "Astrology in the Middle Ages," *History Compass* 8 (2010): 888–902.

347. After seeming to proceed to 1187, Rigord has returned to a prediction for 1186.

348. Job 1:19.

And the wind will sweep up the sand and dust from the surface of the earth and will cover the cities of the plains and especially those in sandy areas, that is, in the fifth climate zone.[349] And Mecca, Basra, Baghdad, and Babylon will be completely destroyed, and nothing will be left but what is covered with earth; and they will be destroyed with sand and dust, so that the regions of Egypt and Ethiopia will be made uninhabitable. And from the West the destruction will stretch all the way to areas of the East. In the western regions, indeed, strife will arise, and unrest among the people. And one from among them will gather armies without number and will wage war along the banks of the waters, in which such heaps of slaughter will be accomplished that the flow of pouring blood will be equal to the swelling waves. Let it be known for certain, however, that the coming conjunction points to the upheaval of kingdoms,[350] the superiority of the Franks, doubt and ignorance among the Jews, the destruction of the Saracen people, and the greater holiness and exaltation of Christ's law, as well as a fuller lifetime for those who will be born hereafter, *if God will have wished it.*"[351]

[55] Again, another letter about the same thing.[352]

"The wise men of Egypt have foretold the signs which will arise in the time when the planets come together, the tail of the Dragon being with them in the sign Moranaim, in the month of Elul,[353] on the twenty-ninth day of the same month, in the year 4946 from the beginning of the world according to the Hebrews, on Sunday. And on the following night, *about midnight,*[354] the following signs will begin and they will continue up until the following Wednesday at noon. From the great sea will arise a great strong wind, shaking the hearts of men, and it will sweep up sand and dust from the surface of the earth to such an extent that it will cover trees and towers; and this is because this conjunction of the planets will be in Libra, that is, in a clearly atmospheric and windy sign. And according to the judgment of these wise men, this conjunction points to a most powerful wind, smashing mountains and cliffs; crashing and *thunder and voices* will be heard in the air,[355] striking

---

349. One way medieval geographers envisioned the earth was as a series of climate zones in bands moving northward from the equator toward the arctic circle.

350. Cf. Daniel 2:21.

351. 1 Corinthians 4:19.

352. Unlike the first letter, this one is known only from Rigord's text.

353. This passage foregrounds Hebrew names for a sign of the zodiac (Libra) and a month (Elul is the sixth month of the Jewish calendar).

354. Acts 27:27.

355. Apocalypse 8:5.

fear into the hearts of men, and all the cities—that is, in the fifth climate zone—will be buried in sand and dust. For the wind will begin from a corner of the West and will extend to the corners of the East, seizing all the cities of Egypt and Ethiopia; that is, Mecca, Basra, and Raham and Alep, and Sinnaar and the lands of the Arabs, and all the land of Elam, Rama, Kirman and Segesta, and Calla and Norozatan, and Chebil and Tanbrasten, and Barach,[356] because all these cities or regions are embraced under the sign Libra, as are also the lands of the Romans.

And after such an onslaught of winds will follow five miracles. First, there will arise from the East a certain man, most wise in foreign wisdom; that is, in the wisdom which is above man. And he will walk in justice and teach the law of truth, and call back many men from the shadows of ignorance to upright morals, and from disbelief to the road of truth, and he will teach sinners the *paths of justice,*[357] and he will not be exalted by this so that he will be counted among the prophets. Second, a certain man will come out of Elam, and he will bring together many strong armies and cause great carnage among the peoples, and he will not live long. Third, there will arise a certain other man, saying that he is a prophet, holding in his hand a book and saying he is *sent by God,*[358] and by his prophecies and foretelling he will lead many people astray. And he *will seduce* a great many *nations,*[359] and what he will have prophesied to the peoples will be turned back upon himself; and this man will not live long either. Fourth, a comet will be seen in heaven; that is, a star trailing long hair or a tail. And this apparition will indicate climaxes and upheavals, harsh battles, withholding of the rains and desiccations of the lands, violent fighting and flowing of blood in the land of the East, and crossing the Hebros River[360] it will reach to the boundaries of the West. Just men and men of faith will be oppressed and endure persecutions to such an extent that their houses of prayer will be demolished. Fifth, there will be an eclipse of the fire-colored sun, such that its whole shape will be darkened. And the darkness over the earth in the time of the eclipse will be like at midnight when the moon does not shine and the rain falls."

Let what has been said about these letters be sufficient for the time being. Now, let us return to the deeds of the sixth year of the reign of Philip Augustus.

---

356. This list concerns cities and regions today in Turkey, Syria, Iran, Israel, and Afghanistan.

357. Psalms 22:3.

358. John 1:6.

359. Apocalypse 20:7.

360. We take this to be the Hebros (better known today as the Maritsa), which flows through the Balkans and in places forms the border between modern Greece and Turkey.

[56] On the war between King Philip of France and King Henry of England.

Then, in that same year discussed above [1186], a dispute arose between the most Christian King Philip and King Henry [II] of England. For from the moment Philip first met Richard,[361] Henry's son and the count of Poitou, [Philip] kept demanding that [Richard] do homage for the whole county of Poitou. At his father's direction, Richard pretended day after day that he would do so. In addition, King Philip was demanding from the king of England the castle called Gisors and other nearby castles which had been given over by his father, King Louis [VII], as dowry for [Philip's] sister Marguerite, when he had joined her in marriage to the famous King Henry [the Younger], son of the elder Henry.[362] This dowry had been granted to [the younger] King Henry on the condition that if he received offspring from her, he would hold the property for his lifetime, but that after his death it would descend to his offspring. If, however, he were to have no children by Marguerite, the dowry would without question revert to the king of France upon the death of [the younger] King Henry. The king of England had often been summoned over these matters by King Philip, but from day to day he repeatedly put off attendance at the king's court for judgment in the matter by offering contrived delays. The most Christian King Philip, however, understood the cunning machinations of the king of England. And very clearly foreseeing that further delay would be harmful to him and his people, he determined to invade the king of England's land with a host of armed men.

[57] The deeds of the seventh year of the reign of Philip, king of France.

It came to pass then, in the seventh year of Philip's reign and the twenty-second year of his age, which is the year 1187 of our Lord's incarnation,[363] that King Philip gathered an army beyond number in the district of Bourges. *With a strong army*[364] he invaded the borders of Aquitaine and plundered that land. And he seized the castle called Issoudun, and Graçay, and a great many other fortifications, and plundered the surrounding lands all the way to Châteauroux.[365] Upon learning of this, Henry, king of England, and Richard, count of Poitou, gathered a great army and boldly advanced

---

361. Future Richard I "Lionheart," king of England, 1189–99.
362. See ch. 22 above.
363. The seventh year of Philip's reign, counting from the death of his father, would be 18 September 1186 to 17 September 1187. Philip passed his twenty-second birthday in August of 1186.
364. 4 Kings 18:17.
365. June 1187.

toward Châteauroux against the king of France, their lord. It was their wish, if they could, to violently expel King Philip and his entire army from the siege of Châteauroux. But seeing the determination and stout resolve of the Franks, they *laid out camp against them.*[366] King Philip was enraged, as were all his warriors, and he called his troops into battle formation against them. They, however, feared the stout resolve of King Philip and the firm bravery of the Franks, and sent to King Philip competent men as well as clerics accompanying the legates of the Roman Church, who at that time had been sent from the side of the supreme pontiff to the regions of France to reestablish peace. These men established by formal pledge on behalf of the king of England and his son Richard that they would fully settle the entire question on all points, in accordance with the decision of the court of the king of France. When this was done a truce was established and everyone returned home.

[58] On the statue of the Blessed Virgin which a mercenary smashed.

While the king was engaged in the siege of Châteauroux, an event worth mentioning occurred.[367] One day Richard, the count of Poitou, had sent a large detachment of mercenaries to help Châteauroux. While they were assembled there in the town square in front of the church of the Blessed Virgin Mary, they began to play a game of dice. Among them was one of the *sons of the devil,*[368] filled with a demon. Since he was losing badly the money which he had gotten badly, he broke forth with blasphemous abuse of God and the Virgin Mary. Furiously raging in anger, *lifting up his eyes,*[369] he saw above the church portal a statue of the Blessed Virgin Mary holding the child Jesus in her arms, a stone sculpture as is often found in churches to stimulate thoughtful devotion in the people. As he beheld this, with wild and bloodshot eyes, redoubling his blasphemous curses with fearful boldness against God and our Lady—oh, for shame!—this woebegone Judas, before everyone's eyes, hurled a stone at the statue and most wickedly smashed off the arm of the statue of the child Jesus and knocked it to the ground. Now, from this break, as we have heard from many people who were at the siege,

366. 3 Kings 20:27.

367. These events actually took place in Déols (north of Châteauroux) on 30 May 1187. See Jean Hubert, "Le miracle de Déols et la trêve conclue en 1187 entre les rois de France et d'Angleterre," *Bibliothèque de l'École des chartes* 96 (1935): 285–300. Other chroniclers such as Gervais of Canterbury and Gerald of Wales report this miracle as well.

368. 2 Kings 3:34.

369. John 11:41.

blood came flowing freely down to the ground, and many there gathered it up and were rewarded by being cured of various diseases. John, who is called Lackland, the younger son of the king of England,[370] who was on a mission for his father, arrived by chance and carried off with him the still bloodied arm of the statue in reverent honor as a relic. The wretch of a mercenary, however, who had so shamefully smashed the statue of the Blessed Virgin, was seized that same day by the demon that had earlier driven him on, and he *ended his life* most pitifully.[371] The other mercenaries who saw what had happened were *struck with fear.*[372] And *praising God,*[373] who leaves no wicked deed unpunished, they departed from Châteauroux, exalting the Virgin Mary, Mother of God, with the highest praises. The monks of that place, seeing the miracles which God was there bringing about day by day, took this statue inside the church because it was not knocked to the ground, amid hymns of praise, where *unto this day*[374] many miracles are occurring to the honor of our Lord Jesus Christ and the Blessed Virgin Mary.

[59] On the envoys sent from Jerusalem to the king of France.

Now, *while these things were happening,*[375] envoys came from Outremer to King Philip. They told him with sighs and groans that, on account of the sins of the Christians, Saladin, the king of Syria and Egypt,[376] had invaded the lands of the Christians of Outremer and had most pitifully slaughtered many thousands of Christians. He had cruelly *slain with the sword*[377] many Templar and Hospitaller brothers, together with the bishops and barons of the land, and had captured the Holy Cross and the king of Jerusalem.[378] And, after a few days time, as the evil spread, [Saladin] had brought under his control the

---

370. The future king John of England, r. 1199–1216.

371. 2 Maccabees 10:13.

372. Wisdom 17:6.

373. Luke 2:20.

374. 1 Kings 5:5.

375. 2 Kings 11:2.

376. Saladin (An-Nasir Salah ad-Din Yusuf ibn Ayyub, 1137–93) was the Kurdish general and founder of the Ayyubid dynasty who rose to power in the 1160s and 1170s and, by consolidating authority over both Egypt and Syria, succeeded in encircling the crusader states. He was proclaimed sultan in 1174. See Jonathan Phillips, *The Life and Legend of the Sultan Saladin* (New Haven: Yale University Press, 2019).

377. 2 Maccabees 12:6.

378. This paragraph recounts events of 1187. On 4 July Saladin annihilated the Christian army at the Battle of Hattin, during which he took captive the king of Jerusalem, Guy of Lusignan, and after which he executed the entirety of the Templar and Hospitaller contingents. Saladin then marched on Jerusalem. The Christian garrison negotiated a surrender, and Saladin took control of the city on 2 October. Guy of Lusignan was freed after about a year in captivity.

holy city of Jerusalem, and all the Promised Land except Tyre, Tripoli, and Antioch, and a few particularly strong castles which he was unable to take.

[60] On the birth of Louis, the son of Philip Augustus.

In the year of our Lord's incarnation 1187, on the fourth day of September, in the third hour, there was a partial eclipse of the sun in the eighteenth degree of the Virgin, and it lasted for two hours. On the following day, that is, the fifth day of September, Louis was born, the son of Philip Augustus, the famous king of the Franks, on a Monday in the eleventh hour of daylight.[379] Upon his birth the city of Paris, where he was born, was filled with such joy that every night for seven days, by the light of flaming torches, the people of the whole city ceaselessly offered due praise to their Creator and led choruses in song. At the very hour of his birth, messengers were dispatched *through all the provinces*[380] announcing to the far corners of the kingdom the joys of such a king. They were overflowing with joy, *praising and blessing God,*[381] who deigned to bring forth such and so fine an heir to the kingdom of the Franks.

[61] On the frequent death of popes.

In the same year, on the feast of St. Luke, in the month of October, Pope Urban III went to the Lord,[382] having held the see for a year and a half. Gregory VIII followed him for one and a half months.[383] Clement III, a Roman, came after him that same year.[384] Now observe that such a frequent change of supreme pontiffs could not happen for any reason unless by their own sins, and by the disobedience of their subjects unwilling to return [to them] by the grace of God.[385] No one returns from Babylon—that is, from the welter of sinners—by his own powers of knowledge, unless the grace of return

---

379. Louis VIII was actually born on 3 September 1187, which was a Thursday. Rigord's Latin phrasing is intended to indicate that in a day divided into twelve equal hours between sun up and sun down, Louis was born at the eleventh hour after dawn. We thank Walter Simons for consultation on this point.

380. Esther 2:3.

381. Luke 24:53.

382. The feast of St. Luke is 18 October. Urban III was pope from 25 November until his death, which actually occurred on 20 October 1187.

383. Gregory VIII reigned 21 October to 17 December 1187.

384. Clement III reigned 19 December 1187 to 20 March 1191.

385. Rigord may be alluding to the continuing battles between popes and Emperor Frederick I (r. 1152–90), but he is notably hostile to both camps.

is lavished upon him from on high. For the world itself grows old; indeed, all practice of government grows old and falls into old age, and it slips back as though into childhood to pour forth a flood of its wishes.

And note that in the very same year of our Lord when the Lord's Cross in Outremer was captured by this same Saladin, babies who were born since that time have only twenty-two teeth, or only twenty, when before then they would usually have thirty or thirty-two.[386]

[62] That with the inspiration of God, King Philip and King Henry of England take the cross.

At the arrival of the feast of St. Hilary, which falls on the thirteenth day of January, a meeting was held between King Philip of France and King Henry of England, between Trie and Gisors.[387] And here it came to pass, contrary to everyone's expectations, through the miraculous agency of the Lord, that these two kings, who had been sent to the same location by heaven through the prompting of the Holy Spirit, took up the sign of the Holy Cross[388] for the liberation of our Lord's sepulcher and the holy city of Jerusalem. And many archbishops, bishops, counts, dukes, and barons did so with them; that is, Walter the archbishop of Rouen,[389] Baldwin the archbishop of Canterbury,[390] the bishop of Beauvais,[391] the bishop of Chartres,[392] the duke of Burgundy,[393] Richard count of Poitou, Philip count of Flanders, Thibaut count of Blois, Rotrou count of Perche,[394] William des Barres count of Rochefort,[395] Henry count of Champagne, Robert count of Dreux,[396] the count of Clermont,[397]

---

386. This sentence appears only in *P*; it is absent in *V*.

387. This meeting occurred on 21 January 1188, rather than 13 January as Rigord has it. The castle of Gisors stood west of Paris at the frontier with Normandy. Trie-Château is just east of Gisors. In other words the two kings met at the frontier between their respective lands.

388. The phrase "taking up the cross" generally meant taking a vow to go on crusade. The vow entailed both obligations and certain protections.

389. Walter of Coutances (r. 1183–1207).

390. Baldwin of Forde (r. 1184–90).

391. Philip of Dreux (r. 1175–1217), a grandson of Louis VI. See Baldwin, *KLL*, 31–35.

392. Renaud of Bar (r. 1182–1217).

393. Hugh III of Burgundy (r. 1162–92).

394. Rotrou IV of Perche (r. 1144–91).

395. William II des Barres (d. 1234); his status as count of Rochefort seems uncertain aside from Rigord's reference. See Baldwin, *KLL*, 51–52; Baldwin, *GPA*, 114.

396. Count Robert II of Dreux (r. 1184–1218), another grandson of Louis VI and brother to Philip of Dreux. See Baldwin, *KLL*, 31–35.

397. Raoul I of Clermont (r. 1161–91), constable of France. Baldwin, *GPA*, 32–33.

the count of Beaumont,[398] the count of Soissons,[399] the count of Bar,[400] Bernard of Saint-Valéry,[401] Jacques of Avesnes,[402] the count of Nevers,[403] William of Mello, Dreux of Mello,[404] and many others afire with the zeal of God whose names it would take long to include here. And on this very spot these two kings devoutly erected a wooden cross in memory of these events, founding a church. And they struck a treaty between themselves, and called the spot the Holy Field, because it was there that they had been signed with holy crosses. And from the report of many people we have learned that they allocated an income sufficient for two priests to serve God there, and they granted that the church, with everything pertaining to it, should be held in perpetuity by the nuns of Fontevraud.[405]

[63] The deeds of the eighth year of the reign of Philip, king of the Franks.[406]

In the year of our Lord 1188, in the month of March, in the middle of Lent,[407] King Philip held a general council at Paris, calling together all the archbishops, bishops, abbots, and barons of the whole realm. And there a host of knights and soldiers beyond count were enrolled in the crusade. And, because of the *present necessity* regarding the city,[408] for the king was very anxious to leave for Jerusalem, he decreed, with the consent of the clergy and the people, that a certain tithe would be collected from everyone, just for that year. This was called the Saladin tithe, which we will set down in this book. [409]

---

398. Matthew III of Beaumont (d. 1208). See Baldwin, *KLL*, 28–29, 150–52.

399. Raoul of Nesle (r. 1180–1237).

400. Henry I (r. 1170–91).

401. Bernard IV, lord of Saint-Valéry (d. 1200).

402. Lord of Avesnes (r. 1171–91).

403. Peter II of Courtenay, another grandson of Louis VI, future Latin emperor of Constantinople (r. 1216–17).

404. William and Dreux of Mello were members of the royal entourage; Dreux would hold the office of constable after 1191. See Baldwin, *KLL*, 45–46; Baldwin, *GPA*, 104–5.

405. Fontevraud was in Anjou and hence under the control of Henry II.

406. The eighth year of Philip's reign, counting from the death of his father, ran from 18 September 1187 to 17 September 1188.

407. Mid-Lent was 27 March this year and so indeed 1188 for Rigord (who began the year with 25 March).

408. 1 Corinthians 7:26.

409. The Saladin tithe is usually described as a 10 percent tax on all landowners, levied in England and France in support of the Third Crusade. The details below demonstrate that its provisions were actually rather more complex. The following three "chapters" are actually Rigord's copy of the royal decrees concerning not only exactions (ch. 66) but also protections for crusaders and their families (chs. 64 and 65). The language of these decrees is notably more legalistic than Rigord's own prose. For context on the challenges of funding the larger passages, see Fred Cazel Jr., "Financing the Crusades," in *A History of the Crusades,* general ed. Kenneth Setton (Madison: University of

[64] Enactment of the tithe.

In the name of the holy, undivided Trinity, amen. It has been enacted by Lord Philip, king of the Franks, upon the advice of the archbishops, bishops, and barons of his land, that the bishops and prelates, the clergy of conventual churches, and the knights who have taken the sign of the cross, shall have relief from repaying debts [contracted with] Jews as well as Christians before the king took the cross, starting from the next feast of All Saints following the day of our lord king's departure and lasting for two years;[410] such that, specifically, on the first feast of All Saints the creditors will have a third of the debt owed, and on the following feast of All Saints another third of the debt owed, and on the third feast of All Souls the final third of the debt owed. Interest, however, will not accrue on prior debts for anyone, starting from the day on which that person took the cross.

If a knight taking the cross is a legitimate heir, a son, or a son-in-law of a knight not taking the cross, or of any widow, and if he is a dependent of his father or mother, then his father or mother will have the relief of his or her debt in accordance with the enactment made.

If, however, their son or son-in-law, their legitimate heir taking the cross, is outside the family,[411] or indeed if he is not a knight and has not taken the cross, his parent will not have this relief.

Debtors who have lands and revenues will assign to their creditors lands and revenues from which the creditors may receive what is owed them at the above-stated times. [They will do this] within fifteen days of the next feast of St. John the Baptist,[412] according to the process just described, through the agency of the lords in whose dominion the lands subject to debt may lie. The lords may not refuse the assignments unless they themselves will have satisfied the creditor from their own funds. Let those individuals who possess no lands or revenues adequate to make an assignment covering their debt [instead] execute for their creditors a promise, through sworn guarantors or pledges, to pay the debt at the stated times. And if,

---

Wisconsin Press, 1989), vol. 6, ed. Harry W. Hazard and Norman P. Zacour, 116–49. For Philip's part in the levy (which he apparently renounced a year later, unremarked by Rigord), see Baldwin, *GPA,* 52–54.

410. That is, starting from 1 November 1189 and lasting until 1 November 1191.

411. This clause may refer to the legal concept of "forisfamiliation," meaning literally "putting out of a family"; that is, portioning off an heir's inheritance in such a manner as to exclude further claim of inheritance from the family. The point is that in that case the heir's parents would have no right to the benefits spelled out here.

412. That is, by 9 July; fifteen days following 24 June 1189.

within fifteen days of the next feast of St. John the Baptist, they
have not made their promise to pay through assignment of land,
or through guarantors or pledges if they have no land, as is thus
required, they will not have the relief granted to others.

If one of the clergy or a knight taking the cross is in debt to
a cleric or a knight taking the cross, he will have this relief from
his debt until the next feast of All Saints, provided good security
is posted for so doing at that time.

[65] On the same.

If anyone who has taken the cross eight days before the Purification of the Blessed Mary[413] or thereafter will have assigned
to another gold or silver or grain or other movable pledge, the
creditor will not be required to give the relief with respect to this.

If anyone buys crops of the land for a year at a fixed price from
someone not taking the cross, [that price] remains good.

If a knight or cleric has pledged or assigned for some years his
land or revenue to any townsman who has taken the cross, or to
a cleric or knight who has not taken the cross, the debtor in this
year will take the crops of the land or revenue; and the creditor, after the term of years for which the pledge or assignation
was due to apply is complete, will hold it for one year [more] in
compensation for that year, in such a manner, however, that the
creditor will have half of the crop in this [additional] year for his
cultivation if he has cultivated the pledged lands or vineyards.

All contracts made since the eighth day prior to the Purification of the Blessed Virgin, or made thereafter, will be valid.

Concerning all debts for which the relief is given, the debtor
will be obliged to provide a sworn guarantee just as good or better
than that which he had previously given. And, if a disagreement
should arise as to the guarantee, a sworn guarantee just as good or
better than before will be given, upon the advice of the lord of the
creditor. And, if the sworn guarantee is not corrected by the lord,
it must be corrected upon the advice of the prince over the land.

If there is a lord or prince in whose jurisdiction the said creditors and debtors will have been unwilling to carry out, or to arrange to be carried out, the prescribed measures concerning the

---

413. The feast of the Purification is 2 February. Thus, anyone who takes the cross before
January 25.

relief to be given to debtors or assignments to be made, and if he has been warned by his metropolitan or bishop and within forty days has still not corrected it, he will be subject to excommunication by the same [metropolitan or bishop].

However, so long as the lord or prince will try to show, in the presence of his metropolitan or bishop, that he has not failed the creditor or indeed the debtor in this matter, and if he is ready to carry out what is there prescribed, the metropolitan or bishop may not excommunicate him.

No one having taken the cross, either cleric or knight or any other person whatsoever, is answerable as to the source of his right to a property, from the day that he takes the cross until the day that he returns from his promised journey, unless it concerns a matter in which he was involved before he had taken the cross.

[66] On the same.

The main points concerning the tithe enactment are that all persons not having taken the cross, whoever they may be, will pay this year at least one-tenth of the value of all their movable property and revenue, except those of the Cistercian order, the Order of the Carthusians, the Order of Fontevraud, and those of lepers, as to their own property.

No one will lay a hand on any commune unless he will have been the lord of this same commune.[414]

Such right, however, as anyone previously had in any of the communes he will continue to have.

He who exercises high justice over an area of land will have the tithe of this land. It will be understood that those who are going to pay the tithe from the whole value of their movable property and revenues will pay the tithe, making no exception for debts previously incurred. For indeed after the payment of the tithe they can pay the debts from what is left.

All the laity, both knights as well as others, will give the tithe bound by the prescribed oath and subject to anathema, and the clergy will pay their tithe subject to excommunication.

---

414. The noun used in this and the following sentence is *communia*, which could refer to a town holding a charter of self-governance (as the editors of *HPA* assume), but could also refer to properties held in common (as by a chapter of cathedral canons), or even the "common" grazing land or pasturage of a village. We have preserved the simplest English translation of "commune" without wishing to exclude the various possibilities of meaning.

who has not taken the cross, who is the liege man of
has taken the cross,[415] will give [his lord] a tenth of
le property and of the fief which he holds of him. If,
ie holds no fief from him, he will give his liege lord a
iis movable property. He will give a tenth of each fief
which ... holds to each individual from whom he holds the fief.
And, if he has no liege lord, he will give the tenth of his movable
property to the person in whose fief he resides.

If a person imposing the tithe on his land should encounter
the property of a person upon his land other than one whom he
may tithe, and the owner thereof can prove his legal ownership,
then he will be unable to subject that property to the tithe.

A knight who has taken the cross, who is the legal heir as son
or son-in-law of a knight who has not taken the cross, or the
widow of such, will have the tithe of his father or mother.

No other person will seize property pertaining directly to archbishops or bishops or chapters or churches, save only the archbishops
or bishops or chapters and churches which directly control them.

If bishops collect the tithe, they will give the same to those to
whom they ought.

Whoever has the ability to pay a tax or tithe as required, and is unwilling to do so, may be seized by the person to whom he should pay
the duty or tithe, so that then he would make satisfaction. He who
will have seized him for this purpose cannot be excommunicated.

Whoever will have given his tithe piously, lawfully, and without coercion will receive his reward from God.[416]

[67] On the breaking of the treaty done by Count Richard.

Two or three months after these things occurred, that is, between Pentecost
and the feast of St. John,[417] Richard, count of Poitou, having assembled an army,
entered the land of the count of Toulouse, which [the latter] held from the
king of the Franks, and he seized Moissac and other castles which belonged
to the count of Toulouse.[418] When he heard of this, Raymond, count of Toulouse, sent his envoys to the most Christian King Philip, explaining to him all the

---

415. A knight might have several lords to whom he had pledged his loyalty. His liege lord was the
lord to whom he owed principal loyalty in the event that those loyalties came into conflict.

416. This is the beginning of the idea that one can share in the spiritual benefit of crusading by
participating financially, even if not militarily in person.

417. Between 5 and 24 June 1188.

418. Raymond V of Toulouse (r. 1148–94) was married to Louis VII's sister Constance.

wrongs that had been done to him by the count of Poitou, contrary to justice and to the established treaty. For Count Richard was breaking the treaty which had been made the previous year, between Chaumont and Gisors, and confirmed by oath,[419] between Philip king of the Franks, Henry king of England, and Richard himself, which was as follows: That each one's land should remain unchanged from the state it was in when he took the cross, until such time as he should return to his own land, in joy, when his service to the Lord overseas in the Holy Land would be complete. When King Philip, ever Augustus, learned of the breaking of the treaty which the two kings had struck between themselves, filled with anger he gathered a host of soldiers and suddenly invaded their lands. He seized the noble castle Châteauroux, and Buzançais, and Argenton, and he laid siege to a fourth castle which is called Levroux. While the king was briefly occupied by the siege, something occurred which is indeed worthy of mention.

[68] On the miraculous swelling of a certain stream.

There was a certain stream in front of the abovementioned castle [of Levroux], in which sufficient water could usually be found when it rained. It had dried up, however, because of the excessive summer heat. Yet when the king and his whole army were suffering greatly from lack of water and great thirst—for it was indeed summer—suddenly, from out of the bowels of the earth, without any rain, the water of the stream miraculously swelled so much that it rose up to the saddle straps of the horses, and the whole army and the animals were refreshed. The people who witnessed this were overjoyed at such a miracle, and *praised God,*[420] *who has done all things* that he wished *in the sea and in all the depths.*[421] And the water lasted as long as the king was involved in the siege. After a few days, he took the castle, that is, Levroux, and he gave it as a gift to his cousin Louis, the son of Count Thibaut.[422] Upon his departure the waters returned *to their former place*[423] and have not appeared since.

[69] On the destruction of Montrichard.

Departing from there,[424] they came to Montrichard and laid siege to it. There the king took some time in the siege. Having surrounded the place with his siege

---

419. See ch. 62.
420. Joshua 22:33.
421. Psalms 134:6.
422. This Louis was son of Thibaut V of Blois.
423. Exodus 14:27.
424. Numbers 33:7.

engines, he captured it with great effort, burned the whole town, and utterly destroyed a very strong tower with fifty knights in it. From there, King Philip captured Palluau, Montrésor, and Le Châtelet, and he brought under his control La Roche Guillebaud, Culan, and Montluçon and whatever rights the king of England held in all of Berry and the Auvergne.[425] Learning of this, the king of England was *exceedingly angry*,[426] and led his army back through the Norman borderlands toward Gisors.[427] When Philip, king of France, learned of this, he followed him; and as he passed he captured Vendôme, and pursued [King Henry] to the castle which is called Troo. He chased the king of England, together with his son Richard, out of this castle in disgrace, and then burned down the whole town. The king of England, crossing the abovementioned borderlands [of Normandy], then burned the castle of Dreux, and on his way he destroyed many villages in the countryside all the way to Gisors. Finally, with the arrival of winter, a truce was agreed upon, and both sides rested from the war.

[70] That Richard, count of Poitou, rendered homage to King Philip.

While all these things were going on, Richard, count of Poitou, asked his father for the wife who was his by right;[428] that is, the sister of Philip, king of the Franks. She had been given to [Henry II] to be her guardian, by King Louis [VII] of good memory, and with her [Richard] also asked for the kingdom. Indeed, it had been agreed that whichever of the king of England's sons should marry her would also receive the kingdom when the king himself died. Richard was asserting that this was his by right, for after his brother Henry, he was the eldest son. In response, the king of England, greatly upset, decreed that he would never do this. For this reason, Richard, count of Poitou, clearly angered, turned away from his father and went over to the most Christian king of the Franks. And *in the presence of his father*,[429] he rendered homage to King Philip and confirmed the treaty by oath.

---

425. The sites mentioned are all in what is now central France, between the cities of Tours and Clermont Ferrand. At the time, they were on the border between lands held by the Plantagenets and lands held by the Capetians.

426. Exodus 11:9; 2 Kings 3:8.

427. Gisors is in Normandy, in territory that in 1188 was held directly by the king of England, just on the border with lands held by the French king.

428. Alix (b. 1160), daughter of Louis VII and his second wife, Constance of Castile. She had been engaged to Richard and raised at the court of Henry II since the age of eight or nine. Henry was not only delaying the marriage but refusing to have Richard co-crowned as king of England as had been done with Richard's now-deceased older brother Henry.

429. Numbers 3:4. The biblical phrase is used literally. These events took place while Philip II, Henry II, and Richard were meeting at Bonmoulins (Normandy) on 18 November 1188.

[71] Happenings.

In this same year 1188, on the second day of February, a Thursday,[430] there was a total eclipse of the moon in the fourth hour of the night and lasting for three hours. Also four before the Ides of February,[431] when I was at Argenteuil,[432] in the full moonlight,[433] shortly before dawn, on a very calm night, the moon, which stands for the Church, was suddenly seen to come all the way down to earth and, after a brief pause, as though reinvigorated, to climb up again by degrees all the way to the place from which it had descended. This was seen by certain religious brothers, Robert of Gisors, prior of this same church [of Argenteuil], and J. of Chartres, sacristan of the church of the Blessed Denis, and many other brothers, who related it to us.

[72] Verses of a certain person.

In this same year verses about King Philip were spoken as though prophetically by a certain poet:

> This young small lion now outshines parental lights
> Serving his God always, renewing his people's delights.
> For him, of his cubs' four swords Brutus has the keep,
> When Romulus hears them clank the goose will be asleep.
> Babylon will rejoice, new folk with oil anointing.
> With the help of Gaul will Silo, too, be rejoicing.
> This lion will go forth and subdue the world around
> Rejoicing he will see the weapons of war put down.
> This lion, crow, and sheep Jebu's walls will mend.
> Five fasts also he'll add when all our days do end.[434]

---

430. 2 February 1189 by modern reckoning.

431. 10 February 1189.

432. This is Rigord's first use of the first person since the prologue. Saint-Denis had a priory at Argenteuil, which is ten kilometers (about six miles) to its west.

433. Rigord seems to have a full moon occurring on 2 February and again on 10 February; perhaps the second reference (*in plenilunio*) is not meant literally.

434. In general, this poem in rhyming hexameters makes Philip II the heir to several lines from Troyes (Brutus the mythical founder of Britain and Romulus the mythical founder of Rome), and the king of the end-time, when infidels will accept baptism, peace will reign, and the walls of Jerusalem will be rebuilt in preparation for the Second Coming. See Jerzy Pysiak, "Philippe Auguste: Un roi de la fin des temps?," *Annales: Histoire, sciences sociales* 57, no. 5 (2002): 1165–90, at 1184–85; and Elizabeth A. R. Brown, "La notion de légitimité et la prophétie à la cour de Philippe Auguste," in *La France de Philippe Auguste: Le temps des mutations*, ed. Robert-Henri Bautier (Paris: Éditions du CNRS, 1982), 78–110, at 85.

[73] Deeds of the ninth year of Philip, king of the Franks.[435]

In the year of our Lord 1189, in the month of May, King Philip, ever Augustus, led his army at Nogent[-le-Rotrou] and then seized La Ferté-Bernard along with four other very strong castles. And *with a strong army*[436] he captured the most powerful city of Le Mans, from which he expelled Henry, king of England, with seven hundred armed knights, in disgrace; and he pursued him with chosen warriors all the way to the castle called Chinon.[437] Returning to Le Mans, he set his sappers to work *undermining the wall,*[438] for he always brought them along in his train, and after great effort he captured the very strong, well-fortified tower. A few days later he led his army toward the city of Tours. There, *having pitched his tents*[439] on the banks of the Loire, the king went alone to survey the river. And by testing the depth of the river with his spear, he found a ford—a thing unheard-of for ages—and he marked it by posts on the right and the left in the river, so that his whole army could wade over, behind him, between the two markers; and he crossed the Loire first, at the head of all the others. When the whole army then beheld the lowering depth of the river which had miraculously come about, they at once pulled up stakes, folded tents, and one and all, *from the least to the greatest,*[440] followed their king through the ford. When all the arms and baggage train were gathered across, the river immediately returned to its former depth. The citizens of Tours saw this and *feared the king.*[441] This came to pass on the vigil of St. John the Baptist.[442] And then, truly, as the king was surveying the weaknesses of the city's defense, his ruffian retainers, who usually launched the first assaults on fortifications, charged the city. And as he looked on, they scaled the walls with ladders and took the city by surprise. Hearing this, the king and his whole army took back the entire city, *setting guards* there.[443] And in that very place, for some days, they gave solemn thanks to God.

---

435. The ninth year of Philip's reign, counting from the death of his father, began 18 September 1188 and ran until 17 September 1189.

436. 3 Kings 3:28; 4 Kings 18:17.

437. These fortifications were further inside English territory. Rigord is narrating Philip's increasing encroachment into English lands.

438. Cf. Genesis 49:6.

439. Genesis 33:17.

440. Genesis 19:11.

441. 3 Kings 3:28.

442. 23 June 1189.

443. Cf. Judges 16:2.

[74] On the death of Henry, king of England.

Twelve days later, that is, on the octave of the apostles Peter and Paul, Henry king of England died at Chinon.⁴⁴⁴ He ruled successfully in every respect up until the time of Philip, king of the Franks, whom the Lord sent as a bit in his mouth, to vindicate the blood of the blessed martyr Thomas of Canterbury,⁴⁴⁵ so that through grief He might give him understanding and return him to the bosom of the mother church. [Henry] was buried at Fontevraud, in a certain abbey of nuns.⁴⁴⁶

Richard his son, the count of Poitou, succeeded him. In that same year, when he first arrived at Gisors the whole castle went up in flames. And as he left the fortification the next day, as all his company was crossing over in disarray, the wooden bridge collapsed beneath his feet, so that Richard, horse and all, plummeted into the moat. A few days later, the peace which had been discussed between King Philip and Henry, king of England, now no more, was concluded and established between King Richard and King Philip.⁴⁴⁷ Then, for the sake of peace, King Philip gave back to Richard, king of England, the cities of Tours and Le Mans, and also Châteauroux with all its fiefs. In exchange, King Richard delivered to Philip, king of the Franks, and to his successors, forever free and clear, the entire fief pertaining to Graçay, and the entire fiefs pertaining to Issoudun, and the entire fief that he held in Auvergne.

[75] On the death of the queen, the wife of Philip, king of the Franks.

In that same year 1189, in the tenth year of the reign of Philip,⁴⁴⁸ on the Ides of March,⁴⁴⁹ Queen Isabelle, wife of Philip, king of the Franks, died. She was buried in the church of Notre-Dame at Paris. The venerable Maurice, bishop of Paris, erected an altar in her memory in that same church.⁴⁵⁰ And the most Christian king, ever Augustus, motivated by piety, for the sake of her soul and the souls of all their predecessors, founded there a living for two

---

444. Henry II died 6 July 1189, two days after meeting with Philip II and agreeing to a humiliating peace, with his sons Richard and John arrayed on the side of the French king.

445. See ch. 47 above.

446. Henry's tomb can still be seen at Fontevraud.

447. 22 July 1189.

448. The tenth year of Philip's reign, counting from the death of his father, began 18 September 1189 and ran until 17 September 1190.

449. Queen Isabelle of Hainaut died giving birth to stillborn twins, 15 March 1190.

450. On Maurice of Sully, see ch. 2 above.

perpetuity, and set aside fifteen Parisian pounds per year for each
..., forever.[451]

[76] That King Philip received the scrip and staff of pilgrimage in the church
of the Blessed Denis.

In the year of our Lord 1190, on the feast of St. John the Baptist,[452] King Philip
went with an enormous retinue to the church of the blessed martyr Denis to
receive permission [to depart]. From ancient times it was the practice of the
kings of the Franks that whenever they campaigned against their enemies
they would take the battle standard from above the altar of the Blessed Denis
and carry it with them, for care or protection, and they would unfurl it in the
foremost rank of battle. Time and again, the enemy, terrified upon seeing it,
turned and fled. And so the most Christian king, humbly prostrate in prayer
upon the marble pavement before the bodies of the sainted martyrs Denis,
Rusticus, and Eleutherius, commended himself to God, the Blessed Virgin
Mary, and the holy martyrs and all the saints. Finally, in tears, he rose from
prayer and with great devotion received there his pilgrim's scrip and staff from
the hand of Archbishop William of Reims, his uncle and legate of the Apostolic See.[453] Then he received with his own hands, from above the bodies of the
saints,[454] two magnificent silk standards and two great battle flags emblazoned
fittingly with gold-embroidered crosses in memory of the holy martyrs, for
protection as he was going forth to fight the enemies of the cross of Christ.[455]
Finally, commending himself to the prayers of the monks and having received
the blessing of the nail, the Crown of Thorns, and the arm of Saint Simeon
the Elder,[456] he departed, and on the Thursday after the octave of St. John
the Baptist, together with Richard, king of England, he arrived at Vézelay.[457]
And there, receiving permission from all his barons, he entrusted the care and
guardianship of the whole kingdom of the Franks, together with his beloved

---

451. That is, Philip endowed a chaplaincy which paid enough to support two clerics to say
masses for the sake of Isabelle's soul in perpetuity.

452. 24 June 1190.

453. On archbishop William, see ch. 3 above. The reception of the scrip (or wallet) and staff was
the formal liturgical ceremony of departure on pilgrimage. Since crusade was conceived of as a type
of pilgrimage, the liturgical rite was soon adapted for departing crusaders.

454. That is, from above the altar where they were buried.

455. The cross was the standard symbol of the crusader, and was often placed upon crusader
battle flags.

456. These were, after the bodies of Denis, Rusticus, and Eleutherius, the monastery's prize
relics. Tradition had it that they were given to Saint-Denis by Charles the Bald. The story of the gift
was probably based on a forgery from the last decades of the eleventh century.

457. 5 July 1190.

son Louis,[458] to his most beloved mother, Adele, and to his uncle, Archbishop William of Reims. A few days later he came to Genoa, where he had arranged that ships and their requisite supplies and weapons should be most carefully made ready. Richard, king of England, and all his forces, however, set sail from Marseille.[459] And thus the said catholic kings, entrusting themselves to the winds and the sea, to defend holy Christianity and out of their love of our Lord Jesus Christ, arrived at Messina[460] after many great perils.[461]

But before King Philip departed the kingdom of the Franks,[462] assembling his friends and close associates in Paris, he executed his testament and set in order the whole kingdom in this fashion.[463]

[77] In the name of the holy and indivisible Trinity, amen. Philip, by the grace of God king of the Franks: It is the duty of kings to plan for the well-being of their subjects in all ways, and to place the public good before their own. Therefore, since with deepest longing and all our strength we are taking up our vow of pilgrimage for the aid of the Holy Land, by the prompting of the Most High, we have decided how the business of our kingdom which must be carried out in our absence ought to be handled; and, should something befall our mortal self, how the final affairs of our life should be arranged.

Therefore, we first instruct that our *baillis* install for each *prévôt* within our jurisdiction four prudent men, who are lawful and of sound reputation;[464] and that no business of the place be carried out without their advice, or the advice of at least two of them, except that at Paris we have appointed six lawful and upright men whose names are these, T. A. E. R. B. N.[465]

---

458. Future Louis VIII.

459. For the details of Richard's route, see John D. Hosler, "Embedded Reporters? Ambroise, Richard de Templo, and Roger of Howden on the Third Crusade," in *Military Cultures and Martial Enterprises in the Middle Ages: Essays in Honour of Richard P. Abels*, ed. John D. Hosler and Steven Isaac (Woodbridge: Boydell, 2020), 177–91.

460. Philip arrived in Sicily 16 September, and Richard six days later.

461. Rigord's first version of the text probably ended here, as does *V* (the Vatican manuscript).

462. Between 25 March and 24 June 1190.

463. On this *testamentum* or *ordinatio*, known only from Rigord's inclusion of it here, see Baldwin, *GPA*, 102–4; and Bruno Galland, *Philippe Auguste: Le bâtisseur du royaume* (Paris: Belin, 2014), 73–78.

464. *Prévôts* were local royal agents who handled financial and judiciary matters (see Baldwin, *GPA*, ch. 3). *Baillis* were a newly created higher level of royal official overseeing *prévôts* on a regional level. The ordinance of 1190 makes their precedence clear, and gives them this temporary power to appoint four men to advise each *prévôt* (see Baldwin, *GPA*, 125–36).

465. The first four can be identified as Thibaut le Riche, Athon de la Grève, Ebroin le Changeur, and Robert of Chartres. The last two might be Baldwin Bruneau and Nicolas Bocel. Baldwin, *GPA*,

And in our lands we have assigned our *baillis*, labeled by their individual names, who in their *bailliages*[466] will establish each month one day which is called the day of assize, when all those who bring a claim will receive their legal rights through them and justice[467] without delay, and we will receive our legal rights and our justice, and the forfeits which are properly ours will be recorded there.

Furthermore, we wish and direct that our most beloved mother, Queen Adele, establish, together with our most beloved uncle the faithful William, archbishop of Reims, one day every four months at Paris, when they may hear the claims of the people of our kingdom, and they may decide them to the honor of God and the good of the kingdom.

We instruct, moreover, that on this day our *baillis* from each of our areas who will hold assizes will be present before [the queen and archbishop], so that they may report to them personally the affairs of our land.

If, however, any of our *baillis* will have done wrong, except in a case of murder or rape or homicide or treason, and this becomes known to the archbishop and the queen and the others who will be present, we direct them to hear the misdeeds of our *baillis*, so that each year, and here three times a year, they may inform us in their letters to us on the abovementioned days[468] which *bailli* has done wrong, and what he has done, and what money or gift or service he received, and from whom, because of which our people have lost their right or we ours.

In a similar fashion let our *baillis* inform us about our *prévôts*.

However, the queen and the archbishop will have no power to remove our *baillis* from office, except for murder, rape, homicide, or treason; nor the *baillis* the *prévôts*, except for one of these offenses. We, however, with the guidance of God, will punish him, after the abovesaid persons have told us the truth of the matter, in a way that will reasonably deter others.

103; John W. Baldwin, *Paris, 1200* (Stanford: Stanford University Press, 2010), 36.

466. That is, the district overseen by each *bailli*.

467. *HPA* contains the typographical error *justicia* where the manuscript (P) correctly reads *justiciam*.

468. The Paris manuscript reads *duobus predictis*, but we have assumed that *duobus* is a scribal error for *diebus*. Henri-François Delaborde, *Recueil des actes de Philippe Auguste, roi de France*, vol. 1 (Paris: Imprimerie nationale, 1916), 418 made this emendation, and the editors of *HPA* must have reached the same conclusion, since they translate as *au jours susdits* without commentary.

Likewise the queen and the archbishop will report to us three times each year concerning the state and affairs of the kingdom.

If by chance an episcopal see or a royal abbey should fall vacant, we desire that the canons of the church or the monks of the vacant monastery come before the queen and the archbishop, just as they would come before us, and ask them for a free election. And it is our desire that they grant this to them without objection. Indeed, we warn the canons, as well as the monks, to select a shepherd who would be pleasing to God and useful to the realm. Let the queen and the archbishop, however, keep the regalia in their hands until such time as the person chosen is consecrated or blessed, and then let the regalia be returned without objection.[469]

Moreover, we instruct that if prebends or ecclesiastical benefices will become vacant, when the regalia have come into our hands, the queen and the archbishop should bestow them upon upright and educated men as best and most rightly as they can, with the advice of Brother Bernard,[470] always, however, respecting dispositions we have previously made to certain others as shown by our letters patent.

And also we forbid that any church prelates or any of our men should pay *taille* or *tolte*[471] as long as we will be in the service of God. Should the Lord God work his will with us and our death come about, we strictly forbid that any person of our land, whether clergy or laity, pay *taille* or *tolte* until our son—may God see fit to keep him safe and sound in his service—shall reach the age when he will be able to rule the kingdom by the grace of the Holy Spirit.

Should some person choose to war upon our son and his own income does not suffice, then let all our people help him with their person and their property, and may the churches render to him such aid as they have been accustomed to do for us.

We forbid our *prévôts* and *baillis* to seize any man or his property, so long as he wishes to provide good bondsmen for his pursuit of justice in our court, unless it be for homicide, murder, rape, or treason.

---

469. "Regalia" refers to royal rights, but also the symbols of those rights. "Regalian" churches and monasteries were those that belonged to the king insofar as he had the right to their revenues during a vacancy of bishop or abbot, and the right to oversee the election of the next bishop or abbot. During such a vacancy the king or his representative kept physical control of the symbols of episcopal or abbatial power. At this time Philip held about sixty-five regalian abbeys and twenty-five regalian bishoprics (Baldwin, *GPA*, 49, 65–72).

470. See above, ch. 9.

471. *Tailles* and *toltes* were arbitrary taxes levied in Philip II's reign. Baldwin, *GPA*, 53, 158–59.

Moreover, we instruct that all our income and services and profits be brought to Paris at three times: first, at the feast of St. Remi; second, at the Purification of the Virgin; third, at Ascension,[472] and let it be delivered to our abovementioned townsmen and to Peter the Marshal.[473] Should it happen that one of these should die, William of Garland should choose another in his place.[474]

At [these three] receipts of our property our cleric Adam will be present,[475] and he will record them. Let each one have their key and to each chest in which our property will be placed in the Temple,[476] and let the Temple have one key. From this, our property, so much will be sent to us as we specify in our letters.

If it should happen that we die on the path we have taken, we instruct that the queen and the archbishop and the bishop of Paris and the abbots of Saint-Victor[477] and Cernay[478] and Brother Bernard will divide our treasure into two parts. Let them distribute one half, according to their judgment, for the repair of churches which have been destroyed during our wars, so that the service of God may be performed in them. From the same half they will give to those who have been impoverished from our *tailles,* and they will give what is left to whomever they wish and whom they believe to be most in want, all this for the good of our soul and the souls of our father, King Louis, and of our predecessors. Concerning the other half, we instruct the guardians of our property and all the men of Paris that they guard it for the use of our son until he reaches an age and understanding when, with God's aid, he will be able to rule the kingdom.

If, however, it should happen that both we and our son die, we instruct that our property be distributed by the hand of the aforesaid seven, for our soul and the soul of our son, in their best judgment. Immediately upon certitude of our death we wish that our property, wherever it should be, be taken to the house of the bishop of Paris and there be kept under guard and thereafter with it will be done as we have directed.

---

472. These dates are 1 October, 2 February, and the fortieth day after Easter.
473. Associated with the court by 1179. Baldwin, *GPA,* 103.
474. Baldwin, *KLL,* 38–39; Baldwin, *GPA,* 113–14.
475. Probably canon of Noyon. Baldwin, *GPA,* 103.
476. The stronghold of the Templars at Paris, just northeast of the city (outside the walls described in the next chapter). The Temple often served as the de facto royal treasury. Baldwin, *GPA,* 57.
477. Abbey of canons regular on the Left Bank in Paris.
478. The Cistercian abbey of Vaux-de-Cernay.

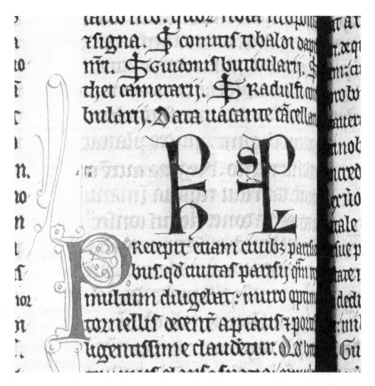

FIGURE 11. Simulacrum of Philip's monogram, placed at the end of the transcription of Philip's testament-ordinance. Paris, Bibliothèque nationale de France, MS lat. 5925, fol. 270vb. Used by permission of the Bibliothèque nationale de France.

We also instruct the queen and the archbishop that they should keep within their own power all the offices which, while they are vacant, belong to our gift, and which they are honestly able to hold, as of our abbacies, deanships, and other such worthy positions, until we will have returned from service to God. And those which they are unable to keep, let them bestow them according to God and award them upon the advice of Brother Bernard, and let them do this for the honor of God and the good of the kingdom. If, however, we die along the way, we wish that they should give these offices and worthy positions of the church to those persons who seem to them to be more worthy.

So that it may remain sound and lasting, we instruct that the present act be confirmed by the authority of our seal and the monogram of the royal name written thereunder. Done at Paris in the year of the Incarnate Word 1190, in the eleventh year of our reign, in our palace, in the presence of those whose names are placed hereunder and signed: Count Thibaut [of Blois], our

seneschal; Guy, butler;[479] Matthew, chamberlain;[480] Raoul, constable.[481] Done while the office of chancellor was vacant."[482]

[78][483] He also instructed the citizens at Paris that the city of Paris, which the
king greatly loved, be enclosed with the very best wall, with towers and gates
properly and carefully arranged. This was accomplished in a short space of
time, and we have seen the completed work.[484] And he ordered that the same
thing be done in other cities and castles throughout his realm.

Now let us return to the deeds which were accomplished between the said
kings at Messina and the state of affairs in the lands beyond the sea.

[79] When King Philip came to Messina in the month of August [1190] he was
honorably received in the palace of King Tancred.[485] And King Tancred gave
him abundantly from his stores of food, and he would have given him gold
without end if he could have married one of his daughters to either Philip
or his son Louis. But out of his friendship for the emperor Henry [VI],[486]
King Philip passed over both offers of marriage. Afterward, a dispute which
the king of England had with King Tancred over the dowry of [the king
of England's] sister[487] was put to rest by the mediation and effort of King
Philip, in the following way: The king of England received from King Tancred forty thousand ounces of gold, of which Philip received a third. He was
due half, but for the sake of the peace among them he agreed to a third. On
behalf of the king of England, certain nobles also pledged, on oath, one of
the daughters of King Tancred in marriage to Arthur, who was to be duke
of Brittany.[488] Then Philip, king of the Franks, celebrated the birth of our
Lord at Messina,[489] and bestowed many great gifts upon the impoverished
knights of his land who had lost all their property when a storm had arisen
at sea: to the duke of Burgundy he gave a thousand marks; to the count of
Nevers, six hundred; to William des Barres, four hundred marks; to William

---

479. Guy of Senlis. Baldwin, *KLL*, 39.
480. Matthew of Beaumont. Baldwin, *KLL*, 28–29, 150–52.
481. Count Raoul of Clermont.
482. Philip purposely left the formerly powerful office of chancellor vacant after 1185.
483. Rigord ceased including chapter titles in the second section of his work.
484. Note the evident passage of time necessary for Rigord to say this work has been completed.
485. Tancred of Lecce, king of Sicily (r. 1190–94).
486. Emperor Henry VI was married to Constance of Sicily and was Tancred's rival for the
crown.
487. King Richard's sister Joan had married Tancred's predecessor William; following William's
death, Richard wanted the return of Joan as well as her dowry or an indemnification.
488. Son of Richard's late brother Geoffrey, who had married Constance, the heir to the duchy
of Brittany; Arthur was only three years old at this point.
489. Christmas 1190.

of Mello, four hundred ounces of gold; to the bishop of Chartres, three hundred; to Matthew of Montmorency, three hundred; to Dreux [of Mello], two hundred,[490] and he gave two hundred to many others, the names of whom would take long to relate. Everything found for sale there at that time was very expensive. A bushel of grain cost twenty-four Angevin sous, a bushel of barley eighteen sous, wine fifteen sous, and a chicken twelve deniers. For this reason the king sent to the king and queen of Hungary for help in provisioning.[491] Afterward, he sent to the emperor at Constantinople[492] for passage to the Holy Land; and if the king, God willing, should return through the land of the emperor, that the emperor should provide him safe passage, and the king should provide good guarantee of peaceful entry and exit of his lands.[493]

[80] A few days later, the king of the Franks pushed the king of England to be ready to sail in mid-March, to cross the sea together. [The king of England], however, answered that he was unable to make the crossing until August. Again, however, the king of the Franks issued orders and warned him, as one of his own men, to cross the sea with him just as he had sworn. And, if he so wished, [the king of England] should marry the daughter of the king of Navarre, whom the mother of the king had brought along,[494] at Acre. If, however, he was unwilling to make the crossing, then he would marry [Philip's] sister as he was bound by oath to do.[495] The king of England then flatly declared he would not do the one or the other. Then the king of the Franks imposed upon the others, who were bound to him by oath, to do as they had sworn. Geoffrey of Rancon and the viscount of Châteaudun[496] answered on behalf of the others and agreed to do as they had sworn and would go whenever he wished. Then the king of England was *exceedingly angry*[497] and swore that he would disinherit them. The course of events proved this to be true. From this moment, disharmony, envy, and enmity began to grow between the two kings.

---

490. See ch. 62 above for identifications. On Matthew of Montmorency, see Baldwin, *KLL*, 36–37.

491. Recall that Philip's sister Marguerite had recently taken King Bela III of Hungary as her second husband, after the death of Henry the Young King of England.

492. Isaac II Angelos, r. 1185–95, and again briefly, during the Latin siege of Constantinople in the Fourth Crusade, in 1203–4, along with his son Alexius IV.

493. For a short summary of the Third Crusade from Philip's perspective, see Baldwin, *GPA*, 77–80.

494. Eleanor of Aquitaine (Richard's mother) brought Berengaria of Navarre to Messina.

495. In the event King Richard refused to marry Alix, Philip's sister, to whom he had long been engaged. Richard and Berengaria were married on 12 May 1191 in Cyprus. See Kathleen Nolan, "Symbolic Geography in the Tomb and Seal of Berengaria of Navarre, Queen of England," in *Moving Women Moving Objects (400–1500)*, ed. Tracy Chapman Hamilton and Mariah Proctor-Tiffany (Leiden: Brill, 2019), 59–85.

496. On Geoffrey of Rancon, see Baldwin, *GPA*, 410; the viscount of Châteaudun is Hugh IV or his son Geoffrey IV, both of whom had previously allied with Philip against the English king.

497. Deuteronomy 9:20.

However Philip, king of the Franks, greatly desired to complete the journey which he had begun, and he set sail in the month of March. And after a few days, with favorable winds, on the eve of Easter he sailed into Acre with all his forces.[498] And like an *angel of the Lord*,[499] he was welcomed with hymns of praise, great weeping, and with extreme joy by the entire army which had sat in siege of Acre for a long time. At once he *pitched his tents*[500] and made his headquarters near the walls of the city, such that the enemies of Christ could fire arrows from bows and bolts from crossbows as far as his headquarters and even beyond. Then, bringing up his catapults, stone slings, and other engines, he had so damaged the walls of the city before the arrival of the English king that nothing was left to do to take the city, except for the assault itself. The king of the Franks did not want to assault the city without the king of England. But as soon as the king [of England] came,[501] the king of the Franks told him that everyone was agreed upon an assault. The king of England, speaking from the bottom of his heart, advised that the assault be carried out, and that he would commit all the forces he could. The next morning, King Philip wanted to begin the assault with his men, but the king of England would not allow his forces to go, and he forbade the Pisans, who were sworn to him, to make the assault, and thus the assault failed. After this, however, upon the recommendation of both sides, general commanders were chosen from each side, wise men of experience, by whose advice and judgment the combined army would be directed. And by the faith which they owed to God and their pilgrimage, the two kings swore and promised to the commanders that they would do whatever they advised. Thereafter these mediators announced that the king of England should send his troops to the assault, place a garrison at the barricades, and see that his catapults and other engines were brought to bear, because the king of the Franks was doing all of these things. Since [the king of England] flatly refused to do this, King Philip absolved his forces from the oath he had made as to the command of the army.

The king of England and his forces, as they were coming by sea, crossed by way of the island of Cyprus, and they seized the island with its emperor and his daughter and carried away all their treasure.[502] At last their ships spread their sails before the wind, leaving the island well garrisoned with [the king's] forces. And Richard encountered head-on one of Saladin's ships,

---

498. Philip set sail on 30 March and arrived in Acre on 20 April 1191, six days after Easter. See John D. Hosler, *The Siege of Acre, 1189–1191: Saladin, Richard the Lionheart, and the Battle That Decided the Third Crusade* (New Haven: Yale University Press, 2018).

499. *Angelus Domini*, a common phrase in both the Old and New Testaments.

500. Exodus 19:2.

501. Richard arrived 8 June.

502. Isaac Ducas Comnenus had ruled the island of Cyprus as an independent kingdom since 1184. His daughter's name is unknown.

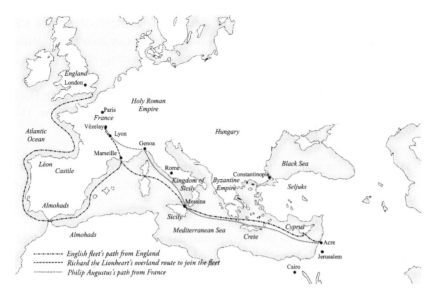

MAP 4. The Third Crusade. © M. Cecilia Gaposchkin

which was amazingly well supplied and heading to the relief of the city [of Acre]. On board there were countless glass jugs full of Greek fire,[503] 150 siege engines, and a vast abundance of bows and weapons, as well as the bravest of warriors. The king of England and his forces killed them all, and the battered ship sank.[504] Our forces seized another of Saladin's ships at Tyre, because it ran out of wind. On board was a supply of weapons and a few men, and it likewise was on its way to the relief of the city of Acre.

[81] In this same year [1190], Frederick [I], the most Christian emperor of the Romans and of the Germans,[505] coming with his son the duke of Bohemia and all his army to Outremer, went the way of all flesh between Nicaea, a city of Bithynia, and Antioch, leaving no little grief for all Christians and leaving his entire army to his son, the duke of Bohemia.[506] He escaped the land of the Turks with a few men and came with them to Acre, where he

---

503. The Byzantines had developed an incendiary weapon, known as Greek fire, that could be delivered with a projectile. By the period of the Crusades, authors often spoke of any powerful incendiary as "Greek fire."

504. 7 June 1191.

505. The emperor Frederick I Barbarossa (r. 1152–90) took the overland route to join the crusade, but drowned while crossing the Saleph River on 10 June 1190.

506. Frederick Barbarossa's second son, also named Frederick, was duke of Swabia, not Bohemia. He died 20 January 1191.

shortly *finished his life* in the course of nature.[507] The emperor Frederick was succeeded by his son Henry [VI],[508] a man vigorous in accomplishments, fierce to his foes, and generous and kind to all approaching him.

[82] In the year of our Lord 1191, fifteen before the Kalends of May, Pope Clement [III] died. He had been pope for two years and five months. The Roman Celestine [III] succeeded him.[509]

[83] In that same year, in the months of August, June, and July, the weather was so wild, due to excess rains, that crops in the fields sprouted ears and leaves before they could be harvested.

[84] In that same year, on the twenty-third day of June, the vigil of St. John the Baptist, while the kings were engaged in the siege of Acre, there was an eclipse of the sun in the seventh degree of Cancer, the moon then being in the sixth degree of the same sign, and tail of the Dragon in the twelfth, and it lasted for four hours.

In the next month, ten before the Kalends of August,[510] Louis, the son of King Philip, fell sick with a most grave illness. The doctors called it dysentery, and everyone despaired for his life. The holy monastery of the Blessed Denis, by common agreement, after fasting and giving prayer in deep devotion, carrying with them the nail and our Lord's Crown of Thorns and the arm of Saint Simeon the Elder, with a procession of the clergy and the people barefoot and tearfully praying to the Lord, came to the church of Saint-Lazare near Paris.[511] There, after prayer and an offering by the people who were following them, they were met and joined by the whole assembly of Parisian religious houses and Maurice the venerable bishop of Paris, with his canons and clergy and a host without number of students and people joining together carrying the relics and bodies of the saints with them, everyone barefoot and crying and weeping.[512] And assembled all together, singing

---

507. 2 Maccabees 10:13.

508. Henry VI (r. 1190–97).

509. Rigord's date for the death of Clement III would be 17 April 1191, but Clement III actually reigned as pope from December 1187 to his death on 20 March 1191; Celestine III (from the noble Roman family of the Orsini) then reigned from his election in late March or early April 1191 to 8 January 1198.

510. 23 July 1191.

511. Situated north of Paris, on the road to Saint-Denis.

512. The monks of Saint-Denis had come south toward Paris, and the bishop had come north, meeting at Saint-Lazare outside the city walls. The combined group then crossed the Right Bank and the Seine to arrive at the royal palace on the Île-de-la-Cité.

FIGURE 12. Procession from Saint-Denis to Prince Louis's sickbed. London, British Library, Royal MS 16 G VI, fol. 351v. Used by permission of the British Library.

with *much lamentation* and sighs,[513] they came to the palace of the king, where the boy lay ill. And there a sermon was preached to the people, with a vast outpouring of tears. As the people earnestly prayed to the Lord for him, and as the boy's whole stomach was touched with the sign of the cross by the nail, the Crown of Thorns, and the arm of Saint Simeon the Elder, that very day he was freed from the threatening danger. And his father, King Philip, then in Outremer, that same day and hour was cured of a similar sickness.

Then, after the boy Louis kissed the relics and received the blessing, all of the processions came to the church of Notre-Dame. Having completed their prayers and offerings to the Lord there, the procession of Notre-Dame with all the other processions led the monks of the Blessed Denis with hymns and praises and great *thanksgiving to the Lord*[514] all the way to the gate of the town. And there they blessed one another with the relics, and everyone returned home. The canons of Notre-Dame returned with the people, rejoicing, because in their own time these relics of the Blessed Denis had been carried down to Paris.[515] For it is nowhere recorded in any written record that until that time for any imminent danger were they ever carried beyond the town of the Blessed Denis. Nor should we pass over in silence the fact that on that same day, because of the prayers of the clergy and the people, calm and

---

513. 1 Esdras 10:1.

514. Leviticus 22:29.

515. That is, the relics of the nail, (a branch from) the Crown of Thorns, and the arm of Saint Simeon, which belonged to the monastery of Saint-Denis (not the relics of Saint Denis himself, which will be referred to in ch. 87).

temperate weather was restored to all the land. For the Lord had rained over the land for a long time, due to the sinfulness of men.

[85] In that same year the bishop of Liège,[516] fleeing the face of the emperor Henry, stayed a short while at Reims. He was received with honor by William, the reverend archbishop of Reims, who lodged him in his own residence and supplied his every need. But after a few days, at the instigation of the devil, some knights arrived, sent by the emperor to the said bishop of Liège. In truth they were minions of a satanic plan. The bishop, however, as a kind and holy man, received them with honor and sat them down at his own table like friends and members of his household. They claimed that they had been unjustly exiled from their lands by the emperor, and they spoke heart to heart, in guile and cunning. For they had *conceived a plot*, and soon they *carried out* this *iniquity*.[517] After a few more days had gone by, they led the bishop out beyond the city, as though going for a walk. And whipping out their swords, they most foully slew the anointed of the Lord, for he had been canonically elected and duly consecrated, albeit against the wishes of the emperor. The knights took flight and returned, as fast as they could, to the emperor.

[86] In that same year Count Thibaut the pious and merciful seneschal of the king of the Franks, the count of Clermont, the count of Perche, the duke of Burgundy, and Philip the count of Flanders all went the way of all flesh, summoned by the Lord at the siege of Acre.[518] The land of the count of Flanders, for he had no other heir, passed to his nephew Baldwin, the son of the count of Hainaut, who subsequently was made emperor of Constantinople.[519]

[87] In that same year, eight before the Kalends of September,[520] upon the advice of Lord William the archbishop of Reims, Queen Adele, and all the

---

516. Albert of Louvain, elected bishop of Liège 8 September 1191, against a candidate supported by Henry VI. Albert was murdered 24 November 1192.

517. Cf. Job 15:35.

518. The seneschal Thibaut of Blois, the constable Raoul of Clermont, Duke Hugh III of Burgundy, Count Rotrou IV of Perche, and Count Philip of Flanders all died on crusade between 1191 and 1193.

519. Count Philip's sister Marguerite was married to Count Baldwin V of Hainault, who now became count of Flanders as well. After Marguerite's and Baldwin's deaths in 1194 and 1195, their son Baldwin VI inherited both counties. Baldwin VI would participate in the Fourth Crusade and was elected as the first emperor of the Latin Empire of Constantinople in 1204. Here Rigord looks ahead to this event (see below, ch. 146). Unless this sentence was added later, it would suggest that Rigord did not write this passage until after 1204.

520. 25 August 1191.

bishops, the bodies of the most blessed martyrs Denis, Rusticus, and Eleuth-rius, with the most exquisite silver reliquaries in which they were contained, very carefully sealed, were brought out and placed upon the altar. And beside them were joined the bodies of other saints that rested in the same church, so that all the faithful assembled for the holy sight, with groans and sighs, *lifting up* their pure *hands* with *Moses*,[521] might pour forth prayers to the Lord for the liberation of the Holy Land, and for the king of the Franks and all his host. For Christians do not place their faith in the power of weapons, but in the power and mercy of Christ; they realize power not in themselves but in God, overcoming infidel peoples and annihilating enemies of the cross of Christ.

On the next feast of the Blessed Denis,[522] when the silver reliquary that contained the body of the most sacred martyr Denis was opened in the presence of the venerable bishops of Senlis and of Meaux,[523] Adele the queen of the Franks, and many abbots and men of religion, the whole body was found, along with the head, as we have said before, and it was displayed most piously to all the faithful of God who had come from far-off places to pray. And in order to be rid of the error of the people of Paris,[524] the head of the holy martyr Denis was reverently retained and placed in a silver casket, while the bodies of the saints with their reliquaries were piously put back in the marble tomb under the altar from whence they had been brought forth. The head, however, was displayed all year long to all pilgrims, in order to arouse the devotion of the faithful. And on the next feast of the Blessed Denis it was placed back in its reliquary with the body.

[88] While these things were happening in France, Philip, king of France, with the aid of those faithful to God, was attacking Acre. He had so smashed the walls of the city with his trebuchets and mangonels that he forced the enemies of the cross of Christ[525]—that is, Saladin's guards who were within, specifically the satraps Limathosius and Carachosius[526] with a host of their

---

521. Cf. Exodus 17:11.

522. 9 October 1191.

523. See above, ch. 46.

524. Rigord is here referring to an episode wherein another "head" of Saint Denis was discovered at the church of Saint-Etienne-de-Grés sometime before 1191.

525. *Inimicos crucis Christi*, a common phrase for the crusade adversary, has its root in Philippians 3:18.

526. Carachosius was Bāha' al-Din al Asadī Qāraqūsh, a commander in Saladin's army in charge of the Muslim garrison in Acre. Limathosius was Sayf al-Din 'Ali ibn Ahmed al-Mashtūb, the Kurdish emir of the city installed by Saladin in 1190.

soldiers—to surrender the city under terms.[527] Bound by solemn oath of
their law, they promised that in exchange for being allowed to leave in safety
they would return without fail the true cross of our Lord, which Saladin possessed, to the king of the Franks and the king of England, before being freed
by these kings, and [they would return] all the Christian captives who could
be found in their land.

In the battle, Albric,[528] a great-hearted man and marshal of the king of the
Franks, a mighty combatant, was caught by the pagans within the town gate
and slain.[529] The tower known as the Maudite,[530] however, which for a long
time caused much misery for our forces, had been undercut by the king's sappers, and their tunnel was held up only by wooden supports, so all that was
left to do to bring down the tower was to set fire to them. When the pagans
saw that they could not hold out against the kings, princes, and other Christians, they held a conference with the kings and princes and, upon the above
terms and with the promise of safe conduct, they turned over the city of
Acre, with all its weapons, arms, and abundant supplies of provisions, to our
kings and princes in the month of July. The Christian people entered the city,
and weeping for joy and tearfully raising both hands to heaven, they said in a
clear voice, *"Blessed be the Lord, our God,*[531] who has *beheld* our efforts and our
labors and has *humbled* beneath our feet the enemies of the Holy Cross *pre-
suming in their own strength."*[532] The Christians divided among themselves the
provisions found there, giving the greater part to the contingents with many
troops and the smaller to those with fewer. The kings, however, received all
captives by lot, dividing them between themselves in equal scale. But the
king of the Franks assigned his part to the duke of Burgundy, with a large
amount of gold and silver and vast supplies of provisions, and entrusted to
him all of his armed forces.[533]

For the king was then suffering from a grave illness, and moreover he was
extremely suspicious of the king of England, because [the king of England]
was frequently sending messengers to Saladin and exchanging gifts with him,
without informing the king [of France].[534] Philip thus held a general council
with his leading men, put his troops in order and, crying with tears in his eyes,

---

527. 12 July 1191.

528. Albric Clément died 3 July, before the surrender of Acre. Baldwin, *GPA*, 34, 79, 113.

529. Medieval Christian authors routinely referred to Muslims as "pagans." See Tolan, *Saracens*.

530. That is, the "cursed" tower.

531. Genesis 9:26.

532. Judith 6:15.

533. Hugh III of Burgundy led the French contingent after Philip's departure, but died 25
August 1192.

534. Rigord mentions Richard only to imply his untrustworthiness. In fact, Richard had been as
sick as Philip, but had insisted in taking part in the siege of Acre anyway. Philip's decision to leave

received approval from his men and entrusted himself to the winds and the sea.[535] He embarked on just three galleys which had been prepared for him by Rufus of Genoa, and as God so willed, he was carried to the region of Apulia.[536] When he had to some small degree recovered his health, though certainly still weak, he took to the road with a few followers. Crossing through the city of Rome, he visited the shrines of the apostles and received the blessing of the Roman pope Celestine [III], before returning to France around the time of our Lord's nativity.[537]

[89] The king of England, who remained in Outremer, was constraining the captives whom he held himself, that is, Limathosius and Carachosius, and others whom other princes held, to do as they had promised—to restore to holy Christendom, without delay, our Lord's Cross which Saladin possessed, as well as all Christian captives, just as they were bound to do by the oath of their law. But because they were unable to accomplish what they had sworn to do, the king of England, *exceedingly angry*,[538] had some five thousand or more pagan captives taken outside the city and beheaded.[539] But he kept back those of rank and wealth, for whom he gained a vast amount of money in ransom and then set them free. Indeed he sold the island of Cyprus, which he had seized during his crossing, to the Templars for twenty-five thousand silver marks. Later it was taken back from them, and he sold it again to Guy, the former king of Jerusalem, to have forever.[540] He utterly destroyed the city of Ascalon, at the request of the pagans who were offering a large amount of gold.[541] He seized the battle standard of the duke of Austria from a certain prince outside of Acre, smashed it most wickedly, and threw it into a deep latrine to insult and dishonor the duke.[542] But, since we have not intended to

---

Acre after its capture was probably influenced by his rift with Richard, and occasioned a fair amount of criticism by French and English sources alike. Richard stayed in the East until October 1192.

535. 31 July 1191.

536. Philip reached southern Italy 10 October 1191.

537. Christmas 1191.

538. Deuteronomy 9:20.

539. 20 August 1191.

540. Richard initially placed the island under Angevin leadership, but soon sold it to the Templars (for one hundred thousand bezants), who shortly after returned it to Richard. In 1192 Richard sold Cyprus to Guy of Lusignan, who established a ruling dynasty on the island that lasted until the sixteenth century.

541. Rigord is misleading; Richard was planning an attack on Ascalon (modern Ashkélon, Israel), a critical port on the route to Egypt, and Saladin determined to forestall the tactic by destroying the city walls, rendering it essentially valueless.

542. Leopold V of Austria participated in the siege of Acre and assumed leadership of the German forces following the death of Frederick I's son Frederick of Swabia. Leopold was denied a share of the spoils upon the taking of the city, and his rights were symbolically disdained by throwing down

write the history of the king of England or his deeds, let us turn our pen to those matters we are covering concerning our king, Philip.

[90] After Philip, king of the Franks, had returned to France, he observed the birth of our Lord at Fontainebleau.[543] Then, after a few days, he hastened to the church of the blessed martyr Denis to pray. There the holy monastery assembled with their abbot Hugh and led [the king] into the church in procession with hymns of praise. After praying, he lay flat down before the bodies of the saints and gave thanks to God and the blessed martyrs, because He had freed him from such great dangers, and upon the altar he made an offering of a silken mantle of finest quality as a mark of loving charity.

In the same year, a few months later, fifteen before the Kalends of April,[544] when he was staying at Saint-Germain-en-Laye,[545] he learned of the scandalous death of a certain Christian brought about by the Jews. And, in deep feeling for the Christian faith and religion, he suddenly set off, though no one in his household knew where he was headed, and at top speed he came flying to the castle called Brie.[546] There he garrisoned the castle gates, rounded up eighty or more Jews, and had them burned. The countess of this castle[547] had been corrupted by the large gifts of the Jews, and had handed over to them a certain Christian whom they had falsely charged with theft and homicide. Moved by ancient hatred, the Jews tied his hands behind his back, crowned him with thorns,[548] flogged him through the town, and, thereafter *hanged him on a gibbet*,[549] even though they themselves had said at the time of our Lord's passion, *It is not lawful for us to put any man to death.*[550]

[91] In that same year, on the eve of the Ides of May,[551] at Nogent in Perche,[552] battle lines of knights were seen descending from the sky to the ground where,

---

his battle standard, perhaps at Richard's command. Leopold thereupon immediately departed the Holy Land. Rigord will describe Leopold's revenge below.

543. Seventy kilometers (forty-three miles) south of modern Paris.

544. 18 March 1192.

545. Twenty-five kilometers (fifteen miles) west of modern Paris.

546. The place-name could refer to Bray-sur-Seine, 110 kilometers (sixty-eight miles) southeast of Paris, in the county of Champagne (outside the royal domain). But Jordan (*French Monarchy and the Jews*, 35–37), and others have shown the likelihood of Brie-Count-Robert, thirty-five kilometers (twenty-two miles) southeast of modern Paris.

547. If Brie-Count-Robert is indeed the correct location, the "countess" in question would have been Agnes of Baudemont, widow of Robert I of Dreux and mother of Robert II (still on crusade).

548. Cf. Matthew 27:29; Mark 15:17; John 19:2.

549. Cf. Genesis 40:22.

550. John 18:31.

551. 14 May 1192.

552. Nogent-le-Rotrou is about 125 kilometers (seventy-eight miles) southwest of Paris, on the route to Le Mans, in the county of Perche.

FIGURE 13. Philip II making his offering to Saint-Denis. London, British Library, Royal MS 16 G VI, fol. 353v. Used by permission of the British Library.

after a marvelous combat, they suddenly vanished. The local inhabitants observing this were *struck with great fear*[553] and returned *beating their breast.*[554]

[92] In the year of our Lord 1192, on the twentieth day of November,[555] there was a partial eclipse of the moon after midnight, in the sixth degree of Gemini, which lasted two hours. In the following month of May, six before the Ides of that month,[556] during Rogation time,[557] a certain priest, an Englishman named William, mighty in the holiness of his life and ways, passed to the Lord at Pontoise.[558] A the time of his death, as the Lord brought it about, many miracles came to pass at his tomb; the blind were enlightened, the lame cured. Others indeed were restored from various diseases back to good health. The fame of such a man, spread throughout the world, caused many people from far-flung regions to come on pilgrimage to the place of his burial.

[93] In that same year, as wickedness grew among the Christians, letters were brought from Outremer to King Philip at Pontoise, to the effect that Assassins were being sent to kill King Philip at the instigation and order of

553. Genesis 45:3.

554. Luke 23:48.

555. From this point Rigord begins to waver between the older Roman dating style of days to the Kalends/Nones/Ides, and the more modern system of numbered days of the month.

556. 10 May 1193.

557. Rogation days asked (*rogare* means "to ask" in Latin) God's blessing on the spring planting. The major rogation was fixed to April 25, and the three minor rogations were celebrated on the Monday, Tuesday, and Wednesday immediately before Ascension Thursday. In 1193 this would have been 3–5 May.

558. Little is known about this William beyond Rigord's brief account.

Richard, king of England.[559] For at that time in Outremer they had killed the marquis,[560] a relative of the king, a vigorous warrior who had ruled the Holy Land by his strength and might with great effort before these kings [of France and England] came there. Now King Philip was extremely angry after hearing these letters. He left that castle at once and was very upset for many days. Since the mind of the king was much disturbed by such rumors and he became more and more anxious each day, he acted upon the advice of his household and sent his own envoys to the Old Man, the king of the Assassins, so that he might more fully and carefully learn the truth from him. Meanwhile the king [of France], for greater caution, instructed his bodyguard to have brass-bound clubs always in hand, and to stand a rotating watch over him through the night. When his envoys returned, the king learned from the Old Man's letters and from the report of his envoys and the careful investigation made by them as to the truth of the matter: that the rumors were indeed false. And now that the false rumor was dismissed, his mind was relieved of the false suspicion.

[94] The king of England, now intending to return to his own land, handed over to his nephew Henry, a very fine young man,[561] all the lands which the Christians then held in Outremer, and gave his army to him as well. [The king of England] set sail[562] and a storm arose. It happened that the wind took the ship he was in toward the region of Istria to a spot between Aquileia and Venice. He was shipwrecked there, as God allowed, and escaped with just a few followers. A certain Mainard of Görtz[563] and the people of that area heard that he was in their land. Carefully considering the discord this king had caused in the Promised Land in the accumulation of his own damnation, they pursued him, intending to take him prisoner, contrary to the customs afforded all pilgrims traveling in peace through whatever Christian lands.[564] As the king took flight they captured eight of his knights. Thereafter

---

559. The "Assassins," led by the figure known as the "Old Man of the Mountain," were a dissident Shi'ite Muslim group in northern Syria which used the threat of assassinations to preserve its independence from Christians and Sunni Muslims alike. The fear their tactics produced is amply demonstrated by Rigord's account.

560. Conrad of Montferrat. He had married Isabella, heir to the Kingdom of Jerusalem, in November 1190. On 24 April 1192 he was chosen king of Jerusalem (supported by Philip II and against the wishes of Richard of England), but on 28 April he was assassinated.

561. Henry II of Champagne (r. 1181–97), son of Henry I and Marie of France. See Evergates, *Marie of France*, 67–73; and Cast of Characters.

562. 9 October 1192.

563. A vassal of Leopold of Austria.

564. Rigord refers not only to customary treatment of pilgrims but more specifically to legal protections offered to crusaders.

the king traveled to a town in the archbishopric of Salzburg which is called Friesach, where Frederick of St. Sowe[565] seized six of [Richard's] knights as the king hurried to Austria by night, with only three knights. Duke Leopold of Austria, however, a blood relation of the emperor, posted watch over the main road and put guards everywhere.[566] He took the king into custody in a suburb outside Vienna, in a house that was being watched, and he seized all his possessions. The following month, December [1192], he handed him over to the emperor [Henry VI]. Richard was unjustly imprisoned by him for almost a year and a half, and there he was saddled with a multitude of costs and much expense. In the end he paid a ransom of two hundred thousand silver marks to the emperor, and crossed the sea to England.[567] He was afraid that he might be again captured by the king of France, whom he had deeply offended, if he traveled through his country.[568]

[95] Henry, the count of Champagne, *an ingenious youth,*[569] was a famous man and nephew to both kings through their sister.[570] When he saw the land of Outremer so abandoned by the departure of these two kings, he was moved, by the inspiration of God, by paternal piety, and by the prayers of the many who remained there in the service of God, to stay there with his forces, and by great effort and sweat and in the greatest want to carry on the honor of Jesus Christ, and if the occasion should arise, to lay down his soul for Christ, rather than to return in shame to his own country without hav- ing visited the Lord's tomb. Realizing this, the knights of the sacred Temple and the Hospital of Jerusalem and the many other pilgrims who had come together to liberate the Holy Land, who appreciated the count's heartfelt, unshakable constancy in the Lord, unanimously elected him king of the supreme city of God. And they gave him the daughter of the king of Jeru- salem as his wife,[571] *praising and blessing* the Lord[572] who had raised up from the blood of the kings of the Franks a savior and liberator of the Holy Land.

---

565. Brother of Mainard of Görtz.

566. Recall that Richard had insulted Duke Leopold at the siege of Acre (ch. 89 above).

567. Freed February, arrived in England March 1194.

568. These fears were well founded; Philip had done everything he could to keep Richard in captivity as long as possible.

569. 3 Kings 11:28.

570. Since his mother, Marie of France, was the daughter of Louis VII and Eleanor of Aquitaine, Henry II of Champagne was nephew to both Richard I and Philip II.

571. Henry married Isabella, the widow of Conrad of Montferrat, 5 May 1192 (see ch. 93 above).

572. Cf. Luke 24:53.

[96] In the year of our Lord 1193, on the eve of the Ides of April,[573] King Philip with his assembled forces seized Gisors, and quickly brought under his control all of the Norman Vexin which the king of England was holding unjustly.[574] Once Gisors had been conquered and the entire march of Normandy returned to his control, King Philip restored Châteauneuf to the Blessed Denis, since Henry, king of England, and then his son Richard, had occupied this place by force for a long time.

[97] At that time Saladin, king of Syria and Egypt, passed away at Damascus.[575] His two sons succeeded him: one named Saphadin controlled Syria; the other, named Meralicius, Egypt.[576]

[98] In that same year, on the feast of the Blessed Denis,[577] a certain boy who had died suddenly was most piously carried by his parents to the church of the most blessed martyr Denis. With tears and lamentations they placed him on the altar before the bodies of the saints, and cried out, "Saint Denis, help us!" And through the intercession and merits of the holy martyrs, the little boy was brought back to life by God, before the whole assembled people.

[99] At this time, King Philip sent a venerable man, Stephen, bishop of Noyon,[578] off to Cnut, king of the Danes,[579] to ask and beseech him that he might consent to send him one of his sisters, whom he would make his lawful wife. Considering this request, Cnut, king of the Danes, happily agreed, and he handed over to the envoys of the king of the Franks his very beautiful sister, Ingeborg,[580] a saintly girl adorned with a good character, and he honored her with fine gifts. Given leave to depart, they entrusted themselves

---

573. 12 April 1193.

574. Philip, allied with Richard's brother John, took advantage of Richard's imprisonment to capture areas in Normandy that bordered on Capetian holdings. Richard had received these areas as part of the agreement of marriage with Alix of France. Since Richard had ultimately refused the marriage, Philip claimed that these lands should rightfully return to him. For Rigord, however, the most important outcome was that the monastery of Saint-Denis recovered one of its priories.

575. 3 March 1193.

576. Rigord is confused about the division of power after Saladin's death. Saphadin was actually Saladin's brother (Al-Adil), not his son. Meralicius was apparently Al-Aziz Uthman, his son, who later reconsolidated much of the Ayyubid kingdom.

577. 9 October 1193.

578. Stephen, bishop of Noyon, 1188–1221.

579. Cnut VI of Denmark (r. 1182–1202).

580. B. 1175. On Ingeborg and her calamitous marriage to Philip Augustus, see George Conklin, "Ingeborg of Denmark, Queen of France 1193–1223," in *Queens and Queenship in Medieval Europe*, ed. Anne Duggan (Woodbridge: Boydell, 1997), 39–52; also Baldwin, *GPA*, 82–84.

to the wind and sea and arrived at Arras. Philip, king of the Franks, sped there with great joy, accompanied by the bishops and foremost men of the kingdom, and he married in lawful wedlock the long-desired Ingeborg, and had her crowned queen of the Franks.[581] But—a strange thing! On that very day—by the work of the devil!—the same king, snared, as it is said, by the spells of sorceresses, began to loath the wife whom he had for so long desired. A few days later, after a line of consanguinity through Charles, count of Flanders, was worked out by the bishops and barons, this marriage was annulled by a church judgment.[582] Queen Ingeborg, however, was unwilling to return to the Danes, and resolved to remain in religious places in areas of Gaul, preferring to preserve marital chastity for the rest of her life rather than stain her first bonds of matrimony by marrying another.[583] But, since it was alleged that in this way the marriage had been unjustly nullified, the Roman pope Celestine [III], at the insistence of the Danes, sent his legates into France; that is, Melior the cardinal-priest and Cencius the subdeacon.[584] They came to Paris and convened a council of all the archbishops, bishops, and abbots of the whole kingdom, where they sought the reestablishment of the marriage between King Philip and his wife, Ingeborg.[585] But because they had become *dumb dogs not able to bark,*[586] afraid for their own hide, they *brought nothing to perfection.*[587]

[100] In that same year, four before the Ides of November,[588] there was a total eclipse of the moon in the first hour of the night, and it lasted for two hours.

[101] In that same year a certain possessed person was miraculously cured in the church of the blessed martyr Denis.

[102] When the month of February [1194] arrived, King Philip assembled his army and again entered Normandy. He took the city of Evreux, brought

---

581. Philip and Ingeborg were married 14 August 1193, at Amiens not Arras. She was crowned the next day.

582. On 5 November 1193, a compliant group of bishops led by William of the White Hands endorsed the fiction that Philip and Ingeborg were too closely related to have been legitimately married.

583. In fact Ingeborg was actively marshaling her family's resources to fight this annulment.

584. Melior, cardinal-priest of St. John and St. Paul; and the apostolic notary Censius.

585. 7 May 1196, at Paris. Rigord has jumped ahead of his narrative, showing that he was writing several years after these events transpired.

586. Isaiah 56:10.

587. Hebrews 7:19. Rigord, who called Ingeborg *puella sancta* (saintly or holy girl) and continued to refer to her as *regina* (queen) after the annulment, here begins to criticize Philip in a way not seen earlier in the text.

588. 10 November 1193.

Neubourg and Vaudreuil and many other strongholds under his rule, and destroyed a large number of them; and he captured many knights and laid siege to Rouen.[589] But, considering the fortifications of the place and the loss of his men, and realizing that he would accomplish nothing there, *inflamed with a great fury*,[590] he burned his mangonels, trebuchets, and other siege engines, and left. Finally, as Lent arrived, he ended his campaign.[591] Then John, called Lackland, brother of the king of England, entered into a treaty with Philip, king of the Franks.[592] But [John] did this in deceit, as the result of the affair later made clear.

[103] In the year of our Lord 1194, Michael, dean [of the cathedral chapter] of Paris, was elected patriarch of Jerusalem. But the Lord arranged things otherwise, and fifteen days later he was elected once again, [this time] by the clergy of Sens as archbishop, with the agreement of King Philip and of all the people of the city, and he was consecrated as archbishop eight before the Kalends of May.[593] It is not in our power to explain here to what extent and how well he prospered before becoming archbishop, in terms of the management of the schools at Paris and the distribution of alms and many other goods.

[104] In that same year, a little three-year-old boy from Courneuve who had happened to drown was brought back to life by the prayers and merits of the blessed martyr Denis.

[105] Three months later, six before the Ides of May,[594] King Philip once more assembled his army and entered Normandy and laid siege to Verneuil. After three weeks, when he had battered down a part of the walls, news came that the city of Evreux, which the king had fortified and was holding, had been

---

589. Rigord is returning to the military narrative at the time when Philip and his ally John were attacking King Richard's holdings in Normandy, while Richard was still in captivity. Recall that Richard returned to England in March 1194. He then quickly crossed to France to defend his interests there.

590. Esther 1:12.

591. Lent began on 23 February in 1194.

592. John and Philip had in fact agreed to a formal treaty of alliance before these events, in January 1194. The terms of this treaty granted some of King Richard's lands in Normandy to Philip. Under those terms Philip could claim to be asserting possession of lands now rightly his.

593. 24 April 1194. Michael of Corbeil was archbishop of Sens 1194–99 (Sens was the archiepiscopal seat for the diocese of Paris). As canon and chancellor of Notre-Dame of Paris from 1192 to 1194, Michael of Corbeil had the authority to license masters, permitting them to teach at the nascent university of Paris. It is possible that Michael of Corbeil was Philip Augustus's almoner. See further ch. 137.

594. 10 May 1194. Rigord's "three months later" is not very exact.

captured by the Normans. The king's knights had been taken prisoner there and many had been disgracefully beheaded. On hearing this, the king, upset and *inflamed with a great fury,*[595] left the siege [of Verneuil]. He drove off the Normans and leveled the city [of Evreux] and in his violent mood he even destroyed God's own churches.[596] His army which had remained at the siege [of Verneuil], seeing that the king was gone and that the enemy was coming on, suddenly pulled up tents and folded pavilions and went off following the king, leaving behind the greater part of its provisions. Those who had been besieged then came out and were enriched by all the provisions and spoils of the Franks which had been abandoned in their haste.

[106] In that same year, seventeen before the Kalends of June,[597] William, count of Leicester,[598] a brave and greathearted man, was taken prisoner by King Philip and imprisoned at Étampes. Meanwhile the king of England with his army took [the castle of] Loches and expelled the canons of Saint-Martin of Tours, violently plundered their possessions, and did much wickedness to God's churches in those regions.

[107] In that same year, in the region of Beauvais, between Clermont and Compiègne, there occurred such rain, thunder, lightning, and storms as was beyond the memory of anyone alive. Stones falling from the heaven the size of eggs, square and triangular, mixed with rain, utterly destroyed the fruit trees, vines, and crops. In many places villages were destroyed by lightning and burned. Crows in great numbers were seen in a storm of this sort, flying from place to place carrying live coals in their beaks and setting fire to houses. Individuals of both sexes were killed by thunderbolts, which presented a miraculous sight to observers, and many other frightful things were shown on that day. A prodigious event ought well to terrify men and keep them from wickedness. We have heard that on the same day the castle of Chaumont in the bishopric of Laon was destroyed by lightning.

In that same year the church of Notre-Dame at Chartres caught fire and burned.[599]

---

595. Esther 1:12. Rigord's use of the same biblical phrase as in ch. 102 to describe Philip's enraged departures suggests something of the king's recurring frustration in these inconclusive military ventures.

596. The king in the last few chapters has abandoned his marriage, suffered several blind rages, and now even attacked churches. The hero of the first part of Rigord's text has lost some of his luster.

597. 15 June 1194.

598. Robert (not William) of Leicester had been defending Rouen.

599. On 9–10 June 1194 a major fire destroyed most of Chartres cathedral, followed by the rebuilding of one of the most famous Gothic edifices of the period. See Baldwin, *KLL*, ch. 10.

In that same year a certain man of Vierzon was freed from prison at Rouen by the prayers of the Blessed Denis.

[108] Philip, king of the Franks, upon learning that the king of England had expelled the clergy from the church of Saint-Martin of Tours and had plundered their goods, in turn seized all of the churches which were in his land but belonged to bishoprics or abbeys which were in the power of the king of England. And at the prompting of certain wicked men, he threw out the monks or clergy who were serving God there, and he turned their revenues to his own use. And indeed he severely oppressed his own churches in his own kingdom at that time with heavy and unaccustomed financial burdens. He heaped up many stores of wealth in various places, content to spend only modestly, saying that the kings of the Franks, his predecessors, lived as poor men who in times of need spent nothing on their hired troops and so, amid pressing warfare, had suffered no modest loss to their kingdom. In amassing this wealth, however, the king's primary goal was the liberation of the Holy Land of Jerusalem from the pagans, and the restitution of the Christians, and the vigorous defense of the kingdom of the Franks from its foes—even though some individuals who understood less, not knowing the will and intent of the king, accused him of excessive greed and grandeur. But, because he had learned from wise men that there is a *time to gather* and *a time to scatter* what has been gathered,[600] as opportunity came his way, he gathered much so that *in time of need*[601] he might distribute the most to a greater number. He made this very clear in the fortification of cities, the repair of walls, and the construction of countless castles.

[109] Afterward, while King Philip and his army were crossing the land of Count Louis [of Blois],[602] the king of England with a large force of armed knights quite unexpectedly charged out of the woods and forcefully carried off King Philip's packhorses, which were loaded with money, much silver, and various equipment.[603] While these things were going on in the land of Count Louis of Blois, John Lackland, Count David, and the count of Arundel[604]

---

600. Cf. Ecclesiastes 3:5.

601. Ecclesiasticus 8:12, 29:2.

602. Louis, count of Blois and Chartres, following the death of Thibaut IV. See ch. 68 above.

603. The Battle of Fréteval, 3 July 1194. It was in this battle that Philip lost all the documents that his itinerant court was carrying, leading to the beginning of the stationary royal archives in Paris known as the Trésor des Chartes.

604. David of Scotland, Earl of Huntingdon (1152–1219), and William of Aubigny, Earl of Arundel (r. 1193–1221).

with their army and the citizens of Rouen laid siege to Vaudreuil, which King Philip had fortified and was holding.[605] A week later, at night, King Philip arrived with a few crossbowmen, and at the break of day he charged their castle. The Normans flew off in haste and headed into the woods, abandoning their trebuchets, mangonels, and other apparatus of war, along with a huge supply of provisions. Quite a few of the Normans were killed in battle while fleeing, and more were captured and ransomed.

[110] In the same year the emperor Henry brought under his rule the whole of Apulia, Calabria, and Sicily, which pertained to him by the law of inheritance on behalf of his wife.[606]

[111] In the same year, Raymond [V] of Toulouse died. He was succeeded by his son Raymond [VI], a relative of the king of the Franks through Constance, the sister of King Louis [VII].[607] In an unusually disturbed spell of weather, tornadoes, storms, and hail destroyed the vineyards and harvests; and a fierce famine ensued in the following year.

[112] In the year of our Lord 1195, in the month of July, the truce was broken by the king of England and war was renewed. Then King Philip completely leveled the town of Vaudreuil, which he had fortified and had been holding. A few days later, that is, thirteen before the Kalends of September,[608] he gave his sister Alix, whom the king of England, Richard, had repudiated, to the count of Ponthieu in marriage.[609]

[113] At that time, Emir Momelin, king of the Moabites,[610] that is, "king of the faithful," invaded Spain with a vast number of Moabite warriors and plundered the lands of the Christians. Alfonso [VIII], the king of Castile,[611] rode out against him with a host of troops. Battle ensued, and he was defeated and

---

605. See ch. 102 above.

606. When Tancred of Lecce died in 1194 (see ch. 79 above), Henry VI successfully claimed the inheritance of his wife, Constance.

607. Raymond V of Toulouse had married Louis VII's sister Constance.

608. 20 August 1195.

609. William IV, count of Ponthieu 1179–1221. Alix died about the same time as her husband, ca. 1220.

610. In fact the Almohad dynasty, which Rigord gives the biblical name "Moabites." "Emir Momelin" was Abu Yusuf Ya'qub-al-Mansur (1184–99), who was successful in pushing back the Christian advance in southern Spain. Christian authors sometimes used the term Moabites (rather than Saracens or pagans) to distinguish Muslims of Iberian or Berber extraction (such as the Almohads or the Almoravids) from those in the Levant.

611. R. 1158–1214.

escaped with only a few Christians.[612] It is said that in this battle more than fifty thousand Christians were slain. This misfortune befell the Christians because King Alfonso ruthlessly oppressed his knights while empowering peasants. For this reason, when the knights were at a loss, having neither horses nor weapons, the peasants, unskilled in arms, turned and fled. And as they fled in haste, the Moabites cut them down from behind in pitiful slaughter.

[114] While these things were happening in Spain, Richard, king of England, assembled his forces from all over and besieged the castle called Arques, which the king of the Franks had fortified and was holding. But, after the passage of a few days, the king of the Franks arrived with six hundred chosen French knights, drove off the Normans, destroyed the village called Dieppe, led away the men, and burned their ships. But as King Philip was returning with his men and crossing the woods, which are commonly called forests, the king of England, completely unforeseen, suddenly emerged from these forests with his troops and slew some men of the rear guard. Mercadier, who was then leader of [Richard's] mercenaries,[613] with his forces destroyed the outskirts of Issoudun, in the area of Bourges, and took the fortification and strengthened it with his men to the advantage of the king of England. After a short while a truce was arranged, and each king ceased the campaign.

[115] In this same year there was such unseasonable weather with such pouring rain that the crops germinated in the ears and hull before the time of harvest. With the havoc of the unseasonable weather the previous year and then the uncontrolled flood of rain, such a period of scarcity followed that a bushel of wheat was sold at Paris for sixteen sous, of millet for ten sous, a mixture [of the two] for thirteen or fourteen sous, and a bushel of salt for forty sous. For this reason King Philip, moved by piety, gave orders that far greater alms be distributed to the poor from his own resources, and by earnest correspondence he pressed the bishops and abbots and the general populace to do the same. The monastery of the Blessed Denis distributed to the poor all the silver which it was able to lay hands on.

[116] In that same year a certain priest named Fulk [of Neuilly] began to preach in Gaul.[614] And by means of his preaching and frequent warnings to

---

612. The Battle of Alarcos, 18 July 1195.

613. Mercadier was an infamous mercenary captain who joined Richard's forces by 1184, accompanied him on the Third Crusade, and continued to fight against Philip II until his death in 1200.

614. Fulk of Neuilly (d. 1201) was a famous preacher from the Paris basin, best known for his preaching of the Fourth Crusade.

the populace, many were called away from their usurious practices, and the interest [they had collected] was returned to poor Christians.

[117] In the following month of November [1195], as its term was reached, the truce ended and war began again. Philip gathered his forces in the region of Berry near Issoudun. Opposing him there was the king of England and his army. Just as each army was girding for imminent battle, against the expectations of all who were there, by the miraculous work of the Lord—who changes when He wills the plans of kings and *brings to nothing the designs* of people,[615]—it happened that the king of England laid down his arms, and with a few followers swiftly approached the king of the Franks. There, before all, he did homage to King Philip for the duchy of Normandy and for the counties of Poitou and Anjou. After that, in the same place, each king swore an oath to maintain the peace. And for the rest, a conference was planned between the kings concerning the establishment and strengthening of peace, [to be held] during the octave of Epiphany,[616] between Vaudreuil and the castle of Gaillon. And thus each of their armies returned home rejoicing. King Philip, not unmindful of his patron and protector, the Blessed Denis, hastened to the church of the most blessed martyr as quickly as possible. There he humbly offered upon the altar a cloak of costly silk, in token of his love and in thanks to God and the blessed martyrs.

[118] Indeed when the month of January [1196] came, on the fifteenth day of that month, at a gathering of archbishops, bishops, and barons from both sides, at the same place, peace was reestablished most firmly between the two kings. And it was confirmed by oaths and exchange of hostages as surety from both sides, in accordance with the understanding contained in the original agreement.

[119] In the year of our Lord 1196, in the month of March, a huge, sudden flood of waters and rivers in many areas destroyed many villages, killed the inhabitants, and smashed the bridges of the river Seine. The clergy and people beheld the threatening prodigies of the Lord, which were then in the heaven above, and *the signs on the earth beneath.*[617] And fearing another fresh cataclysm, the faithful populace devoted to God *cried to the Lord*[618] with

---

615. Cf. Job 5:12.

616. The next octave of Epiphany was 13 January 1196. The next chapter indicates the conference was actually held on 15 January 1196.

617. Act 2:19.

618. Judges 3:9.

groans, tearful lamentations, and constant fasting and prayers as they advanced in barefoot procession, so that He might spare them when they had reformed, and deflect mercifully from them the lash of this wrath, and deign to hear them with pity in their penance and fitting amends. King Philip, as though but one of the people, followed behind these processions, humbly sighing and crying. The holy monastery of the Blessed Denis, carrying the nail of our Lord and the Crown of Thorns and the arm of Saint Simeon the Elder, came with sighs and tears *crying to the Lord*[619] and blessing the waters in the sign of the cross, saying,

[120] "By these signs of his holy Passion may the Lord send these waters back to their own place." And, after a few days, when the Lord was appeased, *the waters returned into their channel.*[620]

[121] In that same year, in the month of May [1196], John, prior of the church of the Blessed Denis, was made abbot of Corbie.[621]

[122] In that same year, in the month of June, Baldwin, count of Flanders,[622] did homage to King Philip at Compiègne in the presence of William, archbishop of Reims, and Marie, countess of Champagne,[623] and many others.

[123] In that same year and month, King Philip took a wife, Marie by name, the daughter of the duke of Méran and Bohemia, the marquis of Istria.[624]

[124] A short time afterward, Richard, king of England, made war upon Philip, king of the Franks, without regard to the oaths and treaties mentioned above. He seized by trick the castle of Vierzon, in the region of Berry, and leveled it. He had sworn to the lord of Vierzon that he would do him no harm. Because of this, the king [of France] assembled his army and forcefully besieged the castle which is called Aumale. While King Philip was engaged

---

619. Judges 10:10.

620. Joshua 4:18.

621. John of Brustin was abbot of Corbie (the venerable Benedictine abbey founded by the Merovingian queen Balthilde) from 1196 to 1198. Rigord wrote his *Cronica* at John's request.

622. See ch. 86 above.

623. Marie (Philip's half sister) was overseeing Champagne while her son Henry II was in the Holy Land (see chs. 94–95).

624. Philip married Agnes of Méran in June 1196. Her full name may have been Agnes-Marie, since Rigord, like several other contemporary chroniclers, refers to her as "Marie." Rigord's desultory commentary here is notable; Philip's ongoing attempts to nullify his marriage to Ingeborg were highly dubious.

there, the king of England took back the castle called Nonancourt by trick and treason, for he paid off the garrison of knights. Then, placing his own knights and crossbowmen there, well supplied with arms and provisions, [King Richard] turned back toward the king [of France] with his Norman troops and mercenaries. Now the king of the Franks had surrounded the abovementioned castle [of Aumale] with his trebuchets and mangonels, and assaulted it vigorously for more than seven weeks. Those inside, for their part, were staunch defenders who were fiercely resisting the Franks, and they sometimes made no small slaughter of them. One day, as the king of England was attacking the enemy, he was surprised by the sudden arrival of the Franks and he turned and fled. As the king of England took flight, Guy of Thouars,[625] a man powerful in war and fierce in combat, was taken prisoner with other knights. The Franks returned to the siege and attacked the castle more fiercely by day and night. Finally, after the tower was broken and the walls smashed by the trebuchets and mangonels, the warriors within gave King Philip a sum of silver, having agreed to terms allowing them to depart unharmed, in peace, and with their property, horses, and weapons. This was done, but some of the Franks, not knowing the king's objective and will, said it was a mistake. When these [defenders of the castle] had departed and been led back to their own forces with their property in safety, King Philip destroyed the castle right down to the ground. Finally, a few days after coming to Gisors, they laid siege to Nonancourt. Surrounding it with siege engines and attacking it fiercely by day and night, in a relatively short time, in a marvelous battle, he took the oft-mentioned castle together with its fifteen knights, eighteen crossbowmen, many other prisoners, and an ample supply of provisions. He entrusted all this to the care of Count Robert.[626]

[125] In this same year, three before the Ides of September,[627] Maurice, of venerable memory, bishop of the Parisians, father of the poor and orphaned, went happily to the Lord.[628] Among his innumerable good deeds, he founded four abbeys and endowed them most piously with his own funds—that is, Hérivaux, Hermières, Yerres, Gif[629]—and many other things which would be long to relate. At the end he bestowed all his wealth upon the poor. Because he believed fervently in the resurrection of the body, about which he had in

---

625. Guy was the brother of Aimery VI, viscount of Thouars. Baldwin, *GPA*, 95, 238–39.
626. Robert II of Dreux (see ch. 64 above).
627. 11 September 1196.
628. On Bishop Maurice of Sully, see ch. 2 above.
629. Maurice of Sully supported each of these four monasteries without being the true founder of any of them.

his life heard many experts express doubts, and desiring at his death to call them back from their disbelief, he ordered[630] that a scroll be written containing this text: "I believe *that my Redeemer lives and on the last day I shall rise out of the earth and in my flesh I will see my Savior. Whom I myself shall see, and not another, and my eyes shall behold. This, my hope, is laid up in my bosom.*"[631] In his final moments, he instructed that this scroll be unrolled upon his breast by his faithful friends and followers, so that all literate men gathering at his burial on the day of his death and reading this holy text would believe most fervently in the shared resurrection of all bodies, and would doubt no more thereafter.

Eudes of Sully, the brother of Henry the archbishop of Bourges, succeeded him,[632] a man most unlike his predecessor in life and morals.

[126] In the year of our Lord 1197, Baldwin, count of Flanders, openly abandoned his allegiance to the king of the Franks and allied himself to Richard, king of England. He violently attacked the king of the Franks and his land. In a similar fashion, Renaud, the son of the count of Dammartin, allied with the king of England.[633] The king of the Franks had given him in marriage the countess of Boulogne with her county, out of his great love and friendship for him. But—inspired by the devil—scorning the homage he had sworn, violating pacts and oaths, he attacked his lord, the king of the Franks, in war. Allied with mercenaries and other enemies of the kingdom of the Franks, he plundered lands, took spoils, and brought much evil to the kingdom of the Franks.

[127] That same year, nine before the Kalends of November,[634] a Saturday, Hugh Foucaud, abbot of the Blessed Denis, passed away, at the third hour of the morning.[635] Hugh of Milan, prior of Notre-Dame of Argenteuil, succeeded him.[636]

---

630. *HPA* contains the typographical error *mandavi* where the manuscript (*P*) reads (and the grammatical context demands) *mandavit*.

631. Job 19:25–27.

632. Eudes of Sully, bishop of Paris 1196–1208, was not related to Maurice. He and his brother Henry, archbishop of Bourges from 1180 to 1200, were cousins of the king.

633. Renaud became count of Boulogne from 1190, at the time of his marriage to Ida of Boulogne, to his death in 1227. He became count of Dammartin at his father's death in 1200 and was a key ally of King John in 1214.

634. 24 October 1197.

635. That is, around 9:00 a.m.

636. Hugh of Milan, abbot of Saint-Denis, 1197 to 1204.

[128] In that same year, Henry [VI], emperor of the Romans, passed away.[637] By this time he had brought Sicily under his rule through tyranny, having crushed many great and noble men there and butchered archbishops and bishops in violation of the Christian religion. Like his predecessors, he had always exercised his tyranny against the Roman Church. For this reason Pope Innocent III[638] opposed the promotion of [Henry's] brother Philip [of Swabia], and excommunicated all of his supporters. [Innocent] himself forcefully supported Otto, the son of the duke of Saxony, and had him crowned king of Germany at Aachen.[639]

[129] At this time, Henry [II], count of Troyes, died at Acre.[640] He had been made king of Jerusalem in Outremer after the return of the two kings. Thibaut, his brother, succeeded him in the county of Troyes.[641]

[130] In that same year, six before the Ides of January,[642] Pope Celestine III went to the Lord. He was succeeded by a Roman, Innocent III, who previously had been called Lothar.[643]

[131] In March of that same year, Marie, the famous countess of Troyes, died.[644] She was the sister of Philip, king of the Franks, by her father; and sister of Richard, king of the English, by her mother. And she was the mother of the two men mentioned above, that is, Henry, king of Jerusalem, and Thibaut [III], count of Troyes.

[132] In that same year, that is, in the third year after the priest Fulk [of Neuilly] started to preach,[645] the Lord Jesus Christ began to perform many miracles through this priest. He restored sight to the blind, hearing to the

637. 28 September 1197.

638. Innocent would not be elected pope until January 1198.

639. After Henry VI's death and Innocent III's election, Innocent supported Otto of Brunswick's claim to the imperial throne, in order to prevent Henry VI's family, the Hohenstaufen, from uniting Germany to the kingdom of Sicily. Since Henry VI's son Frederick was only three years old at his father's death, the main Hohenstaufen claimant was Henry's brother Philip of Swabia. The latter was supported by Philip Augustus, while Otto of Brunswick was a close ally (and nephew) of King Richard of England.

640. Henry II of Champagne (see ch. 95 above) died by falling out of a window in 1197. See Cast of Characters.

641. Thibaut III of Champagne (1197–1201). See Cast of Characters.

642. 8 January 1199.

643. Lothar dei Segni was elected the day of Celestine's death and reigned as Innocent III until 1216.

644. Marie of France, countess of Champagne, died 11 March 1198.

645. See ch. 116 above.

deaf, speech to the mute, walking to the lame,[646] all by means of prayer and the laying on of the priest's hand. And he did many other things which it would be long to relate here, and which we pass over because of people's excessive mistrust.

[133] In the year of our Lord 1198, the oft-mentioned Fulk joined with another priest in the office of preaching. His name was Peter of Roissy, also from the diocese of Paris,[647] a man quite well educated and, as it appeared to us, *a man full of the spirit of God.*[648] He was dedicated to daily divine preaching and brought back many people from the sin of usury and called back a host of men from the stench of wantonness. He redirected into chaste marriage women who had been living in brothels and exposing themselves to all who crossed their path, not out of personal inclination but shamelessly for vile gain. Other women, refusing marriage and devoutly desiring to serve only God, were brought together and took on the habit of regular religious observance in the new abbey of Saint-Antoine at Paris, which had been established at that time for their sake.[649] But should someone wish to know with what purpose each one will have preached, let him await the end. For it is the end which most clearly proclaims the purposes of men: your goal defines the end of your effort.[650]

In addition to these two, Herluin, a monk of the Blessed Denis at Paris, a man deeply learned in Holy Scripture, preached in the villages on the coast of Brittany. Because of his ministry and work of preaching, a vast host of Bretons received crosses from his hand;[651] and suddenly, ahead of other pilgrims,[652] having crossed the sea, they came to Acre, led by this same monk. But there they broke into many factions and, having no one to direct them, they accomplished nothing.

---

646. Cf. Matthew 11:5.

647. Peter of Roissy (d. ca. 1213) was later chancellor of Chartres. See Baldwin, *Paris, 1200*, 11.

648. Cf. Genesis 41:38.

649. Saint-Antoine was founded on the Right Bank, just outside the eastern edge of Philip II's walls, which were then under construction. Although, as Rigord says, it was founded as a house for penitent prostitutes, Saint-Antoine quickly became affiliated with the Cistercian order. See Constance Hoffman Berman, *The White Nuns: Cistercian Abbeys for Women in Medieval France* (Philadelphia: University of Pennsylvania Press, 2018), ch. 7.

650. Rigord seems to offer dark hints in these last phrases, pointing to the following short remarks about strange portents and calamitous happenings. These culminate in what was for Rigord Philip II's biggest mistake—allowing the Jews to return to his realm.

651. Fulk of Neuilly and those associated with him were charged with preaching the Fourth Crusade. Perhaps because Philip II showed no interest in joining this crusade, Rigord only hints at the crusading aspect of this preaching campaign.

652. That is, ahead of other crusaders preparing for the Fourth Crusade.

In this year, there appeared new things without number. At Rozay-en-Brie, in the sacrifice on the altar, the wine was seen to change into blood and the bread into flesh.

In the Vermandois a certain knight who had been dead came back to life. And thereafter he predicted many future events to many people, and he lived a long while afterward without food or drink.

In Gaul, around the feast of St. John the Baptist,[653] dew falling from the sky at night imbued the ears of corn with honey, so that many people chewing the ears most distinctly tasted honey.

During a great storm a thunderbolt killed a certain man at Paris, and hail suddenly damaged the crops and vines in other places.

A few days later, in the month of July, such a powerful storm arose that it completely destroyed the crops, vineyards, and woods from Tremblay all the way to the monastery at Chelles and surrounding areas.[654] Stones were seen falling from the sky the size of large nuts, and in some places the size of eggs and even larger, according to rumor.

A popular rumor spread, saying that Antichrist was born in Babylon and the end of the world was near.

During the three preceding years, crop failures due to the great flood of rain denied sustenance to the people, and this brought France into a time of famine.

In this same year, in the month of July [1198], against everyone's advice and even against the king's own edict, King Philip brought back the Jews to Paris and severely beset the churches of God.[655] For this reason, in the following month of September, on the vigil of St. Michael,[656] punishment followed.[657] For while the king of the Franks was unprepared, the king of England with a force of fifteen hundred armed knights, many mercenaries, and a vast host of armed foot soldiers unexpectedly laid waste to the Vexin around Gisors, destroyed the fortress which they call Courcelles, and burned and plundered many rural villages. King Philip, burning with a towering rage, then tried to reach the castle of Gisors with only five hundred knights. But because of the enemy blocking the way, no route was open to him. When he saw this, his brave spirit overtook his equanimity and he launched a furious

---

653. 24 June 1198.

654. The venerable monastery of Chelles stood about twenty kilometers (twelve miles) east of Paris; Tremblay-en-France is some eight kilometers (five miles) north of Chelles.

655. As related in ch. 15 above, Philip had expelled the Jews in July 1182.

656. The feast of St. Michael is 29 September, so the vigil was Saturday, 28 September 1198.

657. For Rigord, Philip's decision to readmit the Jews goes hand in hand with persecuting churches as indications of the king's turning away from God.

charge right into the battle lines of the enemy. With only a few knights, he fought the enemy bravely and *by the mercy of God*[658] he came out unharmed and made it to Gisors, though many of his knights were taken prisoner and many others fled. In fact the names of the men captured in this melee were Alain of Roucy,[659] Matthew of Marly,[660] William of Mello the younger,[661] Philip of Nanteuil,[662] and many others whose names we have not wished to write, for we are too sick at heart. And thus the king of England returned in triumph from this engagement and divided up the spoils.

Now the king of the Franks was greatly upset by what had happened. He assembled his forces, but he did not bring to mind his offense of God.[663] He invaded and laid waste to Normandy all the way to Neubourg and Beaumont-le-Roger, and carried off much plunder. But at once he dismissed his army so that each man went home, and many people thought this hardly a prudent thing to do. When the king of England heard of this, a few days later he carried away great plunder from the district of Beauvais and the Vexin with his mercenaries led by Mercadier. He ambushed and took prisoner the bishop of that very city [of Beauvais],[664] a strong warrior, and William of Mello, who were hotly pursuing him to recover the plunder, and he imprisoned them for a long time. And the count of Flanders also seized Saint-Omer at that time.

[134] Philip, duke of Swabia, brother of Emperor Henry, took control of the greater part of the empire. In opposition to him, Otto, the son of the duke of Saxony,[665] with the help of his uncle Richard king of England, the count of Flanders, and the archbishop of Cologne, was crowned king of Germany at Aachen. The king of the Franks, Philip, now allied himself to this Philip, the German king and duke of Swabia, hoping with his help to subdue the count of Flanders more easily to deal with the king of England.

While these things were going on, Pope Innocent III sent to France his legate, Peter of Capua, cardinal-deacon of Santa Maria in Via Lata, to reestablish

---

658. Cf. Romans 12:1.

659. See Baldwin, *GPA*, 548n176.

660. Castellan of Marly-le-Roi, west of Paris, died on the Fourth Crusade in 1203. Baldwin, *KLL*, 41.

661. William of Mello (the younger), son of Dreux of Mello (see ch. 62 above).

662. This castellan was originally from the Vermandois, and his main lands were at Crépy; he fought at Bouvines. Baldwin, *KLL*, 51–52.

663. For Rigord, allowing the Jews to return to Paris and the kingdom of France was an offense to God.

664. Philip of Dreux, bishop of Beauvais (see ch. 62 above), a royal cousin.

665. See ch. 128 above. Otto of Brunswick's mother was Mathilda, eldest daughter of Henry II and Eleanor of Aquitaine. He was crowned 12 July 1198 by Adolf, archbishop of Cologne.

peace between Philip, king of the Franks, and Richard, king of England. Arriving in France around the nativity of our Lord,[666] this venerable man was unable to reestablish the peace, which seemed beyond repair. But, based on a foundation of faith between the two kings, he obtained a five-year truce from them. But he was never able to secure it by hostages, because of the deceits of the king of England.

[135] The deeds of the nineteenth year of Philip, king of the Franks.[667]

In the year of our Lord 1199, six before the Ides of April,[668] Richard, king of England, died after being gravely wounded outside of the city of Limoges. He had besieged a castle which the people of Limoges call the castle of Châlus-Chabrol. In the first week of Our Lord's Passion,[669] after a certain treasure had been discovered there by a certain knight, Richard, out of excessive greed, hotly demanded that the viscount of Limoges turn it over to him. For the knight who had found the treasure had fled to the viscount.[670] So, while the king was busy besieging the castle and assaulting it vigorously each day, a certain crossbowman, from out of nowhere, fired a bolt and mortally wounded the king of England. And a few days later he went the way of all flesh. He was buried and rests next to his father at Fontevraud in a certain abbey of nuns. The aforementioned treasure, so it was said, was [a representation of] a certain emperor with his wife, sons, and daughters, done in the purest of gold, showing them sitting together at a golden table and providing a clear memorial to their descendants at that time. King Richard was succeeded by his brother John, who was called Lackland. He was crowned at Canterbury on the following feast of the Ascension of our Lord.[671]

[136] At that time the king of the Franks, with matters now turning in his favor, seized the city of Evreux with its surrounding fortresses, that is, Avrilly and Aquigny, garrisoned them with his men, and laid waste Normandy all the way to Le Mans. Arthur, count of Brittany, the nephew of the king of England, then still a boy, invaded the boundaries of Anjou with a strong force

---

666. Christmas 1198.

667. Rigord suddenly returns to his earlier practice of introducing the new regnal year, which had been abandoned after ch. 73. Dating from the death of Louis VII, the nineteenth year of Philip's reign was 18 September 1198 to 17 September 1199.

668. 8 April 1199; in fact Richard died on 6 April 1199.

669. 4–11 April 1199. Richard was actually wounded on 26 March 1199.

670. Aymar of Limoges, a supporter of Philip Augustus.

671. 27 May 1199. The coronation actually took place at Westminster.

and seized the county of Anjou. And when he met the king of the Franks
at Le Mans, he did homage to him and confirmed by oath his loyalty in all
things, as did his mother.[672] While these and other matters were happening
there, Philip, count of Namur,[673] the brother of the count of Flanders, was
taken prisoner by Robert of Belesio and Eustashe of Neuville, together with
twelve knights, in the month of May, near the castle they call Lens. And he
was handed over to King Philip with Peter of Douai, a cleric who had worked
many wrongs against the king.[674] Moreover, the bishop-elect of Cambrai
had been taken prisoner by Hugh of Hamelincourt. For this reason Peter
[of Capua], the aforementioned legate of the Roman Church, placed all of
France under interdict.[675] But, after three months went by, the king, having
received more reasonable advice, returned the said Peter [of Douai] to the
holy church. Eleanor [of Aquitaine], the former queen of England, rendered
homage to King Philip at Tours for the county of Poitiers which came to her
by the law of inheritance.[676] And then the king led Arthur to Paris, six before
the Kalends of August.[677] Three days later, that is, three before the Kalends
of August,[678] [King Philip] went humbly on pilgrimage to the church of the
Blessed Denis. And there in pledge of his love and devotion to God and the
blessed martyrs he humbly laid a silk cloak upon the altar. In the month of
October, the truce between the two kings was reaffirmed by oath [to last]
until the following feast of St. John.[679] The same was also done between
Baldwin, count of Flanders, and Philip, king of the Franks.[680]

---

672. May 1199. On Arthur, see ch. 48 above. His mother was Constance of Brittany. As soon
as Richard died, Philip II began supporting the twelve-year-old Arthur's claims against John. Since
Arthur was the son of John's late older brother Geoffrey, Arthur had a strong claim to be Richard's
legitimate successor.

673. Philip I of Namur (1174–1212), brother of Baldwin of Hainaut.

674. Peter of Douai was actually a knight, and brother of Hugh II, the bishop-elect of Cambrai
referred to in the next sentence.

675. Innocent III placed the kingdom of France under interdict not for this offense against the
person of a churchman, but for Philip II's refusal to take back his lawful wife, Ingeborg.

676. July 1199. Although there is an oblique reference in ch. 80, this is the only time Rigord
mentions the name of the famous Eleanor of Aquitaine, wife of Louis VII of France and then (after
that marriage was annulled in 1152) of Henry II of England, mother (with Louis VII) of Marie and
Marguerite of France, and (with Henry II) of Henry the Younger, Mathilda (mother of Otto of
Brunswick), Richard, Geoffrey, Eleanor (mother of Blanche of Castile), Joan (wife of Raymond VI
of Toulouse), and John. See Bonnie Wheeler and John Carmi Parsons, eds., *Eleanor of Aquitaine: Lord
and Lady* (New York: Palgrave, 2003); and Martin Aurell, *Aliénor d'Aquitaine* (Paris: Presses universitaires de France, 2020).

677. 28 July 1199.

678. 30 July 1199.

679. That is, intended to last until 24 June 1200. The Treaty of Le Goulet was in fact agreed to
on 22 May 1200 (see below).

680. 2 January 1200.

[137] In this same year, Henry, archbishop of Bourges, died.[681] William, abbot of Chaalis, succeeded him.[682] Then in the following month, that is, November, Michael, archbishop of Sens, a theologian filled by God, went to the Lord.[683] He was succeeded by Peter of Corbeil, who had once been the teacher of Pope Innocent [III]. Through [Innocent's] hand and authority he warranted to become first the bishop of Cambrai and then of Sens.[684]

[138] In that same year, in the month of December, on the feast of St. Nicholas,[685] the abovementioned cardinal, Peter [of Capua], convened a council of all the bishops, abbots, and priors of the whole realm, at Dijon. But because he was working against the king of France to place the kingdom under interdict, the king's envoys appealed this to the See of Rome.[686] The cardinal, however, undeterred by the appeal, imposed his sentence in that same place and in the presence of all the bishops, but he decreed that it not be made public until twenty days after the nativity of our Lord.[687] When twenty days had passed after the nativity, the whole land of the king of the Franks lay under interdict. Upon learning of this, the king was fiercely angry that his bishops had agreed to the imposition of the interdict;[688] and he threw the bishops out of their own sees, ordered that their canons and clergy be stripped of their property and thrown out of his land, and confiscated their property. Even the priests who remained in the parishes were all thrown out, and he confiscated their goods. To top off all this wickedness, he shut up in his castle at Étampes his lawful wife, Ingeborg, the holy queen, adorned by every virtue and character, now deprived of the comfort of her whole court.[689] He did one more thing which upset all of France. He levied a third upon his knights, who once were accustomed to rejoice in their freedom, and also upon their men; that is, he forcefully seized a third part of all their goods. And he squeezed unbearable taxes and unheard-of levies from his townspeople.

---

681. Henry of Sully, brother of Eudes of Sully.

682. William of Donjon, abbot of the Cistercian abbey of Chaalis since ca. 1187.

683. Michael of Corbeil died 28 November 1199.

684. Peter of Corbeil, archbishop of Sens, 1200 to 1222.

685. 6 December 1199.

686. The ecclesiastical sanction of interdict forbade the celebration of church services in a designated area. In this case it was applied to Philip II's lands in an attempt to force him to take back his (lawful, in the eyes of the Church) wife, Ingeborg of Denmark.

687. 13 January 1200. Philip's lands were under interdict until September.

688. Not all the bishops of France were willing to apply the legate's decree; but Eudes of Sully, bishop of Paris, was among those who did, along with the bishops of Senlis, Soissons, Arras, and Amiens.

689. This actually occurred in 1201.

[139] The deeds of the twentieth year of Philip, king of the Franks.[690]

In the year of our Lord 1200, in the month of May, on the Ascension of our Lord,[691] peace was reestablished between Philip, king of the Franks, and John, king of England, at a place between Vernon and the island of Andely.[692] Just how and on what terms this peace was established between them, and how the land was divided between them, is more fully contained in the original documents that they executed and duly sealed.[693] And then, on the following Monday, at that same place, Louis, the only born son of the king of the Franks, married Blanche, the daughter of Alfonso of Castile and niece of John, king of England.[694] And upon this wedding John, king of England, gave over to this Louis, and to his heirs in perpetuity, his claim to all the fortifications, cities, castles, and lands that the king of the Franks had seized. And, after his own death, if he himself should die without a legitimate heir, he conceded all his lands on the other side of the sea to this same Louis, all objections notwithstanding.[695]

[140] In the year of our Lord 1201 [*sic*],[696] upon the nativity of the Blessed Virgin, Octavian, [cardinal]-bishop of Ostia and Velletri, came to France as legate.[697] By means of his stern warning the lord king took back his wife, Ingeborg, into some sort of grace, and set aside his concubine[698] for the time being. A council was then convened at Soissons by Octavian and John of Saint-Paul, cardinal-priest and the legate of the Apostolic See. King Philip was there with the archbishops, bishops, and nobility of the whole kingdom in the

---

690. 18 September 1199 to 17 September 1200, dating from the death of Louis VII.

691. 18 May 1200.

692. The Treaty of Le Goulet, by which Philip recognized John as Richard's legitimate heir and confirmed his possession of Normandy, Aquitaine, Maine, Anjou, and Brittany (Arthur was to hold it as John's vassal). John in exchange gave Philip the county of Evreux and a large cash payment, and, most importantly, recognized Philip as his lord for all of these French lands. The island of Andely is in the Seine, just off the spot where Richard constructed his famous Château Gaillard to defend the entrance to Normandy. See ch. 148 below.

693. One of several indications that Rigord had direct access to the nascent royal archives.

694. Blanche of Castile (1188–1252) married the future Louis VIII on 22 May 1200, on John's lands to avoid the interdict on Philip's domain. See Lindy Grant, *Blanche of Castile* (New Haven: Yale University Press, 2016).

695. In other words, according to Rigord, King John made the future Louis VIII his legal heir to all of his continental lands, should John die without legitimate children.

696. The "I" in the Roman numeral "MCCI" is evidently an inadvertent scribal error in the manuscript (P); the date should be 8 September 1200.

697. This was not really the date of the legate Octavian's arrival in France, but the date on which he lifted the interdict as the result of Philip agreeing to take back Ingeborg.

698. That is, Agnes of Méran, whom both Innocent III and Rigord considered Philip's illegitimate mistress or concubine.

month of April [1201],[699] and the issue of confirming the marriage to Queen Ingeborg or ending it was debated for fifteen days. After many and various arguments by the legal experts, the king was at the end of his patience with the endless delay, and he packed up and left with his wife, Ingeborg, early in the morning, leaving the cardinals and bishops there without saying goodbye. He informed them through his envoys that he was taking his wife with him as his wife, and that he no longer wished to be separated from her. When this was known, the council came to an end, and the cardinals and bishops were dumbfounded, for they had come together to arrange a divorce. So John of Saint-Paul went home very much abashed. Octavian, however, remained in France. And so King Philip in his turn escaped the hands of the Romans.

[141] In that same year, nine before the Kalends of June,[700] Thibaut [III], count of Troyes, died at the age of twenty-five. Since he had no male heir, the king of the Franks took his land under his guard and care, along with his wife and only daughter. But shortly thereafter a son was posthumously born to [Count Thibaut], for his wife had been left pregnant at the time of his death.[701]

[142] In that same year, on the eve of the Kalends of June,[702] John, king of England, came to France. He was received most honorably by King Philip, and most gloriously welcomed in the church of the Blessed Denis with hymns, praises, and a solemn procession. Thereafter the king of the Franks led him into Paris with great respect, and he was received with honor by the citizens, lodged in the king's palace, and attended to most devotedly in all respects. All of the different wines of the lord king were set before him and his people, and he was freely invited to drink from them. In addition, King Philip courteously bestowed upon John, king of England, precious gifts, gold, silver, a variety of garments, Spanish warhorses, palfreys, and other very valuable gifts. And so, in sound peace and delight and with the king's accord, he said farewell and took his leave.[703]

---

699. This council actually began in late March 1201. If it was after 25 March, then by Rigord's method of counting it should have been at the beginning of 1201.

700. 24 May 1201. Rigord's use of *eodem anno* fails to mark the transition to 1201.

701. Thibaut III had been married to Blanche of Navarre, who gave birth to the future Thibaut IV on 30 May 1201. On this succession, see Theodore Evergates, "Countess Blanche, Philip Augustus, and the War of Succession in Champagne, 1201–1222," in *Political Ritual and Practice in Capetian France: Studies in Honour of Elizabeth A. R. Brown*, ed. M. Cecilia Gaposchkin and Jay Rubenstein (Turnhout: Brepols, 2021), 77–104.

702. 31 May 1201.

703. By this time King John had already married Isabelle of Angoulême. See ch. 145 below.

Figure 14.   Philip II and John meet in France. London, British Library, Royal MS 16 G VI, fol. 362v. Used by permission of the British Library.

[143] In that same year, before the legate Octavian returned to Rome, the king's concubine, Marie, upon the summons of the Lord, went the way of all flesh.[704] The king of the Franks had a son named Philip and a daughter named Jeanne by her.[705] He had her and kept her for five years, contrary to the law and God's decree. After Marie's death, upon the request of the king of the Franks, Pope Innocent III ordered that these children be [made] his legitimate heirs, and thereafter confirmed this in writing.[706] This deed dissatisfied very many people at that time.

[144] In that same year, King Philip gathered his army and came to Soissons, for he had intended to ravage the land of the count of Rethel[707] and the land of Roger of Rozoi.[708] Through their tyranny they were robbing the churches of God and stealing their goods, and were unwilling to make restitution in accordance with the order which the lord king directed to them by letters and by envoy. But, when they learned of the king's arrival, they hastened to meet him and gave guarantees, with oaths and hostages, that they would

---

704. Agnes of Méran died 18/19 July 1201, giving birth to a son who did not live long.

705. Philip "Hurepel" (1200–35) became count of Boulogne through his marriage in 1224. His sister was not named Jeanne but Marie (1198–1224). She was briefly engaged to Arthur (nephew of King John) in 1202, but after his death married Henry I of Brabant in 1213.

706. 2 November 1201. Since Philip II still had only one male heir (the future Louis VIII) it was essential that his children by Agnes of Méran be regarded as legitimate.

707. Hugh II of Rethel.

708. A knight who fought at Bouvines. See Baldwin, *GPA*, 451.

entirely restore all that had been carried off from the churches, in accordance with the king's desire, and that they would make satisfaction to the lord king for their crimes. The king returned to Vernon and there, between Vernon and the island of Andely, he conferred with the king of England in the following fashion.[709]

[145] The king of the Franks warned John, king of England, as his liege man, that he should come to Paris fifteen days after Easter to answer fully those matters with which the king of the Franks should charge him concerning the counties of Poitou and Anjou and the duchy of Aquitaine.[710] But, since the king of England did not appear himself on the appointed day and chose not to send an adequate response, the king of the Franks, after taking counsel with his barons and leading men,[711] gathered his forces and invaded Normandy. He completely destroyed a certain small stronghold called Boutavant.[712] Then he seized Argueil and Mortemer, and finally he forcibly brought under his control Gournay and the entire land which Hugh of Gournay was holding.[713] In that same place he made Arthur a knight, bestowing on him the county of Brittany, which pertained to [Arthur] by the law of inheritance, and he added the counties of Poitou and Anjou, which [Arthur] would acquire by right of arms. And to help him, [King Philip] gave him two hundred knights with a large sum of money. For this reason the king received Arthur as his liege man forever. With the king's accord, Arthur departed in the month of July. A few days later, because he entered the lands of the king of England too boldly with too few troops, the king of England with a vast host of soldiers overcame Arthur by surprise, engaged him and his men, and took him prisoner,[714] together with Hugh Le Brun, Geoffrey of Lusignan,[715] and a great many other knights. When King Philip received word of this, he

---

709. This meeting took place on 25 March 1202.

710. Easter was 14 April 1202. As Rigord suggests below, at issue was John's marriage to Isabelle of Angoulême (24 August 1200), who had been engaged to Hugh IX of Lusignan "Le Brun," count of La Marche. The twelve-year-old Isabelle, as heiress to Angoulême, was to have brought that county to Hugh; King John had effectively stolen it away from him, and then declined to make any form of compensation. Hugh called upon King Philip, as the overlord of Poitou, to hear his complaint against John.

711. King John was condemned by Philip II's court on 28 April 1202.

712. On a small island below the Château-Gaillard.

713. Hugh V of Gournay (d. 1214) had participated in the siege of Acre. Gournay-en-Bray is twenty-five kilometers (fifteen miles) north of Gisors.

714. 1 August 1202, at Mirabeau, where the castle was defended by Eleanor of Aquitaine. Arthur was never seen again; contemporaries accused King John of having him murdered, and historians have tended to support this accusation.

715. Hugh Le Brun's uncle.

abandoned his siege of the castle of Arques. Coming with his army to Tours, he seized the city and set it on fire. The king of England, arriving once more with his forces, after the departure of the king of the Franks, completely destroyed this same city with the entire castle. Then after some days had passed, the king of England captured the viscount of Limoges and led him away with him. In truth, Hugh Le Brun, the viscount of Thouars, Geoffrey of Lusignan, and the viscount of Limoges were liege men of the king of England. But because [King John] had carried off by deceit the wife of Hugh Le Brun, that is, the daughter of the count of Angoulême, and had done many other foul deeds to the Poitevins, they had renounced their fidelity to him and allied themselves to the king of the Franks by oath and even by rendering hostages. As winter came on, each ceased campaigning, though without peace or truce and with their positions fortified.

[146] We have decided that at this point should be included some noteworthy deeds done at Constantinople by the barons of the Franks; specifically Baldwin count of Flanders,[716] Louis count of Blois,[717] Stephen of Perche,[718] the marquis of Montferrat,[719] and many other great men and mighty warriors.[720] Upon the death of Richard, king of England of great renown, they took up the cross to liberate the Holy Land, having summoned to their side by oath the doge of Venice with his Venetian troops and fleet.[721] So that the chain of events might be clearer to you, we have endeavored to relate the matter more fully in the present text.

In our own time the most holy Emperor Manuel, known for great generosity, was ruling at Constantinople, and he had a son named Alexius, to whom was given in marriage Agnes, the daughter of Louis [VII], the most Christian king of the Franks.[722] After the death of the emperor Manuel, his

---

716. Ch. 122 above.

717. Chs. 68 and 109 above.

718. D. 1205, son of Count Rotrou II of Perche.

719. Boniface of Montferrat (brother of Conrad; see ch. 93 above).

720. Here Rigord begins his account of the Fourth Crusade, which Pope Innocent III had called for in 1199 with his bull *Post miserabile*. The goal was the recovery of Jerusalem and the Holy Land, but, as Rigord recounts here, the crusade became embroiled in internal politics of the Byzantine Empire and was finally diverted to Constantinople, where Isaac II Angelos had been dethroned by his brother Alexius III Angelos in 1195. Isaac's son, Alexius (ultimately Alexius IV), sought the help of the crusading army to restore his father, and ultimately himself, to the throne. See Donald E. Queller and Thomas F. Madden, *The Fourth Crusade: The Conquest of Constantinople*, 2nd ed., with an essay on primary sources by Alfred J. Andrea (Philadelphia: University of Pennsylvania Press, 1997).

721. The doge of Venice was Enrico Dandalo (d. 1205). See Thomas Madden, *Enrico Dandalo and the Rise of Venice* (Baltimore: The Johns Hopkins University Press, 2003).

722. Manuel Comnenus reigned 1143–80; his son Alexis II married Agnes, the daughter of Louis VII and Adele of Champagne. She was thus the only full sibling of Philip II.

uncle Andronic, led by a lust to rule, killed Alexius by having him thrown into the sea. Agnes, his wife, lived on in holy widowhood.[723] Having become emperor in such tyrannical fashion, Andronic ruled for seven years, or a little less. Finally, Isaac [II][724] took him by surprise, had him bound to a post in the crossways at Constantinople as an archery target, and had him shot full of arrows because of his vast wickedness. After this, Isaac was made emperor. He had a brother, Alexius [III], who was a tough warrior but unjust. Isaac entrusted to him, as though to his dearest brother, all the power of the empire, except for the crown itself and the imperial title. At last—and it was the work of the devil!—prompted by envy of aggrandizing command and having solidified the support of the more powerful leaders of the empire by many lavish gifts, [Alexius III] cruelly blinded his lord and brother, the emperor Isaac, and dared to usurp for himself the name of emperor. He gave orders that the son [Alexius IV] of the blinded emperor be blinded. But, *by the mercy of God*,[725] the son was freed from his squalid jail and escaped from Greece, making his way through Germany to his sister and her husband Philip, king of Germany.[726] And this splendid youth [Alexius IV] encountered a Frank coming into Italy. Finally, when the Franks had arrived at Venice, this youth dispatched able envoys who, presenting the very sad case of father and son, proposed, with many entreaties, that if they would restore the throne to the father and son, they in turn would relieve [the Franks] of the debt of thirty-three thousand marks of silver they owed to the Venetians, and they would also pay the amount [the Franks] had paid for the sea transport, and the youth himself with the force of the empire would go with them to liberate the Holy Land, and would sufficiently provision the army from his own funds. He would also submit and unify the Church of Constantinople to the Church of Rome and to the lord pope, just like a body's limb to its head. Therefore the youth was summoned, and he gave a solemn oath to keep to the letter of his envoys' proposals. At once these strong and faithful men entrusted themselves to the winds and the open sea, and with this youth they sailed off through the midst of the sea's waves, landing quite safely at Constantinople.

---

723. The details of Agnes's "holy widowhood" are less than clear after her husband's murder in 1183; she may have been forced to marry his successor (and murderer) Andronic. After his death her whereabouts are obscure, but she was in Constantinople in 1204 (mentioned by the chronicler Robert of Clari).

724. Isaac II Angelos (d. 1204) was emperor twice, in 1185–95, and again in 1203–4. Rigord calls him "Conrezac."

725. Romans 12:1.

726. Irene Angelina (d. 1208), daughter of Isaac II and sister of Alexius IV, married Philip of Swabia, king of Germany, in 1197.

[147] The Greeks who were outside the city observed the boldness of the Franks and their solid trust in the Lord, and they fled without any engagement, retreating within the walls of the city. The Franks tightly and bravely besieged the city by land and sea for seven days, and in many and various engagements were achieving victories. At last, on the eighth day, the emperor [Alexius III], who had been hiding within [the city walls], came forth with fifty thousand horsemen and an innumerable host of foot soldiers and formed his battle lines to engage the Franks. Now the Franks were very few in number compared to the Greeks. Nevertheless, they were eagerly awaiting combat, for they were exceedingly sure of victory. The traitorous tyrant took a good look at the intrepid boldness of the Franks, and at once he ran fleeing with his forces back within the walls, vowing amid many threats that he would fight the next day. But that night he secretly fled, without his wife or his children. The following day the Franks vigorously attacked the city, climbing over the walls with ladders, and those most worthy of praise hurled themselves down from the walls among the Greeks and made no small slaughter of the Greeks. Now, because the Venetian doge had thought that the Greek host was handing the Franks death and destruction, when he heard what was going on, he immediately came vigorously and powerfully with his fleet to aid the Franks, like one most ready for the fight. Among them the doge himself, though an old man weak in body, was still fiery and brave in spirit.[727] He was first to fearlessly take his helmet and join the fighting Franks.

As the Franks realize this, with fresh and renewed energy, fiercely burning for the fray—as the impious traitor and tyrant fled with his heretics, who partook of fermented bread and rebaptized our children[728]—the city of Constantinople is seized by the Franks and Venetians in a mighty effort.[729] The youth's father [Isaac II] is freed from prison, and at once takes over the palace. The youth [Alexius IV] is presented victoriously and hailed with worthy and overdue praises from the clergy and the people, in both the greater church[730] and the imperial palace, and is solemnly crowned with the most precious diadem. As soon as the youth, the son of the blind Isaac, takes command, he

---

727. Doge Enrico Dandalo was reportedly ninety-five years old and blind at the time of the siege of Constantinople.

728. By describing the Greek Christians as heretics, Rigord is essentially equating them with Muslims as enemies of the church, a core precept of crusading. This rhetorical move legitimized the capture of Constantinople within the framework of crusading.

729. At this point Rigord shifts into a breathless historical present, a rhetorical device intended to convey the rushing of events.

730. Hagia Sophia.

immediately releases the Franks from their debts to the Venetians. From the imperial treasury he liberally provisions the army of the Franks. The doge of the Venetians, together with his Venetian forces, swore that they would provide sea transport and maintain their fleet for the Franks, promising that, should God bless the Franks, for which they were doubtless hoping, they would not leave them until the enemies of Jesus Christ had been utterly undone and defeated. They were led to make such a promise by the munificence of the emperor, who had paid them one hundred thousand marks of silver for the service thus far given the Franks, and what was to be provided thereafter.

After the boy emperor [Alexius IV] died in the war, upon the advice of the Venetian doge and the other princes, with the agreement of the clergy and the people, Baldwin, count of Flanders, was elected emperor by the Franks and subsequently crowned.[731] Thereafter the Eastern Church, with the acquiescence and concession of his nobility, was subjoined by this emperor and united to the Holy Roman Church and the lord pope as a limb to its head. We have seen these things written in their letters, and we have read them hoping, God willing, that in the future [they will accomplish] greater and better things in the Holy Land, when one will pursue a thousand, and two will drive away ten thousand.

[148] Deeds of the twenty-second year of Philip, king of the Franks.[732]

In the year of our Lord 1202 [*sic*], within fifteen days after Easter,[733] the king of the Franks gathered his army and invaded Aquitaine, and as the forces of Poitou and Brittany came to aid him, he took many fortifications. Then the count of Alençon[734] joined in league with King Philip and turned over all his land to the king's guardianship. Returning then into Normandy with his army, [King Philip] took Conches, the island of Andely, and Vaudreuil.

---

731. Rigord passes over a series of complicated events. Alexius IV was imprisoned in a coup early in 1204; his father, Isaac II, died shortly afterward. The leader of the coup, Mourtzouphlus, was crowned emperor 5 February, and he had Alexius IV strangled in prison a few days later. In April the crusaders stormed the city and Mourtzouphlus fled. Baldwin was elected emperor on 9 May and crowned 16 May 1204.

732. The twenty-second year of Philip's reign should have been 18 September 1201 to 17 September 1202, dating from Louis VII's death.

733. The dating grows confusing here (some of this confusion might perhaps be due to the mid-thirteenth-century scribe who copied P at Saint-Denis, rather than to Rigord himself). The year of this event should be 1203. Since Rigord indicates that this happened after Easter (6 April 1203), even by his method of counting he should have referred to the next two weeks as falling in the year 1203.

734. Robert III of Alençon (d. 1217).

While these matters were in progress in France, Pope Innocent III sent the abbot of Casamari[735] to the king of the Franks and the king of England to restore peace between them. In accordance with the lord pope's order, joined by the abbot of Trois-Fontaines,[736] they set before each king the apostolic order directing that, having gathered the archbishops, bishops, and leading men of the whole kingdom, preserving the jurisdiction of each king, they should make peace and restore to their original condition the abbeys of monks and nuns and the other churches ruined by their wars. When this order became known, at Mantes, on the octave of the Assumption of the Blessed Virgin Mary,[737] an appeal was lodged by the lord king while the bishops, abbots, and barons were assembling, and they returned the case for the consideration of the highest pontiff.[738]

On the last day of this month,[739] the king of France gathered his army and laid siege to Radepont.[740] After fifteen days, having set movable wooden towers and a large number of other engines around the town, he vigorously attacked and seized it. In the castle he took prisoner twenty knights—tough defenders—and a hundred sergeants and thirty crossbowmen. Recouping his forces and bringing the army up to strength, he laid siege to [the Château] Gaillard. This was a very strong castle built by King Richard on a high rock over the river Seine next to the island of Andely.[741] The king of the Franks and his army spent five months and more on this siege. He was unwilling to storm the castle, out of concern for the loss of his men and also for the destruction of the walls and tower. He preferred to force those inside to surrender because of famine and lack of provisions. But, since he suspected that they would flee, he began to have a great ditch dug around the castle, such that his entire army could pitch its tents inside the ditch, and he raised ten wooden towers around it. Finally, as the feast of St. Peter's Chair arrived,[742] having set up his trebuchets and mangonels and movable wooden towers and rams, he began to storm the castle very fiercely. Those inside looked to

---

735. Gerard, abbot of the Cistercian house of Casamari, in Latium (Italy).

736. Guy II, abbot of the Cistercian house of Trois-Fontaines, in Champagne.

737. 22 August 1203.

738. Philip objected that the pope had no legal grounds on which to interfere in a dispute between the king of France and one of his vassals (John, as duke of Aquitaine).

739. 31 August 1203.

740. About twenty kilometers (twelve miles) southeast of Rouen.

741. A good description of the important "military complex" formed by the Château Gaillard and the island of Andely (and a lively account of much of the military history recounted by Rigord) can be found in Thomas Asbridge, *The Greatest Knight: The Remarkable Life of William Marshal, the Power behind Five English Thrones* (New York: Ecco, 2014), 251.

742. 22 February 1204.

their defense and fought the Franks bitterly. After fifteen days, on the eve of the Nones of March,[743] as the walls were breached and broken, the Franks captured the said castle in a great battle. Thirty-six knights, famous men and strong defenders, were made prisoner there.[744] Indeed, four knights had been killed in the siege.

[149] In the year of our Lord 1203 [*sic*], six before the Nones of May, Philip, king of the Franks, gathered his army and invaded Normandy.[745] He seized Falaise, a very strong castle, and he took Domfront and a magnificent stronghold which people call Caen, with all the surrounding land all the way to Mont-Saint-Michel at Peril de la Mer, bringing it all under his dominion. Thereafter the Normans, seeking pardon of the king, handed over to him the cities which they were guarding; that is, Coutances, Bayeux, Lisieux, and Avranches, with their forts and suburbs (for he already possessed Sées and Evreux). Nothing was left in all Normandy except Rouen, the capital of Normandy, a very wealthy city full of nobility, and Verneuil and Arques, well-fortified towns located in the strongest place and garrisoned by tough warriors. Having first fortified the cities and fortresses, the king then returned from Caen and laid siege to Rouen. The Normans realized that they could not defend themselves, nor were they expecting support from the king of England. Thus they adopted a more reasonable plan, a cautious effort to maintain fealty to the king of England. They humbly sought from the king of the Franks thirty days before he would assault the city [of Rouen], Verneuil, and Arques—that is, those castles allied with the people of Rouen—a period up until the next feast of St. John the Baptist,[746] so that in the meantime they could send envoys to the king of England, asking him to deign to send help to them now in such dire straits. If, however, he did not, they obligated themselves, having given sixty sons of the citizens of Rouen as hostages on these terms, to turn over the city and the named castles to the most victorious Philip, king of the Franks. When the feast of St. John came and went with no relief from the king of England, they handed over to the king of the Franks, just as they had promised, without objection, the most magnificently wealthy city of Rouen, the capital and head of all of Normandy, together

---

743. 6 March 1204.

744. Rigord expresses a certain admiration for these men who defended the castle valiantly, even as it became clear that King John had retreated to England (December 1203) and would do little to defend his Norman possessions.

745. 2 May 1204.

746. 24 June 1204.

FIGURE 15.   Philip II taking Normandy. London, British Library, Royal MS 16 G VI, fol. 365v. Used by permission of the British Library.

with the two named castles.⁷⁴⁷ It had been 326 years since his predecessors, that is, the kings of the Franks, had possessed this city with all of Normandy, in the time of Charles the Simple. The Dane, Rollo, had arrived with his hordes and taken it from [Charles] by right of conquest.⁷⁴⁸

[150] Some while later, on the feast of St. Lawrence,⁷⁴⁹ King Philip gathered his army, invaded Aquitaine, and recovered the city of Poitiers with all the surrounding territory, that is, the castles, fortified towns, villages. And the barons of that land swore fidelity to him as they were accustomed to do to their liege lord. With winter approaching, he gave up on La Rochelle, Chinon, and Loches. Putting a siege in place around Loches and Chinon, he returned to France.⁷⁵⁰

[151] As the celebration of Easter arrived in the year of our Lord 1204 [*sic*],⁷⁵¹ King Philip summoned the counts, dukes, and *officials of the power* of the Franks.⁷⁵² He assembled many thousands of foot soldiers, paid the mounted

---

747. By agreeing to this thirty-day truce, Philip publicly challenged John's will or ability to come to the aid of his supporters in Rouen; when Philip's bet proved correct, he thus scored a double victory of propaganda and politics.

748. See ch. 41 above for Rigord's version of this history.

749. 10 August 1204.

750. That is, the Île-de-France, the region around Paris and Orléans.

751. Easter was 10 April 1205.

752. Judith 2:7.

archers, and had the whole expedition of knights set out, together with those things which would suffice to supply the armies with adequate provisions. Having gone forth he came to Loches with wagons, horsemen, archers, and siege engines beyond count. Placing them around the castle he stormed it forcefully and took it. He took prisoner the fighting force within, about 120 knights and sergeants. He gave the castle to Dreux of Mello,[753] having established fealty and fortified the castle.

[152] He then led his whole army to Chinon, where he pitched tents and mounted his siege engines. And within a few days he forcefully stormed the castle and took it. He transferred the very brave defenders taken prisoner in the garrison—the knights, crossbowmen, and no few foot soldiers—to prison at Compiègne. After having established guards there, King Philip, ever Augustus, returned to France around the time of the feast of St. John the Baptist.[754]

[153] In the year of our Lord 1205, Philip, king of the Franks, as a pledge of his affection and love, conveyed to the church of the Blessed Denis the Areopagite, with dreadful reverence, having fasted and prayed, the most precious relics which Baldwin, emperor of Constantinople,[755] had received from the holy chapel of the emperors, which they called the Boucoleon;[756] specifically, a piece of the Holy Cross from which the Savior of the world hung, about a foot in length and of a size that someone could encircle it between thumb and index finger; some hair of our Lord Jesus Christ when he was a boy; a single thorn from our Lord's Crown of Thorns; a rib of the holy apostle Philip with one of his teeth; a piece of the white linen cloth in which the Savior was wrapped in his cradle; a piece of his purple robe. The Cross was placed in a precious gem-encrusted golden reliquary made to its dimensions. The other relics listed were placed and are kept in another golden casket. The most Christian king of the Franks gave over all of these relics by his own hand to Henry, abbot of the Blessed Denis,[757] at Paris seven before the Ides of June.[758] The abbot received them with tears of joy in his eyes. And

---

753. Son of the constable of France.

754. 24 June 1205.

755. Ch. 147 above.

756. The Bouceleon (or Boukoleon), literally "the Mouth of the Lion," was a part of, and often equated with, the Great Palace of the Byzantine emperors located in Constantinople. Rigord here uses the Latin designation "holy chapel" (*sancta capella*) for the church of the Virgin of the Pharos, the imperial chapel that was part of the palace complex.

757. Henry of Troon had become abbot of Saint-Denis in 1204; Rigord does not mention his election or the death of his predecessor.

758. 7 June 1205.

enthralled by royal generosity, singing psalms and prayers, he proceeded to the Lendit.[759] There a procession of monks of the Blessed Denis, dressed in silk albs and cloaks, barefoot, met them with all the clergy and people. After a blessing with the relics was given there, with hymns and prayers and the ringing of all the bells, they were stored in the church of the thrice-Blessed Denis in large reliquaries covered with pure gold and precious gems, above the bodies of the holy martyrs, with the head of the most precious martyr Denis and the scapula of Saint John the Baptist.[760]

Blessed be God in all things who granted to me, his servant, though unworthy and a frail sinner, now entering old age, to behold these things by divine goodness.[761]

[154] In the year of our Lord 1206 [*sic*], on the eve of the Kalends of March,[762] there was a partial eclipse of the sun, in the sixth hour of the day,[763] in the sixteenth degree of Pisces. The following June, on the eve of the Nones of that month,[764] Queen Adele, the mother of the oft-named Philip, king of the Franks, died at Paris. Thereafter she was buried at Pontigny, in Burgundy, next to her father, Thibaut, count of Troyes and Blois, who founded that abbey, as we have learned from the report of many people.[765]

[155] In this same year, in the month of June [1206], King Philip once again gathered his army and invaded Poitou, for he had heard that John, king of England, had gone to La Rochelle with a strong army. At this time Louis, the only son of King Philip, was ill for some time, but swiftly regained his health through God's mercy. Then King Philip took his army to Chinon and fortified the city of Poitiers, as well as Loudun and Mirebeau and the other places he held there. And having stationed an adequate number of knights and sergeants there, he returned to Paris. John, king of England, then seized the city of Angers and totally destroyed it. The viscount of Thouars forsook his

---

759. The area south of Saint-Denis, famous for its fairs, that marked the boundary between Saint-Denis and Paris.

760. For the charter of indulgence that independently records this relic transfer and gift, see Paul Edouard Didier Riant, *Exuviae Sacrae Constantinopolitanae Fasciculus Documentorum Minorum, Ad Exuvias Sacras Constantinopolitanas in Occidentem Saeculo XIII Translatas, Spectantium, & Historiam Quarti Belli Sacri Imperijo: Gallo-Graeci Illustrantium* (Geneva, 1877–78), 2:64.

761. Rigord's statement that he is "now entering old age" in 1205 suggests that he was probably born between about 1145 and 1150.

762. By his own method of counting, Rigord should have written 1205, which would be 1206 by modern reckoning, in order to lead up to Queen Adele's death in June 1206.

763. That is, around noon.

764. 4 June 1206.

765. Thibaut "the Great" of Blois, Chartres, and Champagne was not in fact the founder of the Cistercian abbey of Pontigny.

allegiance to the king of the Franks and allied himself with the king of England.[766] On learning this the king of the Franks returned with a strong force to Poitou, and positioning his troops as though for combat, he laid waste the land of the viscount of Thouars while the king of England was at Thouars. At last, a truce was established, to begin on the feast of All Saints and last for two years,[767] and King Philip returned to France and John to England.

[156] In that same year, in the month of December [1206], as the sins of mankind required, such a flood of waters and rivers occurred at Paris as had never been seen by men of that time or had been heard of by their forefathers. It knocked over three arches of the Petit-Pont,[768] swept away a host of homes, and wreaked vast damage in many places. Therefore the monks of the Blessed Denis formed a procession with their abbot, Henry, and all the clergy and people; and, going barefoot, they blessed the waters with the nail, our Lord's Crown of Thorns, and the most sacred wood of our Lord's Cross. When the blessing was done, after great shedding of tears, right away *the waters began to abate.*[769] Blessed be God in all things, who preserves those *that hope in Him.*[770]

[157] In the year of our Lord 1207, King Philip gathered his army, went into Aquitaine, and laid waste the land of the viscount of Thouars. He captured Parthenay, overran a host of surrounding strongholds, and left them, now fortified, in the care of his marshal and William des Roches.[771] The king then returned to Paris.

[158] In the following year, that is, 1208, Eudes, bishop of Paris, died three before the Ides of July.[772] He was succeeded by Peter, treasurer of Tours.[773]

In that year, the abovementioned marshal and William des Roches, having mustered nearly three hundred knights, surprised and defeated the

---

766. Aimery VII, viscount of Thouars, 1173–1226. His loyalty wavered between John and Philip in 1204–6. Baldwin, *GPA*, 238–39.

767. 1 November 1206. Other sources give 13 October as the date of this truce.

768. Literally the "small bridge." In Rigord's day this was the only bridge that linked the Île-de-la-Cité with the Left Bank, leading onto the rue Saint-Jacques.

769. Cf. Genesis 8:3.

770. Cf. Judith 13:17. Rigord's own text almost certainly ends by this point. The short chs. 157–60 would have been added by a continuator.

771. The marshal of France was Henry Clémont (d. 1214). William des Roches was seneschal of Anjou, first for the Plantagenets but now (after several reversals of loyalty) in the service of Philip II. See Baldwin, *GPA*, 113–14, 194–95, 234–37.

772. 13 July 1208.

773. Peter of Namur, bishop of Paris 1208–19.

viscount of Thouars and Savery of Mauléon,[774] who had entered the lands of the king with a strong force and were carrying off much plunder. Forty knights or more were taken prisoner in this engagement; specifically, Hugh of Thouars,[775] the brother of the viscount; Aimery of Lusignan, the son of the viscount; Porteclie;[776] and many other bold warriors whose names we do not want to list. They sent all these prisoners to their lord, the king of the Franks, at Paris, under close guard. At length a truce was established and they retired from campaigning.

[159] In this same year, a certain count palatine (who is called a "landgrave" in their language, that is, a count of the palace) slew Philip, the Roman emperor.[777] After his death, Otto, the son of the duke of Saxony, was attempting to acquire the empire through the efforts and authority of Pope Innocent III.

[160] In this same year [1208], Pope Innocent III sent to France his legate, Galon, cardinal-deacon of the title of Santa Maria in Portico, an expert in law, distinguished by his lofty ethics, a most hardworking overseer of all the churches, and devoutly dedicated to the church of the Blessed Denis.[778] In these days Pope Innocent wrote to Philip, king of the Franks, and to all the leading men of his kingdom, ordering and directing that, as true catholic men, faithful to Jesus Christ, they should invade with a strong army the land of Toulouse, Albi, and Cahors, parts of Narbonne and Beziers, and many other neighboring lands, and they should destroy the heretics who lived in those lands.[779] And, should they meet death on the way or in combat against these people, this same pope, on behalf of God and by authority of the apostles Peter and Paul and on his own authority, absolved them of every sin done from the day of their birth for which they will have confessed and not done penance.[780]

---

774. Savery de Mauléon (d. 1236) was alternately loyal to John, Philip, and then John again, and was also known as a poet. Baldwin, *GPA*, 239.

775. Hugh I of Thouars.

776. Porteclie, lord of Mauzé.

777. Philip of Swabia was killed on 21 June 1208.

778. Guala Bicchieri (1150–1227) was cardinal-deacon of Santa Maria in Portico Octaviae (1205–11) and then cardinal-priest of San Martino ai Monti (1211–27).

779. The text thus fatefully closes with Innocent III's call for what became known as the Albigensian Crusade (1209–29). Philip Augustus never participated in this attack on the lands of the count of Toulouse, but Louis VIII would be instrumental in the final victory by Capetian forces fighting in the name of the Church. See Mark Gregory Pegg, *A Most Holy War: The Albigensian Crusade and the Battle for Christendom* (Oxford: Oxford University Press, 2008).

780. That is, Innocent III was offering the crusade indulgence for those who undertook to eradicate heresy from the south. There is no evident break in the manuscript copy (*P*) at this point, halfway down the first columns of fol. 286r, where the text flows uninterrupted into William le Breton's continuation.

Translator's Postscript

The careful reader, but surely the careful translator, comes to know his author, to appreciate his character, his tastes, his desires, and to gauge his achievement. Rigord aspires to depict a virtuous King Philip: to see him grow in holy wisdom, protecting the Church, its aims, its clergy, its property; to note the miracles asserting God's favor; to relate the deeds of the crown and the affairs of state. He would claim his own place in the line of chroniclers of Saint-Denis where rest the bones of kings, where is kept the oriflamme, the battle flag of the Franks, where are the histories of France. A poet tells us that our reach really should exceed our grasp "or what's a heaven for?" But Rigord, though disappointed in some respects, writes well, is interesting and informative, and can sketch a tale that grabs the reader. He is, after all, a chronicler. His work runs on year by year. Long digressions come at a cost.

It is clear that Rigord conceives of his work as a unified whole that has been polished for a final presentation. There is an introductory letter of dedication and a prologue. The words of the prologue suggest that it was written some ten years after he began his work, and it is thought that he offered it to King Philip when the king returned from crusade in the year 1191. Yet his chronicle runs on after this, even up to 1206 (with continuations to 1208). The dedicatory letter is not to King Philip but to his son, Louis, who was only four when his father returned from crusade but is now, most probably, entering young manhood. It may well be that King Philip was simply not impressed or even interested in Rigord's work, and so Rigord dedicated it to Philip's son Louis at a later date.

These two passages, the dedicatory letter and the prologue, are crafted in the traditional fashion: very apologetic, unassumingly modest, sprinkled with learned quotations and serious cant. What a relief it is to find that, straight into chapters 1, 2, and 3, Rigord writes very well when on his own. We rejoice with Philip's father when his son is born and then we sit with the aged royal father as he confers with each of the bishops and abbots about Philip's succession. Then the lad is found riding fast after a boar into the darkening wood, all alone, and there he meets a huge man with an ax. Next the youth is, in all righteous piety, commanding that foul-tongued gamblers be flung into the river and he then lends an eager ear, even more righteous, to learn the supposedly foul deeds of the Jews.

With the air of one informed of daily court affairs, Rigord tells of Philip's first military efforts, campaigns to crush rebellious lords who have abused and plundered the clergy. Our monk of Saint-Denis is overjoyed to see Philip expel the Jews. He lays out the reasons, relates their atrocities, describes their murders, the wretched state of their bonded debtors, the resistance of the wealthy bankers, their bribery of the nobility, and, then, the firm determination of the youthful king whose faith prevails. Rigord is happy to record these victories of the Church and recite the letter of the emperor Heraclius to Dagobert that provides a historical precedent for King Philip. One senses that Rigord speaks from some authority, perhaps of his own making, but valid within his own work.

Knowledgeable of court affairs, Rigord notes how responsibly the young Philip attends to the market stalls at Les Halles and the walls in the forest at Vincennes. He relates the difficulties with Flanders, the obvious miracle of the unforeseen harvest endangered by the campaign. The defense of the churches in Burgundy leads him to the recitation of ancient royal immunities bestowed upon the churches of the Franks. Philip has seized Châtillon. The pious young king is prevailing. Rigord seems, at this point, to have found his stride. We are with him as the king, one day, glances out the palace window and sees that the Paris streets are deep in stinking mud. Of course this will not do. Who, of those who reigned before him, would have dared to undertake the task? Philip will. He gives his orders. The town and roads will all be paved. It will no longer be mudville, Lutetia, but Paris, so named for Paris Alexander, the son of the king of Troy. And so, holding fast to Rigord's hand, we are off to work out the genealogy of the kings of the Franks, the knowledge of which is the treasure of the abbey of Saint-Denis.

Our chronicler has some talent and imagination. One feels, however, that the task of tidying up the threads of time historical, biblical, and mythological is not easy. He escapes from this tangled wood after five chapters, having done his best. Rigord is still in on the events of the day: the king of Hungary's request to wed Philip's sister; the death of Geoffrey, son of Henry II; the walls built for the cemetery at Champeaux; and Philip's rebuke to the wastrel youths who lavish their finery on the immoral traveling players. Rigord shares the several letters now come to court from seers Jewish, Saracen, and Christian, foretelling great winds of destruction. Ill news from Outremer: Saladin now holds Jerusalem and the Holy Cross itself. The campaigns of Philip and Henry II wind down, and both kings come together all of a sudden and take the cross. The Third Crusade should now begin, and Rigord can and will tell us how Philip plans for it, funding it through the tithe of Saladin and arranging by his will that the Franks be ruled efficiently in his absence and be provided for should he die on crusade.

When all is going smoothly we suddenly find that Richard invades the lands of Philip in violation of the truce for the crusade. Philip repels him with God's favor, for this is shown by the miracle of the rising river at the siege of Levroux. Thereafter Richard does homage to Philip for his lands. This also shows God's support.

At this point in our story, chapter 71, when all is going so well, Rigord tells of a total eclipse of the moon on 2 February 1189, and then a strange omen, when, as he says, he was at Argenteuil. The moon, in full moonlight, descends to earth and rises back up again. The moon, we are told, represents the Church. This is immediately followed by "verses of a certain person," a prophetic text of mythic characters pointing to eschatological events. Immediately the story returns to Philip successfully expelling Henry from Tours. Once more he succeeds by God's help. He finds an unknown ford and leads his troops across. Then Henry dies, he to whom God had sent Philip, to be as a bit in Henry's mouth to vindicate the blood of the blessed martyr Thomas of Canterbury and return him to the bosom of the church.

All is now running well. In 1190, in the church of the blessed martyr Saint Denis, Philip receives the battle standard of the Franks to unfurl before the enemies of the cross of Christ. He receives the blessing of the nail, the Crown of Thorns, and the arm of Saint Simeon the Elder. Commended by the prayers of the monks, he marches forth with the flags emblazoned in memory of the Saints Denis, Rusticus, and Eleutherius. This is a high point of the tale told by Rigord. The king is off on his way to Genoa, and Richard, now king of England, sails from Marseille.

Here Rigord inserts the text of Philip's will and his directions to the regency in his absence. This is of vast historical interest but, when it is done, the reader senses that something is now different. There are no more chapter headings describing the deeds of King Philip. One is still uncertain about the strange omens of chapter 71. Did Rigord really mean to say that there were two full moons in February that year, one for the eclipse on 2 February and one for the moon's descent on 10 February? Was this writing done some time after the return of King Philip from his crusade, when Rigord was feeling that his work found, to say the least, little favor with the king?

However this may be, the story continues to unfold. Rigord very deftly relates the facts, the disputes, such success as did occur in Outremer, and then he varies these achievements with the powerful deeds done by the relics of the monastery of Saint-Denis. After moving the rather disunited crusading forces on to Acre and relating the death of Frederick Barbarossa, we hear of the death of Pope Clement III and the election of Celestine, bad harvests and an eclipse of the sun. Back in Paris prince Louis has fallen ill, and all of Saint-Denis goes in barefoot procession to save the child. Rigord is here at his best. The whole monastery of Saint-Denis turns out with the nail, the Crown of Thorns, the arm of Saint Simeon the Elder. They proceed barefoot, in tears, down to Paris to be greeted by the bishop and all the religious houses, the canons, the clergy, the students. They assemble, they sing, they preach, they pray, they sign the cross on Louis's stomach with all the relics. He kisses the relics and he recovers, and, by the way, so does Philip, who has fallen ill in Outremer. Such is the power of the prayers of the clergy and people that calm and temperate weather returns to the land, for "the Lord had rained over the land for a long time, due to the wickedness of men."

Wickedness, indeed! We find no mention of miraculous deeds of Philip overseas. In fact we are next told of the assassination of the bishop of Liège who was foully slain by knights sent from the emperor Henry VI. Again we turn to Saint-Denis and the relics. The archbishop of Reims and Queen Adele have them brought out in great celebration and prayer for the success of the king and army in the Holy Land. Rigord then turns back to Philip and his success at Acre, runs over the main points, and has him coming home with tears in his eyes while Richard remains behind with notable success at Ascalon. When home, Philip rushes to Saint-Denis to lie down flat in prayer and praise of God and the blessed martyrs for their aid.

At this point it is clear that Rigord's heart is with the monastery of Saint-Denis and its relics. King Philip will have to be on his own for a while. All the good that Rigord can say of him is that in a fit of religious faith he rode off to burn at least eighty Jews at Bray-sur-Seine for supposedly hanging a

Christian. We are then treated to more omens: battle lines of knights are seen to come down from the sky to do combat on the ground and suddenly vanish. We then see the fear and seclusion of Philip when news arrives that the Assassins may be coming for him, and feel his relief when the news is found to be false. With his customarily efficient pen Rigord relates the difficult return of Richard the crusader and then tells of Henry, count of Champagne, who stood by the land of Outremer when it was "so abandoned by the departure of the two kings."

It is with the marriage to Ingeborg that Philip reaches his nadir in the eyes of Rigord. Things are on the mend, for the king has recovered all of Norman Vexin and Saladin has died. But the repudiation of Ingeborg, for no apparent reason—surely the work of the devil—and the rapid annulment and the powerless pope, legate, archbishops, bishops, and abbots, now "dumb dogs not able to bark, afraid for their own hide," are appalling to Rigord. From this slough of despond, which he so effectively delineates, our author struggles to recover. Philip and Richard war back and forth, seesawing for control while Rigord reports strange omens: powerful storms, thunder and lightning out of all memory, egg-size stones falling from heaven. Amid the storm fly crows bearing hot coals setting houses aflame. Crops are ruined and people killed. Such prodigies, he says, should terrify men and keep them from wickedness. But wicked they are, for Richard mistreats clergy and so does Philip, expelling monks and stealing revenue.

No more is heard of any virtue from Philip until, during the famine following such evil weather, he is "moved by piety" to give and to encourage others to give greater alms to the poor, and Saint-Denis gives all it has. Things do begin to improve for Philip militarily. Richard does homage for Normandy, Poitou, and Anjou. Peace is struck, and Philip, mindful of his patron, returns to render gifts in thanks to Saint-Denis. Then, in 1196, in the great flood of Paris, as the people and clergy come in prayer and weeping procession, Philip joins in "as though but one of the people . . . humbly sighing and crying," while the monastery of Saint-Denis, with all it relics, leads them blessing the waters, which recede shortly to their old channel. Perhaps the hero of this work, in the eyes of its author, is no longer the king but Saint Denis.

But battles resume. Now up, now down, the forces sway but Rigord follows them efficiently and skillfully. Much preaching is done and some miracles, but they are done by priests not royalty. Prodigies continue: wine and bread visibly become flesh and blood on the altar, a knight returns from the dead. Honey-flavored dew infuses the corn. Crops are destroyed, and more egg-size stones come down. Floods bring famine while rumor tells of the birth of Antichrist in Babylon. As if no worse could occur, Philip brings the Jews back to Paris! The next month, of course, Philip suffers military defeat, is almost captured, "but for the mercy of God," yet he still does not realize "his offense of God." At this point Richard dies, and, as John succeeds him, Philip starts to gain the upper hand, controls Arthur, receives the submission of Eleanor, a peace is concluded, and he returns to give gifts of thanks to Saint-Denis, pledging his love and devotion to God and the blessed martyrs.

Despite this success the papal legate arrives to place the kingdom under interdict. In rage the king lashes out at his bishops, evicts them, and seizes their lands. Peace with John occurs but how and on what terms we are not told. Prince Louis marries Blanche of Castile and under the stern warning of the papal legate Octavian, Philip takes back Ingeborg to wife and sets aside Agnes, his concubine, who dies the next year. To Rigord's evident chagrin, the pope orders her two children by Philip made legitimate. As Philip rises in military dominance, John, his unruly liege man, loses his grip in his French lands.

Now Rigord steps forth and states that he wants, at this point, to relate the deeds done at Constantinople, that is, the events of the Fourth Crusade. These are not the deeds of Philip. Rigord is stepping outside the parameters of his espoused endeavor to render, in excellent, deft, efficient prose, an account culminating in a breathless rendition of battle, given in the classic historical present tense, of the final, crucial engagement when the aged doge dons his helmet, the youth, the son of blind Isaac, takes charge, and the day is won; the Franks are given money, transport, and provisions and sent off to the East. Upon his death Baldwin, count of Flanders, is elected emperor and the Eastern Church surrenders itself to the pope. What a tale! What a splendid success and well told! If one should wonder why, one has only to wait four chapters to find Philip bestowing on the church of the Blessed Denis the Areopagite, "with dreadful reverence," the relics that Baldwin, the emperor of Constantinople, had received and now is giving to the Franks. This paragraph is the soul of our author, writ large. He humbly states, "Blessed be God in all things who granted to me, his servant, though unworthy and a frail sinner, now entering old age, to behold these things by divine goodness."

Perhaps the significance of the writing of Rigord is to be found in a quotation from Ernst Kantorowicz (to which William Jordan directs our attention in his preface to *The King's Two Bodies*) in *Laudes regiae*: "It was St. Louis, who in every respect enriched that treasure of grace on which all his successors would thrive. It was he whose kingship was elevated to transcendancy by the Spiritualist and Symbolists of his age and who, in turn, bestowed the thin and light air of the angelic kingdoms upon his country."[1] This is the story that Rigord truly wanted to write. His subject did not live up to his expectation, and so he turned to his beloved relics. The next time that relics come around, things are different. Walter Cornut picks up the tale of Emperor Baldwin and his descendants. His account of their success is told in his tract "On the Feast of the Translation of the Holy Crown of Our Lord." It is a gripping, fast-moving story written in a style reminiscent of Rigord. When the relics arrive, however, they do not go to Saint-Denis, but are housed in a chapel built for them by the king who will become Saint Louis.[2] This little writing was well known. Indeed, it was incorporated into the liturgical celebration for the Crown of Thorns, and may be the text so mentioned by Geoffrey of Beaulieu in his *Life* of Saint Louis.[3] Hardly thirty years after Rigord finished writing, lessons have been learned. Did the rising Dominicans and Franciscans in their youthful, spirited zeal, and did even the parents, Louis VIII and Blanche, perceive the possibilities to be achieved by good writing and a pious example?

It cannot be said that the writing of Rigord has the sweep of Otto of Freising or the emotional temper of Liutprand of Cremona. But he surely could tell a tale, and quite likely one that showed a path to those who came after him.

---

1. William Chester Jordan, "Preface (1997)," in Ernst H. Kantorowicz, *The King's Two Bodies: A Study in Medieval Political Theology* (Princeton: Princeton University Press, 2016), xxix, note 23, citing *Laudes regiae: A Study in Liturgical Acclamations and Mediaeval Ruler Worship* (Berkeley: University of California Press, 1946), 3–4.

2. M. Cecilia Gaposchkin, "Between Historical Narrative and Liturgical Celebrations: Gautier Cornut and the Reception of the Crown of Thorns in France," *Revue Mabillon*, n.s. 30 (2019): 91–145. There is some question whether the description of the Crown's arrival to the royal palace was original to Cornut's composition.

3. Larry F. Field, trans., *The Sanctity of Louis IX: Early Lives of Saint Louis by Geoffrey of Beaulieu and William of Chartres*, ed. M. Cecilia Gaposchkin and Sean L. Field (Ithaca: Cornell University Press, 2014), 101.

Further Reading

The bibliography listed below offers starting points for readers who wish to delve more deeply into the world of Rigord and Philip Augustus. English-language books are given priority, though some essential French-language titles are listed as well. Further references to additional French and German works and more specialized studies can be found in the footnotes to the introduction and translation.

Capetian France

The best recent introduction and overview is Elizabeth M. Hallam and Charles West, *Capetian France, 987–1328*, 3rd ed. (New York: Routledge, 2020). On the historiography of the Capetian period beginning with Philip II's reign, see Sean L. Field and M. Cecilia Gaposchkin, "Questioning the Capetians, 1180–1328," *History Compass* 12 (2014): 567–85. In French, the most up-to-date surveys are Dominique Barthélemy, *Nouvelle histoire des Capétiens, 987–1214* (Paris: Seuil, 2012) and Jean-Christophe Cassard, *L'âge d'or capétien, 1180–1328* (Paris: Belin, 2011). To situate France in the wider European landscape, see William Chester Jordan, *Europe in the High Middle Ages* (New York: Penguin, 2001).

The Reign of Philip II

John Baldwin's magisterial *The Government of Philip Augustus: Foundations of French Royal Power in the Middle Ages* (Berkeley: University of California Press, 1986) remains unmatched, with Jim Bradbury, *Philip Augustus: King of France, 1180–1223* (London: Longman, 1998) providing a more traditional biography of the king. In French, Bruno Galland, *Philippe Auguste: Le bâtisseur du royaume* (Paris: Belin, 2014) and Jean Flori, *Philippe Auguste: La naissance de l'État monarchique* (Paris: Tallandier, 2007) offer concise narratives, while the formative essays in Robert-Henri Bautier, ed., *La France de Philippe Auguste: Le temps des mutations* (Paris: Éditions du CNRS, 1982) are updated in Martin

Aurell and Yves Sassier, eds., *Autour de Philippe Auguste* (Paris: Classiques Garnier, 2017).

On the aristocracy in this period the works of Theodore Evergates are crucial, including *Henry the Liberal, Count of Champagne, 1127–1181* (Philadelphia: University of Pennsylvania Press, 2016) and *Marie of France, Countess of Champagne, 1145–1198* (Philadelphia: University of Pennsylvania Press, 2019), and the essays (by multiple authors) in his edited volume *Aristocratic Women in Medieval France* (Philadelphia: University of Pennsylvania Press, 1999). Also essential are John W. Baldwin, *Aristocratic Life in Medieval France: The Romances of Jean Renart and Gerbert de Montreuil, 1190–1230* (Baltimore: The Johns Hopkins University Press, 2000) and Baldwin's posthumously published *Knights, Lords, and Ladies: In Search of Aristocrats in the Paris Region, 1180–1220* (Philadelphia: University of Pennsylvania Press, 2019). See also Amy Livingstone, *Out of Love for My Kin: Aristocratic Family Life in the Lands of the Loire, 1000–1200* (Ithaca: Cornell University Press, 2010), and Constance Brittain Bouchard, *Strong of Body, Brave and Noble: Chivalry and Society in Medieval France* (Ithaca: Cornell University Press, 1998).

For queens in this era, see the essays in Kathleen Nolan, ed., *Capetian Women* (New York: Palgrave Macmillan, 2003); Bonnie Wheeler and John Carmi Parsons, eds., *Eleanor of Aquitaine: Lord and Lady* (New York: Palgrave, 2003); Lindy Grant, *Blanche of Castile: Queen of France* (New Haven: Yale University Press, 2016); and Maria Carriere, "Adele of Champagne: Politics, Government, and Patronage in Capetian France, 1180–1206" (master's thesis, University of Vermont, 2021).

The English Monarchs

For the wider cross-channel perspective, see Martin Aurell, *The Plantagenet Empire, 1154–1224*, trans. David Crouch (London: Longman, 2007). For the English monarchy broadly, see M. T. Clanchy, *England and Its Rulers, 1066–1307*, 4th ed. (Malden, MA: Wiley, 2014). Reliable studies of individual English kings include Wilfred L. Warren, *Henry II* (Berkeley: University of California Press, 1973); Matthew Strickland, *Henry the Young King, 1155–1183* (New Haven: Yale University Press, 2016); John Gillingham, *Richard I* (London: Longman, 1999); and Ralph V. Turner, *King John* (London: Longman, 1994).

Rigord and Saint-Denis

In English the starting point remains Gabrielle Spiegel, *The Chronicle Tradition of Saint-Denis: A Survey* (Brookline, MA: Classical Folia Editions, 1978). See also her classic essay on the abbey's relationship to the monarchy in

"The Cult of Saint Denis and Capetian Kingship," *Journal of Medieval History* 1 (1975): 43–69. For Rigord's career the most up-to-date treatment (in French) is the introduction to *Histoire de Philippe Auguste*, ed. and trans. Élisabeth Carpentier, Georges Pon, and Yves Chauvin (Paris: CNRS Éditions, 2006). On the abbey of Saint-Denis a good introduction in English is Sumner McKnight Crosby, *The Royal Abbey of Saint-Denis: From Its Beginnings to the Death of Suger, 475–1151* (New Haven: Yale University Press, 1987). In French, see Elizabeth A.R. Brown, *Saint-Denis: La Basilique* (Paris: Zodiaque, 2001). Most of the English-language scholarship on the abbey has centered on the age of Suger. Still valuable are the essays collected in Paula Lieber Gerson, ed., *Abbot Suger and Saint-Denis: A Symposium* (New York: Metropolitan Museum of Art, 1986). For its place in the thirteenth-century history of the monarchy, see William Chester Jordan, *A Tale of Two Monasteries: Westminster and Saint-Denis in the Thirteenth Century* (Princeton: Princeton University Press, 2009).

The Development of Paris

John W. Baldwin, *Paris, 1200* (Stanford: Stanford University Press, 2010) is a brilliant summation. More recently (and more technical) in French, see Denis Hayot, *Paris en 1200: Histoire et archéologie d'une capitale fortifiée par Philippe Auguste* (Paris: CNRS Éditions, 2018). Even those who do not read French can benefit from Philippe Lorentz and Dany Sandron, *Atlas de Paris au Moyen Âge: Espace urbain, habitat, société, religion, lieux de pouvoir* (Paris: Parigramme, 2006). On the cathedral of Notre-Dame, see the early chapters of Dany Sandron and Andrew Tallon, *Notre Dame Cathedral: Nine Centuries of History*, trans. Lindsay Cook and Andrew Tallon (University Park: The Pennsylvania State University Press, 2020).

The Jews in Capetian France

In English the essential work is William Chester Jordan, *The French Monarchy and the Jews: From Philip Augustus to the Last Capetians* (Philadelphia: University of Pennsylvania Press, 1989). More broadly, a classic study is Robert Chazan, *Medieval Jewry in Northern France: A Political and Social History* (Baltimore: The Johns Hopkins University Press, 1974), with a wider reassessment in Chazan, *Reassessing Jewish Life in Medieval Europe* (Cambridge: Cambridge University Press, 2010). Recent works on the rising anti-Judaism of the period include E. M. Rose, *The Murder of William of Norwich: The Origins of the Blood Libel in Medieval Europe* (Oxford: Oxford University Press, 2015) and Juliette Sibon, *Chasser les juifs pour régner* (Paris: Perron, 2016).

France and the Crusades

Good recent surveys of the crusade movement in English include Thomas F. Madden, *A Concise History of the Crusades*, 3rd ed. (Lanham, MD: Rowman & Littlefield, 2014) and Christopher Tyerman, *God's War: A New History of the Crusades* (Cambridge, MA: Harvard University Press, 2006). For the Capetians and the Crusades in this period, see James Naus, *Constructing Kingship: The Capetian Monarchs of France and the Early Crusades* (Manchester: Manchester Uiversity Press, 2016).

On the Third Crusade the classic survey is Sidney Painter, "The Third Crusade: Richard the Lionheart and Philip Augustus," in *A History of the Crusades*, ed. Kenneth Setton (Madison: University of Wisconsin Press, 1962) 2:45–86; important recent perspectives in English include John D. Hosler, *The Siege of Acre, 1189–1191: Saladin, Richard the Lionheart, and the Battle That Decided the Third Crusade* (New Haven: Yale University Press, 2018); Jonathan Phillips, *The Life and Legend of the Sultan Saladin* (New Haven: Yale University Press, 2019); and Jay Rubenstein, *Nebuchadnezzar's Dream: The Crusades, Apocalyptic Prophecy, and the End of History* (Oxford: Oxford University Press, 2019).

On the Fourth Crusade, see Donald E. Queller and Thomas F. Madden, *The Fourth Crusade: The Conquest of Constantinople*, 2nd ed. (Philadelphia: University of Pennsylvania Press, 1997); and Michael Angold, *The Fourth Crusade: Event and Context* (New York: Longman, 2003).

Index